THE MORALITY OF SECURITY

When is it permissible to move an issue out of normal politics and treat it as a security issue? How should the security measures be conducted? When and how should the securitization be reversed? Floyd offers answers to these questions by combining security studies' influential securitization theory with philosophy's long-standing just war tradition, creating a major new approach to the ethics of security: 'Just Securitization Theory'. Of interest to anyone concerned with ethics and security, Floyd's innovative approach enables scholars to normatively evaluate past and present securitizations, equips practitioners to make informed judgements on what they ought to do in relevant situations, and empowers the public to hold relevant actors accountable for how they practise security.

Dr Rita Floyd is Lecturer in Conflict and Security at the Department of Political Science and International Studies, University of Birmingham. Her books include *Security and the Environment: Securitisation Theory and US Environmental Security Policy* (Cambridge University Press, 2010) and her articles have appeared in journals including the *Review of International Studies, Security Dialogue*, and *The Journal of International Relations and Development*, amongst others.

The Morality of Security

A THEORY OF JUST SECURITIZATION

RITA FLOYD

University of Birmingham

CAMBRIDGE
UNIVERSITY PRESS

CAMBRIDGE
UNIVERSITY PRESS

University Printing House, Cambridge CB2 8BS, United Kingdom

One Liberty Plaza, 20th Floor, New York, NY 10006, USA

477 Williamstown Road, Port Melbourne, VIC 3207, Australia

314–321, 3rd Floor, Plot 3, Splendor Forum, Jasola District Centre, New Delhi – 110025, India

79 Anson Road, #06–04/06, Singapore 079906

Cambridge University Press is part of the University of Cambridge.

It furthers the University's mission by disseminating knowledge in the pursuit of education, learning, and research at the highest international levels of excellence.

www.cambridge.org
Information on this title: www.cambridge.org/9781108493895
DOI: 10.1017/9781108667814

First published 2019

Printed and bound in Great Britain by Clays Ltd, Elcograf S.p.A.

A catalogue record for this publication is available from the British Library.

ISBN 978-1-108-49389-5 Hardback

To my loving family:
  Jonathan,
  Corin Sylvan
  and
  Arwen Romola

Contents

Figures

Acknowledgements

I first had the idea for this book in 2007 at the Political Studies Association's annual gathering in beautiful Bath. My plan – at that point – was to write a book about morality and security by somehow 'going through the sectors'. Although I was never able to explain this idea clearly to anyone, I meant by it that I wanted to devise a separate morality of security for each of the sectors of security, following the pattern I employed in the concluding chapter of my PhD, later published by CUP as *Security and the Environment: Securitisation Theory and US Environmental Security Policy*. Some time later – in about 2009 – I dismissed this idea in favour of writing a book identifying security threats to the core of international society. This book was to identify when, why and how the Western core is permitted to defend against these threats. Later still I realized that before that book should be written (at approximately 30,000 words in), if indeed it ever could, I needed a general theory of morality and security. But even from that insight it took me some time to realize that this could be done by taking inspiration from the just war tradition. This right kind of impetus came from having been invited to 'The Politics of Securitization' conference at Copenhagen University, Center for Advanced Security Theory on 14 September 2010. It was here that I presented some preliminary ideas on the topic, that were later published as 'Can securitisation theory be used in normative analysis? Towards a Just Securitization Theory', in *Security Dialogue*. I would like to thank all participants at the conference for their valuable comments, and especially Ole Wæver for his support of the project and his critical feedback, but also Mike Williams for his encouragement with this project as well as Ulrik Pram Gad and Karen Lund Petersen for inviting me.

During the many years of thinking about and actively researching and writing this book I have incurred many debts. My husband Jonathan Floyd, who is not only a terrific father and a loving husband but also a very fine political philosopher, has been my primary help and sounding board, and I am deeply grateful to him for everything; including, for listening to my endless monologues about the necessity and shape of one or other principle. I could not have done this without him!

I am also especially grateful to Jonathan Herington, a moral philosopher with an interest in security (and now at Kansas State University), who I met when he was temporarily based at the University of Birmingham (UK) (UoB) in 2012, and who has been a source of inspiration and a superb help (including via Skype) ever since. His insights and suggestions have proved invaluable to the overall argument in this book.

I am also very much indebted to my Birmingham colleague in the Philosophy Department, Jonathan Parry, who has not only saved me from a number of major errors, but whose comments have helped me improve Chapters 5 and 6 immensely. To be sure, however, none of these proper philosophers bears any responsibility for some of the inevitable mistakes and oversights regarding ethics in this book.

I am grateful to Cambridge University Press and John Haslam for giving me once again the chance to be published in this esteemed place. I am also extremely grateful to two anonymous reviewers whose extensive feedback and keen eye for detail improved this book in more ways that I can mention.

I could not have written this book without having been appointed Birmingham Fellow in Conflict and Security at the UoB in 2012, which allowed me some time relieved of all teaching and admin-related duties. Professors Tom Sorrel and Karen Rowlingson were on the interviewing panel, and I remain grateful to them and other decision-makers at UoB for awarding me this sought-after opportunity.

Birmingham has provided a wonderful working environment, and I have benefited hugely from the input and support of many of my valued colleagues (past and present), especially: Adam Quinn, Chris Finlay, Mark Webber, Nick Wheeler, Marco Vieira, Pete Burnham, Stefan Wolf, Kevork Oskanian and Felix Heiduk, as well as members of the Security Studies research group who have had to listen to my presentations on this topic on more than one occasion. I have also benefited from the generosity of the School of Government and Society which funded a workshop on the final draft of this book, held on 22 May 2018 at the UoB. I benefited hugely from the many comments, suggestions and criticisms by the participants of the workshop: Chris Brown, Janina Dill, Chris Finlay, Cian O'Driscoll, Ian Paterson and Marc Evans. Their comments have given the book its final shape and I am deeply grateful to each one of them for giving up precious time to read the manuscript, engage with it critically and sit through an entire day of workshop proceedings during the busy exam period.

Stuart Croft has been a mentor and friend to me since before the beginning of this project. I am grateful for his feedback and suggestions, especially in the early stages, but also for his continuous and unwavering support of this project and my career as a whole.

I am grateful to successive cohorts of students on my MA course in Security Studies (G22) for tolerating sessions on ethics and security, as well as for their support and enthusiasm. I am extremely grateful to the following individuals for their written comments on parts of earlier versions of this book: Thierry Balzacq, João Nunes, Richard Falk, Andrew Neal, Phillipe Bourbeau, Barry Buzan, Jonna Nyman and Ian Gough. I am deeply grateful to Juha Vuori and Kamilla Stullarova for reading all of an earlier draft of this book and for their extensive feedback. I am also very grateful also to Darrel Moellendorf for engaging in written email correspondence concerning criterion 9 (the timing of just desecuritization), in the absolute final stages of putting this book together and thus helping me to see things more clearly.

I would like to thank my lecturers – especially James Patterson and Kerry Lock – at the Oxford Institute for Advanced Studies for introducing me to the concept of ecosystem services when I studied for an Advanced Diploma for Environmental Conservation from 2009 to 2011. I am grateful to the British Academy for giving me that opportunity.

Over the years I have presented aspects of this book in many different settings. I am grateful to audiences for their comments and suggestions during the following talks: 'Just and unjust desecuritization' (Warwick University, 24 October 2012); 'The morality of climate security: Should the state securitize?' (Eberhard Karls University, Tübingen, Germany, 12 June 2013) (here especially to Thomas Diez for the invitation and for some challenging questions); 'Justice during securitization' (paper prepared at ISA 2013) (here especially to Lene Hansen and Mark Salter, for their feedback but also for welcoming the idea of just securitization to Securitization Studies); 'The Ethics of Security and the Ethics of Securitization: What exactly is a just cause in just securitization?' (paper presented at BISA 2013) (here especially to Molly Cochran and Toni Erskine for some very insightful comments as well as their enthusiasm for this project); 'Just resort to securitization: Some considerations concerning human beings as valuable referent objects for emergency politics' (paper presented at the Ethics, War and Intervention conference from the Institute of Advanced Studies, University of Birmingham, 30 May 2014); 'Just cause for securitization: Some considerations concerning just reason' (presented at the Laws of Security: Re-conceptualising Security at the Intersections of Law, Criminology, Politics, and International Relations, at the University of Leeds, 12–13 June 2014) (here especially to Adrian Gallagher, Lene Hansen, Didier Bigo, Adam Crawford and Steven Hutchinson for their insightful feedback and critical suggestions); and, finally: 'States, last resort and the obligation to securitise' (presented at the annual POLSIS conference in Kenilworth in June 2017) (here especially to Ole Wæver for his encouragement with this project as well as to Mark Webber for his interest in the project and his support).

Parts of the book have appeared elsewhere during earlier stages in the project. I would like to thank Taylor & Francis for allowing me to reproduce parts of my 2016 article 'Extraordinary or ordinary emergency measures: what, and who, defines the "success" of securitization' which appeared in the *Cambridge Review of International Studies*, in Chapter 2, including the reproduction of Figure 2.1. I am also grateful to Routledge and Taylor & Francis for allowing me to reproduce sections of my chapter 'Just and unjust securitization', published in Thierry Balzacq (ed.) *Contesting Security*, 2015 in Chapter 7, including Figure 7.1. I am grateful to Springer/Palgrave for giving me permission to reuse some sections of my article 'A new standard for the evaluation of solidarist institutions', which appeared in the *Journal of International Relations and Development*, July 2017, in Chapter 4. Finally I am grateful to Sage for allowing me to reuse sections of my article 'Can securitization theory be used in normative analysis? Towards a Just Securitization Theory', which appeared in *Security Dialogue*. I would like to use this opportunity to once again thank everyone – anonymous reviewers and peers and colleagues – for their feedback and suggestions that have helped me improve those published papers at the time and that now feed into the argument presented here.

I would like to dedicate this book to my wonderful family: my husband Jonathan and our two children Corin Sylvan and Arwen Romola. Both of whom were born during the thinking about and – in my daughter's case – the writing of this book. This does not always make for an easy combination, but their love and affection saw me through all of it. One day perhaps, they'll be proud of their mum for having written this book.

RF
Tewkesbury, UK
September 2018

Glossary

The purpose of this glossary is to explain the specialist terminology as developed and used in the book. Many terms are my own; some generic terms such as 'securitization' correspond to the definition of the concepts used and developed in this book.

Agent-benefiting securitization = a securitization where the primary beneficiary of **securitization** is the **securitizing actor**.

Agent-caused threat = refers to a threat that is a consequence of an agent's behaviour, but is not intended by that agent. I differentiate between two sub-types of agent-caused threats: 1) by obliviousness, i.e. when people do not realize that their (combined) actions are potentially threatening to other entities; or b) by harmful neglect, i.e. when relevant agents fail to protect against foreseeable harmful events/consequences.

Agent-intended threat = refers to a threat that is intentionally levelled at another actor, order or entity.

Agent-lacking threat = refers to a threat that does not originate from human agents (e.g. a truly natural disaster).

Aggressor = the agent or agents at the source of an agent-intended threat.

Audience = in **original securitization theory** refers to the entity that has to consent to the threat narrative contained in the securitizing move; in my version of securitization theory it refers to the addressee of the **securitizing move** which is either the agent at the source of a threat and/or the referent object of security.

Counter-securitization = a securitization launched by 'A' in direct response to a securitization by 'B'.

Desecuritization = a sum of actions (a process) referring to the unmaking of **securitization**, involving the termination of security language and **security measures.**

Desecuritized state of affairs = the outcome of **desecuritization,** in which the former securitized issue is either politicized or depoliticized.

Direct lethal threat = a threat to human life regardless of the source of threat.

Evidence relative = refers to the situation when the available evidence suggests decisive reasons that the beliefs people hold about a given situation are true.

Executor of securitization = refers to **security professionals,** e.g. police, border guards, employees of private security firms enforcing security policy. In non-state securitization, divisions are less applicable and executors are (likely to be) the same as **securitizing actors.**

Indirect lethal threat = an existential threat to something other than individuals that carries (the risk of) death to people.

Just cause = in **just securitization theory, just cause** is made up of the **just reason** and the **just referent object.**

Just reason = prescribes the reason when **securitization** is morally permissible. In **just securitization theory,** it refers to the presence of an **objective existential threat.**

Just referent object = designates that a referent object (i.e. the entity in need of protection) is entitled to self-defence or is eligible to defensive assistance only if it is morally justifiable, and specifies that moral justifiability is tied to the satisfaction of **basic human needs.**

Just securitization theory = my variant of a theory of just securitization that focuses on the **moral permissibility** of securitization.

Morally permissible = refers to whatever actors are allowed (permitted) to do from a moral point of view in a certain context.

Morally wicked = refers to a person or collective who intentionally and without excuse deprive(s) innocent others of their basic human needs simply to further their own ends.

Objective existential threat = refers to a threat that is both real in the **evidence-relative** sense and of a magnitude that it threatens either the survival of the referent object or its essential properties/character.

Original securitization theory = refers to the **Copenhagen School**'s version of securitization theory, whereby **securitization** includes a speech act (**securitizing move**), a relevant audience that has to accept the speech act, effects on inter-unit relations and the breaking free from established rules.

Reactionary securitization = a securitization launched in response to (i.e. as a reaction to) **desecuritization**.

Referent object = the thing that is threatened and hence to be protected by **securitization**.

Referent object benefiting securitization = a securitization where the primary beneficiary is the referent object identified as existentially threatened by the **securitizing actor**.

Renewed securitization = refers to a renewed securitization of an issue that was already desecuritized. Renewed securitization can be carried out by a different actor.

Restorative measures = measures put in place by desecuritizing actors in order to ensure that **renewed** or **reactionary securitization** is unlikely.

Securitization = the process whereby an issue is moved from normal politics into the realm of security politics. In this book, successful/complete securitizations tend to involve: 1) a **securitizing move** (an existential threat articulation) plus 2) **security action** (a change of behaviour by a relevant agent (the **securitizing actor** or someone instructed by the same) that is justified by the **securitizing actor** (and sometimes also by the **executor of securitization**) with reference to the declared threat). **Securitization** is possible without 1 but not without 2. However, in most cases 1 will feature even if it is not always traceable for security scholars. Moreover, **security action** can be either non-exceptional or exceptional in nature; Just Securitization Theory is interested only in **security action** as **the exception**. I refer to exceptional security action as **security measures**. Ergo, in **just securitization theory, securitization** is defined as the move from normal politics to the high politics of security, where the issue in question is dealt with using **security measures**.

Securitized state of affairs = the outcome of **securitization** in which the threat is either successfully averted or remains present; either way, security measures are present.

Securitizing actor = the agent whose relevant behavioural change constitutes **securitization**, or who is in a position of power over other agents who can execute security measures.

Securitizing move = generally speaking, the identification of an existential threat; in Just Securitization Theory, relevant securitizing moves are those by **securitizing actors** which amount to either warnings to agents at the source of the threat and/or promises of protection to referent objects.

Securitizing requests = rhetorical moves aimed at persuading others (usually more powerful actors) to securitize, or else make securitizing moves.

Security action = specifies that language alone is not sufficient for successful securitization; instead successful/complete securitization requires that **securitizing actors** act in response to the securitizing move. While the action taken may be either exceptional or non-exceptional, Just Securitization Theory is concerned only with **the exception**. Exceptional means in response to securitizing moves are referred to as **security measures.**

Security measures = the use of exceptional (cf.: **the exception**) means and conduct in response to a **securitizing move.**

Security practitioners = anyone involved in securitization, including the **securitizing actor, security professionals** and **executors of securitization.**

Security professionals = individuals working in the security provision industry (e.g. police, military, private security companies, border guards).

The exception = as far as liberal democratic states are concerned, the exception refers not to the suspension of law altogether, but rather to the situation when (new) emergency laws are passed/put into action and/or (new) emergency powers are granted that seek to govern the insecurity/crisis situation, or when a state's existing security apparatus is employed to deal with issues that are either new, or that it has not dealt with previously.

In non-state actors and autocracies, the exception refers to whatever most reasonable persons would agree constitutes exceptional means and actions, most notably perhaps, in terms of the amount of harm risked/caused or intended, and/or the level of violence employed.

Abbreviations

AfD = Alternative für Deutschland (Alternative for Germany, a political party)

AIDS = Auto Immune Deficiency Syndrome

AZBR = Arizona Border Recon

BBC = British Broadcasting Corporation

CDR = Carbon Dioxide Removal

CIA = Central Intelligence Agency

EU = European Union

HIV = Human Immunodeficiency Virus

IPCC = Intergovernmental Panel on Climate Change

IR = International Relations (the academic discipline)

IS = Islamic State

JST = Just Securitization Theory

LOAC = Laws of Armed Conflict

GCHQ = Government Communications Headquarters (UK)

GDR = German Democratic Republic

MEA = Millennium Ecosystem Services Assessment

NSA = National Security Agency

OSCE = Organization for Security and Co-operation in Europe

SANFFA = Security: A new framework for analysis

SED = Sozialistische Einheitspartei Deutschlands

TEEB = The Economics of Ecosystems and Biodiversity

UK = United Kingdom

UNDP = United Nations Development Report

UNEP = United Nations Environment Programme

UNESCO = United Nations Educational, Scientific and Cultural Organization

UNFCCC = United Nations Framework Convention on Climate Change

US = United States

WHO = World Health Organization

WWII = Second World War

WWF = World Wide Fund for Nature

Introduction

At 2.20 pm on 22 May 2013, off-duty British Army soldier Drummer Lee Rigby of the Royal Regiment of Fusiliers was attacked and brutally murdered in a terrorist attack by two men outside the Royal Artillery Barracks in Woolwich, south-east London. Both men – Michael Adebolajo and Michael Adebowale – were Britons of Nigerian decent, and both were converts to Islam. The perpetrators remained at the scene, leaving no doubt about their intentions, with one of them declaring: 'The only reason we have killed this man today is because Muslims are dying daily by British soldiers. And this British soldier is one. It is an eye for an eye and a tooth for a tooth. By Allah, we swear by the almighty Allah we will never stop fighting you until you leave us alone' (The Muslim Issue Worldwide, 2013). A day after the attack it emerged that both men had been known to British security services for many years, leading to criticism of the services for not preventing the attack, and the latter subsequently faced a Commons enquiry into the matter.

Two weeks later on 6 June 2013 *The Guardian* newspaper together with the *Washington Post* published a number of secret intelligence documents leaked by an American former technical contractor for the United States' National Security Agency (NSA) and former employee of the Central Intelligence Agency (CIA), Edward Snowden. Among other things, the documents revealed the extent of mass surveillance by national intelligence agencies since the onset of the securitization of terrorism. Through the Prism programme, for example, both the United States' National Security Agency (NSA) and its British counterpart the Government Communications Headquarters (GCHQ) have access to millions of emails and live chat conversations held by the world's major internet companies, such as Google, Facebook and Microsoft. The United States and British governments attempted to justify and downplay the extent of surveillance – US President

1

Barack Obama, for example, said that Prism was both targeted and necessary, and claimed that it had prevented some fifty terror attacks (York, 2013). Nevertheless, Snowden's revelations were met with a huge public outcry in the United States, Europe and elsewhere. The issue stayed for weeks on the top of the news media's agenda, Snowden was hailed by many as a whistle-blower, and civil liberty groups everywhere widely condemned the United States for seeking his extradition. This introduction is not the place to pass a verdict on either the security services' role in not preventing the murder of Lee Rigby, nor on the NSA/GCHQ spy-scandal and whether the means used by governments for counter-terrorism were morally justifiable. Instead, these examples serve to illustrate that although sometimes the general public wants certain issues (here, terrorism) to be securitized (which is to say, rendered a top priority and addressed by extraordinary/exceptional means), the same public (or at least large sections thereof) are also deeply sceptical of securitization (of terrorism). This scepticism is sensible, for there are always dangers associated with securitization. Raising an issue out of normal politics and into the realm of exceptional politics, where it is addressed by extraordinary measures, may, for example, result in the systematic infringement of key rights, the loss of civil liberties, an increase in police powers, 'othering'/alienation of suspect individuals and groups, the use of lethal force, and because the issue itself is removed from democratic decision-making, a reduction of the democratic process. Nevertheless, sometimes the general public – depending on context and circumstances – deems securitization permissible and at times even obligatory. Usually this is in order to seemingly achieve security and thus ensure that, for instance, outrages such as the murder of Lee Rigby cannot be repeated.

Although critical security scholars[1] are traditionally concerned with the negative effects of securitization, they are increasingly open to the suggestion that securitization can sometimes be right, or be put to good ends. Yet we do not have a systematic normative theory that theorizes the circumstances when the move out of normal politics is morally permissible, and what considerations ought to inform the choice of security measures used. The development

---

[1] While I use this label here to designate those engaged in the academic study of security who do not prioritize the state as the referent object of security, I agree with Nik Hynek and David Chandler (2013) that it technically is a misnomer as the adjective 'critical' signifies emancipatory content which is absent from many approaches standardly grouped under that label (for a different view, see Vuori, 2014: chapter 1). It is, however, custom to refer to those with emancipatory intent with upper case 'Critical' and to everyone else by the lower case 'critical', yet confusingly the lower case subsumes the upper case (see Peoples and Vaughan-Williams, 2015: 30).

of precisely such a theory is this book's overriding rationale. In the process the book addresses the following pressing issues definitive of the conundrum of security and morality. Does morality count in matters of security? Or is it the case that the threat overrides all moral concerns? Can we meaningfully differentiate between entities (including persons) that are worthwhile securing, and those rightfully subject to securitization? Are there restrictions on the kind of harm securitization may cause, or does just cause side-line all other ethical concerns?[2]

I call the theory I advance throughout this book just securitization theory (JST). This theory takes the form of a set of criteria or principles[3] that determine the justness of securitization and desecuritization. The idea of developing a normative theory of securitization from universally applicable criteria is inspired by the just war tradition (JWT), which for centuries has seen scholars develop criteria determining the morality of war. Criteria or principles usually fall into two areas: *jus ad bellum* (just resort to war) and the *jus in bello* (just conduct in war), while many recent accounts also include criteria specifying *jus post bellum* (just peace). As with the just war tradition, competing theories of just securitization made up of distinct sets of criteria, informed by different objectives (e.g. restrict the occurrence of securitization or else utilize the mobilization power inherent to securitization for desirable ends) are thus a possibility. And consequently this book has the potential to pave the way towards a major new area of research in Security Studies: just securitization studies.

A key advantage of approaching the morality of security by developing principles of just securitization is that it enables scholars of security, who

---

[2] Many philosophers use the terms ethics and morality interchangeably, with both simply referring to right and wrong or good or bad. And while some authors (especially outside of philosophy) distinguish between morality and ethics, no accepted definition exists. *The Penguin Dictionary of Philosophy*, points out, for example, that some (notably Hegel, Bernard Williams, Habermas and Rawls) all distinguish between the two, yet have different ideas about what either might mean. In one sense it is possible to argue that this book follows the distinction (if there is one) implied in Rawls's *Theory of Justice*, whereby 'Ethics is concerned with the good life, morality with right conduct' (Mautner, 2000: 367). Thus for the most part just securitization theory is a moral (normative) theory concerned with right conduct. However, given my specification of a just referent object in terms of the satisfaction of basic human needs and the connection between this and human well-being (see Chapter 4) I venture – at least in this context – into the realm of the ethical. Moreover, the branch of philosophy called ethics (also known as moral philosophy) includes both theories of the right and theories of the good. In other words, ethical consideration on security as a concept or a social and political practice involve both, and the interchangeable use of morality and ethics, as practised here, is permissible.

[3] I use the terms criteria and principles interchangeably in this book. A criterion can be defined as 'a principle or standard by which something may be judged or decided' (Soanes, 2000: 255).

almost inevitably have a view on the value of any given securitization they study, to make better-informed normative[4] judgements about their relative worth. It should be noted here that the study of security is no longer the exclusive business of International Relations scholars; instead, security is increasingly of interest to – among others – law scholars, criminologists, anthropologists, geographers and philosophers. The question of the moral value or disvalue of the security policies (implemented into practice or otherwise) they study unites them all, making this book and its just securitization theory useful to the widest possible interdisciplinary scholarly audience.

Beyond that, just securitization theory and other possible theories of just securitization and desecuritization have at least the potential to guide the actions of security practitioners in concrete situations. This is not merely wishful thinking. Now at last the Snowden affair has shown that there is a need on the part of the practitioner community to consider the normative implications of moving out of normal politics and resorting to using security measures, but to do so they need the right kind of tools; tools that theories of just securitization can offer.

Finally, provided that just securitization took off as a research project in its own right and came to inform the language and behaviour of security practitioners, it has the potential to render security practitioners accountable for their decisions and actions. Rendering practitioners of security more fully accountable than they have been hitherto is necessary because securitization affects not simply those individuals security measures are levelled against, but often also the wider population.[5] In the West, for example, where people are relatively secure in so far as they enjoy high levels of both freedom from fear and freedom from want, security measures were felt most acutely in the aftermath of 9/11, when a number of new laws and regulations impinged upon civil liberties. Ten years later, the NSA/GCHQ spy scandal suggested that no end to this was in sight. While it might be the case that, in the words of former British Foreign Secretary William Hague, law-abiding citizens have 'nothing to fear' from surveillance programmes such as Prism (Hague, 2013), such programmes alter a given states of affairs, deprive individuals of some fundamental rights inherent to the democracies they inhabit and perhaps quite justifiably render people afraid that they'll wind up

---

[4] To be clear, and unless otherwise stated, normativity, in this book, concerns moral rightness and wrongness.

[5] To be sure, even if 'only' aggressors were adversely affected by security policies, moral considerations still matter. Thus the same rules regarding what has to be considered in the resort to and during securitization still apply; the idea of just securitization is not to sanction revenge (cf. Chapter 5, section 5.3).

wrongfully accused and suspected. For proof that this can happen we need but think of the unfortunate Jean Charles de Menezes, the Brazilian electrician, who was wrongly suspected of terrorist activity and simply on his way to work when he was shot dead by armed police in London in 2005. The criminologist Lucia Zedner has summarized the relationship between security and harm aptly in the following metaphor: 'security has all the qualities of a fire engine, replete with clanging bells and flashing lights, whose dash to avert imminent catastrophe brooks no challenge, even if it risks running people down on the way to the fire' (2009: 12).

The potentially wide-ranging negative consequences of securitization mean that its moral permissibility is already in everyone's interest. In an ideal world, for example, a critical mass of the general public would hold their governments accountable for the employment and nature of securitization in any given situation, in the same way as parts of the voting public now routinely question the morality and necessity of warfare. Indeed, while just war theories have sometimes been abused by warmongering politicians to shine a positive light on their dubious activities, the just war tradition has had precisely this positive effect. In liberal democracies, especially as regards the 2003 Iraq war, ideas inherent to the just war tradition inform public debate and the general public was able to hold decision-makers accountable for going to war (Walzer, 2002: 930). The ultimate aim of wider just securitization studies/research must be that just securitization becomes the standard against which decisions and actions are made and informed, while simultaneously equipping the general public with the tools to hold security practitioners accountable, thus making positive change possible.

While few scholars would object to the *desirability* of the latter, many, in particular critical security scholars, will object to working with the just war tradition in order to devise a theory of just securitization. Some will do so because they question the authority of the just war tradition, others will question the possibility of comparing war with securitization, and others still will point to meta-theoretical differences between just war theory,[6] with its focus on real threats, and securitization theory, with its focus on threat construction. Given this, it is necessary to spell out clearly my reasons for working with the JWT here.

As soon as one thinks of normative criteria in connection with security, one cannot ignore the JWT. In a recent edited book on *Ethical Security Studies*, contributor Helen Dexter reminds us that for some security scholars (here

---

[6] I agree with Helen Frowe (2016: 4), contra Alex Bellamy (2006), that there is no difference between the just war tradition and just war theory, and use the two interchangeably.

Stephen Walt), 'the main focus of security studies is the phenomenon of war', consequently 'the ethics of security are easy to identify and can be summed up in three small words: Just War Theory' (Dexter, 2016: 174). While in practice security has moved on from war, and considering that scholars no longer study real or perceived security threats only if they (are likely to) lead to war,[7] Dexter's point still serves to remind us that when it comes to thinking ethically about security (albeit in the limited guise of war), we do have an established body of theory. In my view we cannot ignore the JWT for thinking about the justice of securitization, because although the instruments of war and securitization are distinct concepts, they are similar insofar as both involve extraordinary measures[8] (e.g. large-scale killing and maiming of people, including as collateral damage in war, and the systematic infringement of civil liberties, the violation of fundamental rights and due process, the increase in police powers and even the use of (comparatively small-scale) lethal force in the name of security), not only in order to secure a referent object but problematically to further often dubious political agendas.

Often securitization and war are also sequentially connected, with war the extraordinary measure evoked in the name of security (Wilhelmsen, 2016). Jef Huysmans (2014: 39) argues: 'National security does more than asserting a point in time when decisions will affect the survival of the political order. It mobilises an imaginary of war and enemies to make the struggle for survival concrete and acute.' Moreover, war's changed nature (i.e. away from its Clausewitzian form) blurs the lines between war and securitization; the United States Department of Defense's use of targeted killing via unmanned drones is a case in point. This changed nature of war has meant that Michael Walzer, perhaps the most influential just war theorist ever, (2006 [1977], xv) has argued for the inclusion of *jus ad vim* within the just war tradition, i.e. 'a theory of the just and unjust uses of force' *outside war*.[9] And already some just war scholars are working on issues very close to Security Studies with their interest in 'forcible alternatives to war', including targeted killing, humanitarian rescue missions or international policing missions (Dill, 2016).[10] For the

---

[7]   Migration or environmental degradation, for example are of interest not only because of their potential to lead to violent conflict, but also because of the potential threat they pose to human security, political security or economic security.

[8]   Notably this depends on the definition of securitization – see Chapter 2, section 2.2 – but it is true of the definition of securitization utilized in this book.

[9]   Frowe 2016 refers to this as justice before force, whereby force refers to kinetic force.

[10] A 2017 book on *Soft War: The Ethics of Unarmed Conflict* identifies – among other unarmed conflicts/tactics – cyber warfare, media warfare, economic sanctions and 'lawfare' as applicable domains for just war theory. Soft war is different from securitization chiefly for two reasons: first, because it deals with agent-intended threats only, and second, because only

purposes of this project it is therefore vital to be clear on the differences between war and securitization; notably just securitization theory does not seek to rival the just war tradition. Although securitization may entail the use of lethal force, the abiding difference between war and securitization (apart from scale) is that unlike in war,[11] killing is *not* a necessary feature of securitization, but merely – and far from always – one aspect of it. In short, while I hold that securitization and war are similar, and therefore that the just war tradition can serve as a useful guide for thinking about criteria of just securitization, just securitization theory does not intent to deal with situations of war, whereby the working definition of war includes those grey areas of the *jus ad vim* (notably drone warfare).

The just war tradition has been criticized for a vast number of reasons, above all else for being pro-war. Patricia Owens (2010: 310–311), for example, argues that just war thinkers 'wish to imagine the decision to go to war as an *ethical* choice in itself. In some circumstances, war is *the right thing to do.*' While it is true that especially after the end of the Cold War, a new world order allowed for the inclusion of humanitarian intervention as just cause, historically the goal of the just war tradition has not been the 'elimination of injustice' (Rengger, 2013: 9) but instead 'to restrain both the incidence and the destructiveness of warfare' (Orend, 2006: 31).[12] In more detail: 'Just war theory seeks to minimize *the reasons* for which it is permissible to fight, and seeks to retain and limit *the means* with which communities may fight. Just war theory is *not* pro-war. It is, rather, a doctrine deeply aware of war's frightful dangers and brutal inhumanities' (ibid.: 31 emphases in original). As such, the objective of many just war theorists is actually close to that of many scholars concerned with the ethics of security, as many such scholars are against

---

threats whose impact on civilian human needs is comparable to kinetic war are considered (cf. Wolfendale, 2017: 20–22).

[11] A widely accepted definition of war is that advanced by the Uppsala Conflict Data programme that defines wars as armed conflict with 1,000 battle death per year. While I accept that such exact thresholds come with problems of their own (notably, wars can result mainly in the large-scale destruction of infrastructure and still be largely bloodless: Steinhoff, 2009; Lazar, 2017), I am not sure it is helpful to redefine war so that it can include unarmed conflict (Soft War). After all, it is a boon for just war theorists that – unlike with securitization – their subject of study is well understood and (reasonably well) defined. Note, I do not wish to suggest that just war theory does not have something useful to say about unarmed conflict; but merely that the term war should be reserved for something else.

[12] Cian O'Driscoll notes that theories of the just war adapt and change in light of empirical developments (2008a: 109–114). If he is correct, then we can assume that the problematic aftermath of recent interventions in Afghanistan, Iraq and Libya is likely to shape future accounts of the just war towards a renewed focus on 'the limitation of the destructiveness of war' (Rengger, 2013: 8).

securitization and in favour of democratic decision-making/politicization, a quality said to be lost once an issue is securitized (cf. Chapter 1).

Be that as it may, this still leaves the question of why we can take some of the ideas of how war ought ideally to be restrained (most just war theorists have homed in on some basic ideas concerning just cause, right intention and proportionality) as authoritative? This is important also because as Cian O'Driscoll and Anthony Lang (2013: 8) note, the issue that the authority of the tradition is rarely addressed by just war theorists, but simply assumed. This is controversial because the just war theory emerged in the context of Christian religion, and although contemporary versions have little to do with that heritage, the tradition has a heavy Western focus and as such some regard it as legitimizing certain forms of government and delegitimizing others. According to O'Driscoll and Lang, two arguments in particular justify the authority of the just war tradition. First, is 'the rich historical lineage' argument, which holds that the just war tradition is an exercise in 'communal learning ... It embodies and conveys, from one generation to the next, the wisdom of the ages, the sum of experimental knowledge as it bears on the use of military force' (ibid.: 8). In support of this argument, consider that there is general consensus on what sort of principles matter for the justice of war (cf. O'Driscoll, 2008a: 112), and that even if one or other principle is not explicitly stated by one theorist, the reasons for the omission are generally thoroughly discussed. This general consensus, in my view, not only renders disparate theories of the just war a tradition, it also gives authority to this same tradition as it is unlikely that the countless scholars who have worked within the tradition have been unable to identify at least broadly what matters for the morality of war.[13]

The second source of authority for the tradition, argue O'Driscoll and Lang (ibid.: 8), is its practical usage; that is to say, whether it has had an impact on the policymaking world. Although the just war tradition has been abused by some policymakers to further dubious ends, its principles have come to inform the training of military personal, it has penetrated the discourse of relevant politicians, and it informs specific policies. In summary, we can say that the just war tradition is authoritative for thinking and talking about the ethics of the use of force both because of its historical lineage and because of its usage in practice.

Different theorists of the just war have developed a number of basic ideas informing all just war theories (concerning, for example, just cause, right

---

[13] This intersubjective element ought also to appeal to securitization scholars.

intention and proportionality)[14] into elaborate lists of criteria governing all eventualities of war and now even the just ending of war.[15] In my view, given the similarities of war and securitization as both forms of exceptional politics and political instruments, and considering further that – for me at least[16] – just securitization is about restricting the occurrence and destructiveness of securitization, the criteria of the just war tradition cannot be ignored; instead they can serve as a valuable starting point for developing criteria of just securitization, at least until we have competing theories of just securitization against which criteria can be revised, refined and developed.

While this explains why I draw on the JWT, I have not yet explained why this theory can be combined with securitization theory. This is important, especially seeing that there is a meta-theoretical divide between the JWT and securitization theory concerning the relevance of real threats. Securitization theory was initially proposed by Ole Wæver in 1995[17] and then developed by him and others as part of the Copenhagen School in the seminal *Security: A New Framework For Analysis* (SANFFA) in 1998.[18] Securitization theory holds that security threats do not simply exist 'out there', but rather that security is a highly political process with issues turned into security threats through a sequence of events usually involving a securitizing actor, a securitizing speech act/ securitizing move (whereby a securitizing actor declares a particular referent object threatened in its existence unless urgent action is taken immediately), the audience (which has to 'accept' the speech act, albeit unwillingly), and the enacting of extraordinary measures and thus the breaking of established rules in order to deal with a (perceived) threat.

---

[14] As McMahan (2012) observes, these principles coincide 'closely with the law as codified in the United Nations Charter and the Geneva Conventions'.

[15] I am keen not to overstate the case for consensus. Thus while just war scholars agree on many of the same principles, their relevance is weighted differently.

[16] Theories of just securitization could also focus on the circumstances when securitization is morally obligatory, in the same way as some just war scholars focus on using the tool of war to bring about a better world, notably those scholars who focus on just humanitarian intervention (Pattison, 2010; Fabre, 2012:178ff.).

[17] In a published format; in unpublished works, the idea goes back to at least 1989.

[18] In a 2012 review of my 2010 book *Security and the Environment* I was criticized by Copenhagen School member Jaap de Wilde for conflating Wæver and the Copenhagen School and seemingly attributing Wæver's views to the Copenhagen School. Although I have taken care to be clear on who I mean in this book, Wæver is the authoritative voice on securitization theory within the school; his earlier work on securitization theory informs all parts of SANFFA. In other words, he should be able to speak for the school when it comes to meaning, interpretation and application of the original variant of the theory.

Securitization has been heavily debated in the scholarly community. Among other things much discussion has focused on the issue of whether securitization is satisfied simply by audience acceptance of the securitizing move, or whether it has to involve extraordinary measures (Balzacq, Léonard and Ruzicka, 2015). All securitization scholars accept, however, that security threats are socially and politically constructed, or in other words that: 'Security issues are made security issues by acts of securitization' (Buzan et al., 1998: 204). This has allowed scholars to recognize what Jef Huysmans calls 'the political force of security' whereby '[s]ecurity is a practice not of responding to enemies and fear but of creating them' (2014: 3). An exclusive focus on the constructedness of security means, however, that securitization scholars tend to ignore whether or not the threats that inform securitization are real or otherwise. And as Thierry Balzacq argues, this has had the disadvantage of securitization scholars overlooking the fact that securitizing moves that refer to 'brute threats' are more likely to succeed because, 'to win an audience, security statements must, usually, be related to an external reality' (2011b: 13). Balzacq's observation is important in the context of this book as it goes some way towards paving the way for the inclusion of objective existential threats into securitization analysis. As I will argue in this book, real threats are important for the purposes of just securitization theory as only these may constitute a just reason[19] for securitization.

The Copenhagen School's refusal to 'peek behind [threat construction] to decide whether it is really a threat' (Buzan et al., 1998: 204) and the just war tradition's insistence on real threats as just causes, appear to suggest insurmountable differences at the meta-theoretical level between the two theories. Importantly, however, the Copenhagen School's unwillingness to, as they put it, 'peek behind' threat construction, does not stem from a *denial* that real threats exist (after all Wæver (2011: 472) recognizes that 'lots of real threats exist'),[20] but from the belief that the study of threat construction is ultimately more fruitful than pondering the presence of real threats (Buzan and Hansen, 2009: 213; Buzan et al., 1998: 204). Beyond this, the decision not to try and examine whether security threats refer to real threats is also – at least in part – driven by a strong normative conviction. Thus by focusing on the political force of security as opposed to whether or not threats are real, Wæver and the Copenhagen School

---

[19] As argued in Chapter 3, the just reason is part of the just cause, the other part is the just referent object dealt with in Chapter 4.

[20] As Balzacq, Léonard and Ruzicka (2015, 26–27) observe, 'securitization theory is agnostic as to reality of threats' – but not, I might add, atheistic.

highlight the fact that securitization is/was not inevitable; things could have been treated in a different way (for example, perceived threats could have been criminalized or simply politicized). This enables scholars following this logic to highlight that securitizing actors bear responsibility for framing things in this way. Wæver calls this 'the politics of responsibility' (2011: 472), which he explains as follows: 'The securitization approach points to the inherently political nature of any designation of security issues and thus it puts an *ethical question* at the feet of analysts, decision-makers and activists alike: why do you call this a security issue? What are the implications of doing this – or of not doing it?' (Wæver 1999 cited in Wæver, 2011: 468; emphasis added).

The significance of the fact that securitization is a political choice cannot be overstated; however, it is also the case that decision-makers are likely to consider securitization the *right* political choice when they believe that they are in fact dealing with a real threat. In other words, the possibility of framing the issue differently will not be tempting if they believe that there is a real threat. Given that the Copenhagen School and their followers cannot tell them anything about the actual objective existence of the threat, the framework seems of limited persuasiveness here; it is simply the securitizing actor's belief against the scholar's argument that things could and perhaps should be different. Indeed the Copenhagen School recognizes 'our inability to counter securitization (say, of immigrants) with an argument that this is not really a security problem or that the environment is a bigger security problem' as the securitization approach's 'main disadvantage' (Buzan et al., 1998: 206). I propose that if the ethical goal of securitization analysis is that securitizing actors take responsibility for their actions, then a better strategy is to begin by (helping them in) judging the objective existence of a threat, because unless there is a real threat, securitization is most definitely the wrong political and ethical choice. Importantly, however, as I argue in this book, the existence of a real threat does not automatically necessitate securitization (indeed this remains a political choice), neither does it – by itself – render it morally permissible; the presence of real threats is rather one important requirement for securitization to be justified. In other words, just securitization is informed by the idea that securitizing actors are not only responsible for choosing to securitize, they ought to be responsible for securitizing in an ethical manner. In my view, the fact that the original variant of securitization theory excludes objective existential threats not on ontological, but at least partially on normative grounds means that a variant of securitization theory that includes real threats is at least permissible, provided, of course, that a theoretical framework that shows how we can know that threats are real is delivered. In this book, such a framework is set out in Chapter 2.[21]

JUST SECURITIZATION THEORY: BASIC IDEAS

I now want to turn to the book's overriding rationale which is to develop and defend a particular version of a theory of just securitization, which I refer to by using the capitalized Just Securitization Theory (JST). While many different and competing versions of a theory of just securitization are possible,[22] Just Securitization Theory is about what securitizing actors are – from a moral point of view – *permitted* to do when it comes to security. It is *not* about what

---

[21] Some scholars may object to the possibility of combining insights of opposed theories on the grounds of inconsistency – for example, critical security studies, with its postmodern roots, with insights gained from analytical, moral and political philosophy. Interestingly, Wæver has faced similar charges of inconsistency for combining elements that ordinarily don't go together (notably, Wæver refers to himself as a poststructural realist). To these critics Wæver offers this persuasive riposte: 'This criticism presupposes that these larger groups are internally consistent and mutually isolated. On the contrary, we all know numerous examples of internally consistent theories that draw on several traditions – and many more examples of theories that stay within their "box" and yet are horribly inconsistent. Therefore, investigations of the internal consistency and productivity of research traditions should focus on distinct theories, not loose collections hereof' (Wæver, 2015:124). Generally speaking, I am critical of the tendency to confuse theory with ideology, and thus disallowing and discounting anything outside of one's perceived and tightly regulated theoretical remit. In the past in IR such thinking has led to bad scholarship; thankfully now scholars are working to dispel artificially imposed dichotomies, such as that on the relationship between causation and discourse (Kurki, 2008).

[22] Different rationalist normative theorists generate distinct and sometimes incompatible principles for the world; or put differently, just war theorists disagree with one another. This raises the following question once put to me by Thomas Diez: does the fact that not all of them can be right undermine the rationalist project? While it is true that rationalists disagree, it is important to realize that their disagreements are only at the level of *reasoning* (i.e. they concern the nature of logical inferences). All rationalists agree on the value, possibility and method of what Nagel calls reason (1997: 5), but I prefer to call moral universalism. The latter is evinced by the very fact that all just war theorists recognize and share the need for just such a theory. Disagreements over, for example, whether or not soldiers are morally culpable for partaking in wars that are unjust for *jus ad bellum* violations cannot render the rationalist project void because all just war theorist debating this issue agree that it is possible to develop criteria governing the justice of war in the first place. I would like to go further than this and suggest that disagreement over reasoning is a healthy development and I would very much welcome it with regards to just securitization. Thus not only is a single theory of just securitization unlikely to have all the answers to all of the relevant questions (not least because all such theories are going to be limited in some way), but the long-term aim is to hold security practitioners accountable for securitizing certain issue and how they do so. The latter is more likely to be achieved if just securitization becomes a research project in its own right, ignited by a belief in the same thing, but fuelled by disagreement on reasoning. (Further on this point see also Richard North (2016), who offers a refutation of the view that non-compliance and disagreement renders principles unable to guide actions.)

securitizing actors are morally *required* to do with regards to security.[23] It does not, for example, consider whether the West has an obligation to save residents of small island states from the effects of global climate change, to which it has historically contributed the most. Neither is it about what sort of thing is morally praiseworthy/supererogatory. For example, it does not discuss whether we ought to intervene in the internal affairs of failed states and sacrifice our own soldiers in order to 'save strangers' (Wheeler, 2000).

With its focus on moral permissibility, Just Securitization Theory retains the commitment to studying the politics of securitization intrinsic to original securitization theory (see Pram Gad and Petersen, 2011). Thus JST does not say: 'here is an objective existential threat that ought to be securitized by relevant actors'; it rather looks at whether and when securitization is/was permissible. In its backwards-looking guise it helps scholars to morally evaluate the political decision of actors to securitize and how they did so. As a forwards-looking theory it can guide the actions of security practitioners, yet the decision whether or not to securitize is theirs. Notably, in the variant of securitization advanced as part of JST, security speech alone is not definitive of the success of securitization (cf. Chapter 2, section 2.2).[24]

Although as argued above, the idea to develop criteria of just securitization is in principle compatible with the original variant of securitization theory, I nevertheless propose my own variant of such a theory, one where securitization is defined as the process whereby an issue is moved from normal politics into the realm of security politics. I argue that successful securitizations tend to involve: 1) a securitizing move (an existential threat articulation) and 2) security action (a change of behaviour by a relevant agent (the securitizing actor or someone instructed by the same) that is justified by the securitizing actor (and sometimes also by the executor of securitization) with reference to the declared threat). I hold that securitization is possible without the securitizing move but not without security action; however, in most cases a securitizing move will feature even if it is not always traceable for security scholars. Moreover, while security action can be either non-exceptional or exceptional in nature, just securitization theory is interested only in the latter. I refer to

---

[23] Although the difference between permissibility and obligation is well established in moral philosophy, not all just war scholars draw this distinction; instead many hold that there is a corresponding duty to fight wars one is permitted to fight (cf. Oberman, 2015). This seems to be a function of the fact that the threshold for when a war is permissible is set so high (notably, for many, it must be a last resort) that war is automatically necessary when it is allowed. I argue that securitization is morally permissible before it is a last resort, to wit when securitization is on all available evidence the best option for addressing the threat (cf. Chapter 5, section 5.5.2).

[24] As such, JST retains the functional distinction between securitizing actor and security scholar also championed by the Copenhagen School (Buzan et al., 1998: 207).

exceptional security action throughout as security measures. I will explain my variant of securitization, and within that the meaning of the exception, in some detail in Chapter 2. This will be necessary for two reasons. First, the meaning of securitization is contested, and not all formulations of securitization easily allow a comparison with war. Notably, for some securitization is understood as a multi-layered, multi-faceted process, involving a multitude of actors, rendering it quite different from the decision to go to war and the act of war (Huysmans, 2011; Wilhelmsen, 2016). In other words, the feasibility of a theory of just securitization depends on the meaning of securitization. My variant of securitization retains a decisive moment at which securitization ensues, namely when securitizing actors (or someone else they are in a position of power over) act/change their behaviour in response to the securitizing speech act they themselves uttered; and, precisely by retaining a decisive moment/act it becomes comparable to war. The same is further facilitated by the fact that I focus only on those securitizations that amount to exceptional politics.

Second, the exact definition of securitization influences the nature of the criteria advanced. Most notably my definition does not award a pivotal role to the notion of 'the audience' in securitization; as such, JST does not specify a criterion requiring audience acceptance of the threat narrative and/or security measures for the justice of securitization (contrast with Roe, 2008b; Salter, 2011). With 'the audience' as a central element practically gone from my variant of securitization theory, some may question the validity of calling my proposed theory 'securitization' (impetus for this will no doubt be fuelled by the apparent meta-theoretical differences between securitization theory and the JWT). One reason why the development of new variants of securitization theory that challenge key aspects of the original Copenhagen School variant of the theory is permissible, is that securitization now refers to more than just this variant.[25] Not only does the sociological strand inspired by Thierry Balzacq's work (2011a, b; 2005) rival the Copenhagen School in detail and rigour, but also 'securitization' is now widely used – including in the relevant policy-making world – with people employing this term to describe the process whereby issues become (considered as) matters of security policy; sometimes seemingly without any knowledge of the theoretical debates on the matter going on in the background.[26] In other words it ought to be permissible

---

[25] As Balzacq, Léonard and Ruzicka (2015, 24) put it: 'there is no grand theory of securitization. Instead ... there are various theories of securitization. However, they all negotiate their position within a common framework of thinking'.

[26] As a case in point, see Amnesty International's 2017 report on 'Europe: Dangerously Disproportionate: The Ever-expanding national security state in Europe', www.amnesty.org/en/documents/euro1/5342/2017/en/.

to use the term 'securitization' without being constrained by observations, requirements and beliefs held by the term's originators, i.e. the Copenhagen School.

That said, another reason why I wish to retain the idea of securitization is that like many European scholars of security of my generation, my thinking about security has been influenced and shaped by the Copenhagen School more so than by anyone else. This manifests itself most in what is perhaps best described as a loss of naivety as regards the value of securitization[27] as well as the realization that securitization is possible across a whole spectrum of sectors, levels of analysis and referent objects of security. Notably, I focus on all actors, all types of threats (including those lacking intent) and all referent objects (including non-human species and ecosystems). This is inspired by the School's original securitization theory. Focusing on the social and political construction of security threats, this is the only security theory able to account for the fact that within different 'security sectors' we can locate different providers of security at different levels of analysis, different threat sources, and distinct referent objects of security (i.e. that which is to be defended) (cf. Balzacq, Léonard and Ruzicka, 2015: 3). Environmental security, for example, may refer to both the safeguarding of the nation state from an environmental threat, but also to safeguarding of the natural environment from human behaviour.

Securitization theory has proved extremely popular, and the idea of securitization uniquely captures the diversity of security as a social and political practice. For example, depending on who is to be secured, by whom and from what threats, securitization may involve the banning of industry to deal with an environmental threat; the forceful detention of people believed to be carriers of infectious disease; the building of physical borders (walls and fences), complete with shoot-on-site policies to stop any influx of illegal migrants;[28] the granting of additional powers to the police and military, as well as extensive surveillance to ward of a terrorist threat; and much else besides. Moreover, securitization has the advantage that it marks out security as a political practice, distinct from security as a valuable state of being, more

---

[27] Indeed I came to Security Studies through my interest in environmental problems and how these adversely affect human well-being. Upon first hearing of the concept of environmental security as an undergraduate at the University of Portsmouth, I considered this a promising solution. It was only later that I realized that not all approaches to environmental security aim to save the natural environment for the benefit for human beings (Floyd, 2013b), and hence the realization that a belief in the intrinsic value of environmental security is naive.

[28] India's Border and Security Force operates a shoot-to-kill policy at its border with Bangladesh in order to 'decrease illegal migration, smuggling and terrorism' (Hussain, 2009).

clearly than any other security theory (Herington, 2012), and it is this understanding of security I am interested in for the purposes of JST. In short, the use
of the label securitization is also a way of acknowledging my intellectual debt
to the Copenhagen School.

The just war tradition, and as we shall see specifically the revisionist
school of thought, which differs from traditional versions by – among
other things – questioning the moral standing of states (Lazar, 2017) is of
crucial importance for JST.[29] Its general principles form a useful point of
entry into the uncharted territory of just securitization. Notably I devise
each criterion of JST by reflecting on the relevance of principles informing the justice of war for just securitization, including just cause, right
intention, macro-proportionality, legitimate authority, reasonable chance
of success, last resort, discrimination and micro-proportionality. I argue
that not all of these are relevant for the justice of securitization, and devise
corresponding criteria only where relevance can be established. It should
be noted in this context that while it is this book's purpose to devise a list
of criteria specifying the justice of securitization and desecuritization,
much more can be said on each criterion (including the ones excluded)
than I can offer here. Many of the issues tackled here across a finite
number of pages refer back to vast debates in philosophy. The issue of
macro-proportionality in war and self-defence, for example, has dominated
some philosophers' entire careers and – if my own experiences with
proportionality are anything to go on – quite possibly has broken some
scholars' spirits. All this is not to say that my criteria are not conclusive,
only that we must realize that a project such as the one attempted here is
necessarily limited by time and space constraints, and that much more
can be said on all parts of this study.

The development of each substantive criterion is not completed by putting
forward normative arguments specifying criteria and the form they ought to
take. Instead, normative arguments are supplemented by analytical arguments
(defining key concepts, such as objective existential threats, threat types and
the meaning of desecuritization). Importantly I do not develop the criteria in
the context of one or two elaborate case studies (though the global war on
terror and global climate change are frequently evoked); instead, I use
a multitude of different illustrative examples, including factual and hypothetical ones, and cases involving state and non-state actors drawn from different
sectors of security. This approach is justified because the theory advanced is
a normative theory that builds a case for what ought ideally to be done; its

---

[29]   In spite of this I do not take sides on the justice of war siding with neither camp.

veracity and persuasiveness do not depend on whether a real-life example of just securitization or just desecuritization already exists.

Overall, the principles advanced as part of JST are supposed to be 'universal and exceptionless' (Nagel, 1997: 5). As such, my theory is at odds with much of Critical Security Studies, which rejects the possibility of universal ethics. In João Nunes's words: 'One of the achievements of the critical turn was the recognition that knowledge claims and conceptions of right and wrong are not founded upon self-evident truths or timeless notions of "the good". Rather, these claims are historically situated, resulting from the interplay of actors equipped with their interests and power capabilities' (2016: 91). The debate between moral universalism and relativism is a long-standing one that I am not equipped to settle.[30] What I can do, however, is to explain that my reasons for situating myself in the universalist camp are four-fold. First, there is the argument that moral relativism is self-contradictory. Following Thomas Nagel, on logical grounds it simply makes no sense to say "[e]verything is subjective" [read: relativist][31] for it would itself have to be either subjective or objective [read: universalist]. But it can't be objective, since in that case it would be false if true. And it can't be subjective, because then it would not rule out any objective claim, including the claim that it is objectively false' (Nagel, 1997: 15).

Second, I reject relativism because not only is it much easier to insist that universal principles do not exist than to show what they actually are, but also, because deconstruction without an attempt towards reconstruction (i.e. saying what ought to be the case) is simply not action-guiding. And (as James Griffin tells us) 'Ethics should be concerned not just with identifying right and wrong, but also with realizing the right and preventing the wrong' (2008: 19).

Third, cultural relativism, which is to say 'the idea that conceptions of right and wrong differ from culture to culture' is dangerous and the respect of *all* other cultures is misplaced (Rachels, 1986: 617). While many in critical security studies consider tolerance of all other cultures a virtue, taken to its logical conclusion, cultural relativism does not allow us to condemn a society that is anti-Semitic, misogynistic or racist. Indeed, 'we would not even be able to say that a society tolerant of Jews is *better* than the anti-Semitic society, for that would imply some sort of transcultural standard of comparison' (ibid.: 619 emphasis in original).

---

[30] Perhaps no one is, but for an excellent attempt, see Thomas Nagel, *The Last Word* (Nagel, 1997).

[31] Nagel uses the term subjective for relative.

My fourth reason is that universalism is attainable. After all universalist ethics simply considers humans everywhere as equal and identifies those practices that either hinder or promote *'the welfare of the people affected by it'* (ibid.:26) (emphasis in original).

Having established that moral universalism is both preferable and possible, it is now time to consider the normative basis of just securitization theory. Given that I am writing about just securitization, readers might be tempted to think that I am invoking an account of justice, but this is not what I am doing. In line with most just war theories, just securitization is about how and when an action (i.e. securitization or war) is *justified*[32] or morally right. It generally does not work with or advance a theory of distributive justice which is about what people deserve and how goods should ideally be distributed.[33] Instead, the normative grounds I am appealing to are facts about objective human well-being, which is to say the condition whereby people are able to live minimally decent lives. There is of course disagreement on when this threshold is met and how we can measure, or ensure, it. As I explain in Chapter 4, I hold that objective human well-being pertains to the satisfaction of basic human needs. Following Len Doyal and Ian Gough's influential theory of human needs (1991), I hold that human beings are fundamentally social creatures who cannot live meaningfully as humans if they are unable to participate in social life. They are able to do this if the basic human needs of physical health and autonomy are met (see Chapter 4, sections 4.2 and 4.3). This theory informs my argument that – with the exception of human beings, who I take to be intrinsically valuable – putative referent objects of securitization are morally justifiable and hence eligible for self-securitization or for defensive assistance by third parties only if they facilitate human well-being by satisfying basic human needs. My choice of needs over the vastly more popular (human) rights results in part from the fact that I consider entities (e.g. non-human species) that cannot be examined in terms of whether they satisfy human rights (cf. Chapter 4, section 4.2). However, I also hold that the mere existence of rights does not easily allow us to measure the actual level of objective well-being in a given social and political order. Yet, the idea of basic needs is compatible with rights; not only do many needs inform theories of human rights (Miller, 2007: chapter 7), but also some needs are met/protected through rights legislation (Gasper, 2007; Doyal and Gough, 1991: 224).

---

[32] As Chris Brown pointed out during a workshop on this book when in draft form, the just war theory is really misnamed and ought to be called justified war theory.

[33] There are notable exceptions to this, including Fabre (2012).

RESEARCH QUESTIONS AND SUGGESTED CRITERIA OF JUST SECURITIZATION AND JUST DESECURITIZATION

For ease of understanding it might be helpful to break down the objectives of just securitization theory into a number of guiding research questions. Three such questions present themselves:

1. When, if ever, may an issue be securitized?
2. If an issue is securitized, how should the securitization be conducted?
3. If an issue is securitized, how and when must the securitization be reversed?

In line with these three research questions, just securitization theory breaks down into three parts. First, the just initiation of securitization is concerned with the move from politicization to securitization, and as such is informed by *jus ad bellum* criteria which cover 'the transition from a state of peace to a state of war' (Rodin, 2008b: 54). Second is just conduct in securitization which is concerned with the nature of the security measures used and the obligations and rights of executors of securitization. As such it is informed by the *jus in bello* 'which specifies the rights and obligations of actors once in the state of war' (ibid.).[34] Third is the just termination of securitization, which is broadly informed by the idea of just peace which is commonly referred to as *jus post bellum*. Strictly speaking, however, *jus post bellum* specifies 'the rights and obligations of actors once they have transitioned from a state of war into a state of peace', whereas *jus terminatio*[35] 'governs the transition itself' (ibid.). In other words, the relationship between *jus terminatio* and *jus post bellum* follows the logic of the separation between *jus ad bellum* and *jus in bello*. Just termination of securitization is informed by both *jus terminatio* and *jus post bellum* considerations.

The criteria of just securitization theory developed over the course of this book are as set out in the sections below.

Just Initiation of Securitization

1. There must be an objective existential threat to a referent object, that is to say a danger that – with a sufficiently high probability –

---

[34] To be sure, the divide between just initiation of securitization and just conduct during securitization is necessary because, especially in state-led-securitizations, we deal with distinct groups of people in the different realms (cf. Lazar, 2017: 10).

[35] Also known as *jus ex bello* (Moellendorf, 2008).

threatens the survival or the essential character/properties of either a political or social order, an ecosystem, a non-human species, or individuals.

2. Referent objects are entitled to defend themselves or are eligible for defensive assistance if they are morally justifiable. Referent objects are morally justifiable if they meet basic human needs, defined here as necessary components of human well-being. Political and social orders need to satisfy a minimum level of basic human needs of people part of or contained within that order and they must respect the human needs of outsiders. Ecosystems and non-human species, in turn, need to make a contribution to the human needs of a sufficiently large group of people. Human beings are justifiable referent objects by virtue of being intrinsically valuable; all other referent objects therefore have instrumental value derived from the needs of human beings.

Together, criteria 1 and 2 are jointly and sufficiently necessary for *just cause* for just securitization. Although vital, the just cause alone does not determine the just initiation of securitization, it also includes the following criteria.

3. The right intention for securitization is the just cause. Securitizing actors must be sincere in their intention to protect the referent object they themselves identified and declared.
4. The expected good gained from securitization must be greater than the expected harm from securitization; where the only relevant good is the good specified in the just cause.
5. Securitization must have a reasonable chance of success, whereby the chances of achieving the just cause must be judged greater than those of alternatives to securitizing.

Just Conduct in Securitization

6. The security measures used must be appropriate and should aim to only address the objective existential threat that occasions securitization.
7. The security measures used must be judged effective in dealing with the threat. They should aim to cause, or risk, the least amount of overall harm possible; and do less harm to the referent object than would otherwise be caused if securitization was abandoned.
8. Executors of securitization must respect a limited number of relevant human rights in the execution of securitization.

Just Termination of Securitization

9. Desecuritization of just securitization must occur when the initial and related new objective existential threats have been neutralized, whereas desecuritization of unjust securitization must occur immediately.
10. Desecuritization should ideally be publically declared, and corresponding security language and security measures should be terminated with immediate effect.
11. In order to avoid renewed and/or reactionary securitization, desecuritizing actors should undertake context-specific restorative measures.

It is important to notice that although I argue that the possibility of desecuritization depends on the pre-existence of securitization (see Aradau, 2004); the justice of desecuritization is *not* pre-determined by the justice of securitization, neither is the justice of securitization determined by the justice of desecuritization. In other words, an unjust desecuritization does not render a just securitization unjust, and vice versa. This is discussed at some lengths in Chapter 7. I mention it here because although just desecuritization is strictly speaking part of just securitization theory (in the same way as just peace is part of just war theory), they lead to different kinds of prescriptions. Hence unlike just securitization, just desecuritization is about what desecuritizing actors are *required* to do, not about what such actors are *permitted* to do. This shift from moral permissibility to what is morally required, from a concern with just securitization to a concern with just desecuritization, is a function of the fact that while securitization is not morally required in the presence of a just cause,[36] but depending on circumstances is morally permissible, desecuritization is morally required in the absence of a just cause for securitization, because no securitization is morally permissible in the absence of a just cause.

In the context of the relationship between securitization and desecuritization one further point needs to be made here. Many just war scholars, following St Augustine, hold that the object of a just war (or even war in general) is peace (May, 2012). Given the influence and inspiration the just war tradition has on JST it is easy to assume that the object of just securitization is the achievement of a just and lasting desecuritized state of affairs. For the following reasons I do not hold that view. First, I do not think that the object of (even a just) war is peace. Instead the object of a just war is to right a wrong and to

---

[36] I am not suggesting that this is never the case, only that JST is interested in the broader permissibly of just securitization, not in the comparatively smaller number of cases when securitization is obligatory.

emerge victorious over an unjust threat. Peace – at least the negative kind – goes hand in hand with victory, but it is not the war's aim.

Second, although the relationship between securitization and desecuritization is underdeveloped in the relevant literature, it seems to me that for Wæver at least, the object of securitization is not desecuritization,[37] but rather the object of securitization is to address a threat (Wæver, 1997: 223).[38] The achievement of desecuritization in turn is the objective of the securitization scholar who has a negative view of securitization, and struggles against securitization (ibid.: 221–224).[39]

Third, to say that the objective of a just war is a just peace strikes me as a normative ideal that serves to heighten the importance of the *jus post bellum* vis-à-vis the other branches of the JWT. We can see this clearly in Larry May's (2012) work on justice after war. He argues: 'If the object of war is a just and lasting peace, then all of Just War considerations should be aimed at this goal, and the branch of the Just War tradition that specifically governs the end of war, *jus post bellum*, should be given *more* attention, if not pride of place, as opposed to being neglected as is often the case' (May, 2012: 13; first emphasis in the original, second emphasis added). To my mind the view that the objective of JWT traditionally and war in general – which May strongly believes – is peace, is incompatible with his finding that *jus post bellum* has been systematically neglected by just war theorists. In short, I believe that May would like for the JWT to be about a just peace but he acknowledges that this is not currently the case.

It is of course possible to share May's ambition for JST and to formulate a theory of just securitization so that it has a desecuritized state of affairs in which all relevant parties enjoy sufficient security (as a state of being) as its aim. However, I think that doing this runs the risk of locking one into a position whereby only just securitizing actors could justly undo securitization. But as we shall see in Chapter 7, other actors too can have a duty to undo securitization, while – so I argue – just desecuritization can follow from unjust securitization, and vice versa. More worryingly still, such a formulation ignores that securitization and desecuritization are related but distinct processes with distinct outcomes. The objective of just securitization is to justly address a threat (and given that, the threshold for just securitization is set high: its principal purpose is to reduce the occurrence and destructiveness of

---

[37] Indeed if this was the aim I should think that fewer people would object to securitization.
[38] More sinister reasons abound, including in-securitization (Bigo, 2008: 124–125).
[39] As we shall see (Chapter 1, section 1.4.1), desecuritization has two meanings; beyond this normative strategy it also refers to simply a political process that follows after securitization ends.

securitization); while the object of just desecuritization is to establish a lasting and stable desecuritized state of affairs. Note, however, that while I identify different objectives for just securitization and just desecuritization, my theory identifies a point in time when just securitization is no longer permissible and desecuritization must ensue. In short, we may say that while desecuritization (the process) is not the aim of just securitization, just securitization itself is restricted by the necessity of desecuritization.

OVERVIEW OF ALL CHAPTERS

The argument presented is advanced in seven chapters. Chapter 1 surveys the existing literature on ethics and security, whereby security is understood as either a valuable 'state of being' or as a social and political 'practice' (Herington, 2012: 8 and 2015). I argue that while valuable work has been done on the ethics of security as a state of being, from the point of view of International Relations (IR) theory, what is ultimately more interesting are the moral issues/problems that are generated because of the logic inherent to security as a particular kind of social and political practice, including – in democratic states – the legitimacy to go beyond the democratic process. I demonstrate that while critical security studies has done much to make us receptive to the logic of how security is practised, thinking about the morality of security and what it ideally ought to look like has been systematically shut down by the widespread normative preference for desecuritization. I demonstrate that desecuritization is not a sufficient normative strategy because it rests on a number of flawed assumptions; most importantly perhaps it works only when the possibility of objective existential threats is ignored. I go on to examine a number of works that have pointed to the idea of positive securitization, in the sense of at least the possibility of morally justifiable security policies, where scholars variously consider the consequences of the implementation of such policies, the number and variety of actors involved, or states' obligations towards their citizens. That this type of work remains in an infancy highlights the need for a systematic normative theory of securitization of the kind proposed in this book.

Chapter 2 is this book's conceptual framework chapter. In it I set out the meaning of securitization I work with in developing just securitization theory. As mentioned already, the precise meaning of securitization does more than make a comparison with war, and hence just war theory, either possible or impossible; it also influences the nature of the theory of just securitization advanced. As part of this chapter I engage extensively with securitization studies and argue for a variant of securitization that takes a particular stance on three contested themes: 1) the point when securitization is satisfied (i.e. does it have to involve simply performative/securitizing language or also policy action); 2) the nature and significance of the audience; and 3) the role and nature of the exception, and whether or not securitization needs to involve exceptional measures.

Having thus clarified what I take to be the meaning of securitization, I move on to the method by which principles of just securitization and desecuritization are being derived. I begin by discussing the possibility of deriving such principles via a communicative process commonly known as discourse ethics. In part because discourse ethics is one theory that tells us how actors ought to engage in decision-making, but little about what the decision should be, this approach is rejected in favour of one that borrows heavily from moral, analytical and political philosophy's dominant method: wide reflective equilibrium. I then demonstrate how the just war tradition and in particular its revisionist strand, serves as an entry point into the uncharted territory of just securitization as it allows us to reflect on the kind of considerations relevant for a corresponding theory. The conclusion considers two prominent objections to ethics and force that could also be made of the ideal of just securitization: the pacifist and realist objections.

Chapter 3 is the first of five substantive chapters developing just securitization theory. Following the leading just war scholar Jeff McMahan, I argue that the just cause is the most important principle determining the justice of securitization. Just cause in turn consists of two separate though related principles: the just reason for securitization and the justice of the referent object of securitization (the latter is the subject of Chapter 4). I argue that only objective existential threats permit an exceptional policy response, i.e. securitization. For the purposes of analytical clarity I go on to differentiate between agent-intended, agent-lacking and agent-caused objective existential threats, and demonstrate how users of just securitization theory need to go about verifying the existence of such threats. Part of the discussion of the just reason for securitization is dedicated to the issue of future objective existential threats, that is to say, to the question of whether pre-emptive securitization is morally permissible.

Chapter 4 deals with the just referent object of securitization. I argue that regardless of the magnitude and reality of a threat, not each and every possible referent object is entitled to defend itself or is eligible for defensive assistance, but that both are tied to the referent object's moral justifiability. I argue further that moral justifiability stems from the referent object's record/ability in meeting basic human needs, which I define as necessary components of human well-being. In other words, just referent objects form alongside the just reason the second part of the just cause for securitization. In the remainder of the chapter I discuss what human needs are, how they can be measured and what tying moral justifiability to the satisfaction of basic human needs means for an array of possible referent objects, including social and political orders, ecosystems and non-human species, and human beings.

Chapter 5 specifies three additional criteria for the just initiation of securitization. The first is the sincerity of intention criterion, which holds that the right intention for securitization is the just cause. A further criterion is concerned with the circumstances when it is proportionate to initiate securitization. A third criterion requires that securitizing actors take the decision to securitize in light of the probable consequences securitization might have, specifically in terms of the chances of securitization achieving the just cause. The chapter continues by discussing why legitimate authority and last resort, both of which feature prominently in theories of just war, are not separate criteria in JST.

Chapter 6 is concerned with the just conduct in securitization. I argue that three criteria are relevant here. The first is concerned with the fact that security measures need to be targeted to the threat. Specifically I hold that securitization is morally permissible only in the presence of the just cause; this means that securitizations that utilize security measures that are not appropriate because they exceed the threat and target another issue than that specified in the just cause are not justified. The second principle is concerned with reducing harm. I argue that security measures must aim to cause, or risk the least amount of overall harm possible and do less harm to those it seeks to protect than there would be if securitization was abandoned. A final criterion is concerned with the just conduct of executors of securitization and security professionals; I discuss why just securitization cannot be conducted with total disregard for a number of core human rights, including the right to life, freedom from torture and arbitrary detention.

This chapter then turns to two prominent issues that need addressing in the context of just conduct in securitization. The first is the problem of dirty hands, or in other words the question of whether there are situations in which executors of securitization and security professionals can act unjustly without securitization becoming unjust. A second issue concerns the moral culpability of agents that are party to an unjust securitization. Especially pressing here is the question whether executors of securitization in state-led securitizations, or in other words, security professionals (i.e. police, border guards, immigration officials etc.) who are party to an unjust securitization whose lack of justice arises from just initiation to securitization violations, but not because of anything the security professionals in question have done, are morally culpable for

simply doing their job. The conclusion summarizes the findings and addresses
two outstanding questions. First, whether all criteria have to be met for
securitization to be morally permissible? And secondly, whether
a securitization and a counter-securitization (i.e. a securitization launched
by 'A' in direct response to a securitization by 'B') can both be justified at the
same time.

Chapter 7 is about the just termination of securitization, or in other words,
just desecuritization. The chapter begins with an analysis of the meaning of
desecuritization. I argue that desecuritization, like securitization, ought to be
understood as a sum of actions (i.e. a process); not (as it so often is) as an
outcome. Understood in this way, desecuritization becomes a time-limited
event that can be identified, studied and morally evaluated. The chapter goes
on to discuss who can meaningfully 'unmake' securitization, and then turns to
the tricky issue of who is morally required to do so. I suggest that desecuritizing
actors fall into one of five distinct categories, depending on who they are and
on whether securitization was just or unjust. My argument for the moral
obligation to desecuritize draws heavily on David Miller's (2007) concept of
remedial responsibility and his connection theory; as such, it includes the
possibility of actors being responsible for desecuritization without having been
involved in securitization.

The chapter continues by specifying three criteria that govern the
justice of desecuritization. The first pertains to the last point in time
when desecuritization must be terminated. The second specifies what
actors must undo as part of desecuritization. A third criterion holds that
desecuritizing actors must put in place positive and constructive measures
primarily aimed at restoring relations adversely affected by securitization
or that were the object of securitization. In short, I argue that just
desecuritizing actors must do more than simply to undo securitization if
security (as a state of being) is wanted.

The chapter concludes by discussing whether different types of desecuritizing actors have in comparable situations distinct levels of duty when it comes
to putting in place restorative measures.

Chapters 3 to 7 build logically on each other, but each is written in such
a way that it can be read and understood in isolation; however, the reader is
well advised to read Chapter 2 in order to fully understand the concept of
securitization employed. All chapters are written so that they can be understood by scholars and practitioners of security alike. Where practitioners are
concerned, the criteria serve as guides specifying what matters for the justice of
securitization. Where scholars are concerned the same criteria serve to guide
them in evaluating the justice of past and present securitizations; where

appropriate individual sections tell scholars how to go about testing for the satisfaction of any given criterion.

By way of a conclusion I summarize the argument. I go on to stress that my version of just securitization theory should be seen as the first but definitely not the last word on this topic. I argue that much more work on the moral permissibility of securitization is important, not only because inevitable gaps remain in the account present here, but also only once the concept of just securitization is widely known can the general public use it to hold security practitioners to more ethical security practice, thus fulfilling just securitization's emancipatory potential. I also argue that the theory proposed in this book needs to be supplemented by theories specifying when securitization is morally required or obligatory.

1

Ethics and the Study of Security

1.1 INTRODUCTION

Security Studies is perhaps the most popular subfield of the academic discipline of International Relations (IR). Since the end of the Cold War, it includes – especially in Europe (Wæver and Buzan, 2007) – beyond national security and the military sector, a wide range of security actors (global actors, non-state actors), referent objects of security (including individuals and the biosphere) across a wide range of issues (including terrorism, global environmental change, migration, infectious disease and many more). The latter is often called critical security studies. Interest in security has been helped by a number of pivotal world events, most notably the rise of identity/societal security in the wake of the break-up of the Soviet Union; the events and aftermath of the terrorist attacks of 9/11; the general acceptance of anthropogenic climate change; the financial crisis and the rise of economic insecurity; cyber insecurity manifest in the Wikileaks and the NSA/GCHQ spy scandals; and, more recently, the European refugee/migrant crisis.

While 20 years ago few textbooks and introductions to the subject of Security Studies (critical or otherwise) existed (notable exceptions are Lipschutz, 1995; Terriff et al., 1999; Croft and Terriff, 2000), today students are spoilt for choice. In addition to general introductions (among the best are Williams ed., 2013 and 2008; Buzan and Hansen, 2009; Peoples and Vaughan-Williams, 2015 and 2010; Collins ed., 2016, 2012 and 2007; Fierke, 2007), there are volumes concerned with method in (critical) Security Studies (Salter and Mutlu, 2013; Shepherd ed., 2013; Aradau et al., 2014); huge handbooks on the subject exist (Dunn Cavelty and Mauer, 2010; Burgess, 2010), at least one dictionary of international security (Robinson, 2008) and even introductions to specialized sub-fields within Security Studies, including on gender (Detraz, 2012), environmental and climate security (Floyd and Matthew, 2013); and health (Elbe, 2010). All of these books have in common that they are exceptionally weak on ethics, which is to say they are not concerned with the right and/or the good and connections between these two cornerstones of ethical theorizing (Rawls, 1971: 24) and security. Works on International Relations Theory more generally which include security fare no better. A leading handbook of International Relations, *The Oxford Handbook of International Relations*, edited by Christian Reus-Smit and Duncan Snidal, pays attention to ethics in an unprecedented fashion by tracing the ethics of all major theoretical perspectives to IR, yet security does not occupy a separate chapter in the volume, not to mention its ethics. All of this suggests that as it stands, ethics in Security Studies is *not* a major area of research. This is astonishing because even if – like me – one does *not* subscribe to the Critical Theorist's view that because the researcher's own politics are inescapable, all research is effectively normative,[1] what use is research in IR unless it is action-guiding?[2] Moreover, even if researchers don't own up to it, most researchers make value judgements in their work, often because they aim to influence the actions of practitioners of security. To stand the test of time and be responsible, however, ethical statements have to be properly grounded, something that is amiss not only in Security Studies but also in International Relations at large. The English School for example often operates with a common-sense ethics that often relies on empirical-pragmatic knowledge and is not properly grounded in moral-philosophical knowledge (cf. Cochran, 2008).

In order to be action-guiding, researchers need to be able to make informed claims about either the value of security (including about how (sufficient levels) of security as a state of being can be achieved and what these are), or about the circumstances under which an issue can be moved out of ordinary politics and treated in security mode, and what considerations ought to inform the security measures adopted in securitization.

Increasingly, scholars are recognizing the inescapability and centrality of ethics in Security Studies, and articles embracing ethics and security and/or securitization have been published in major journals of the sub-field (see, for

---

[1] I have elsewhere argued that it is a mistake to label all theory as normative simply because value-neutrality in choosing a research topic is hard to achieve. Instead, 'Normative theory (which includes but is not exhausted by Critical Theory) engages in arguments regarding what should and should not be the case in the world and what we should and should not do within it, while analytical theory engages in arguments regarding what does exist and why it exists, and what people do and why they do it' (Floyd, 2013a; 28).

[2] Richard North (2016: 76) argues convincingly that: 'a theory counts as action guiding when its principles are capable of delivering coherent, consistent, and determinate verdicts on the justness or unjustness of actions, and citizens have the ability to use those principles to derive prescriptions for action that they are able to comply with.'

example, Huysmans, 1998, 2002, 2006; Aradau, 2004; Booth, 1991, 2007; Floyd, 2007a, 2011a, 2017; Browning and McDonald, 2013; Roe 2008a, 2012; Hoogensen-Gjørv, 2012; Burke, 2013; Hynek and Chandler, 2013). More recently, an edited volume on the subject bringing some of these writers together has emerged (Nyman and Burke, 2016).

The task of this introductory chapter is to chart the existing literature on ethics in critical security studies and – where relevant – related subjects. The purpose of this is to point to existing gaps in the literature; gaps which Just Securitization Theory competently fills.

I proceed by separating the existing literature into approaches concerned with the ethics of security (i.e. reflections on the concept of security itself, including what it *should* be), and normative reflections on the practice and value of security as a special kind of politics (we might call this the ethics of securitization, whereby securitization designates security as a process, or a special kind of action as distinct from security as a state of being). It is argued that while perhaps more work has been done on the ethics of security, works on the normative value or disvalue of securitization have been disproportionally influential. Led by the Copenhagen School as the originators of securitization theory, the latter tend to take the form of explicit rejections of securitization complete with normatively driven arguments in favour of desecuritization (Wæver, 1997; Buzan et al., 1998; Huysmans, 2006). It is further argued that the impact of this work has been such that thinking in terms of 'positive', 'morally right' or 'just' securitization in the way proposed in this book is considered by many scholars unthinkable and even undesirable (e.g. Aradau, 2004; Neocleous, 2008; Bigo, 2008 for a different view see Wæver, 2011: 472–473). Only of late have a few authors been bucking this trend, with a number of preliminary works on 'positive securitization' and 'positive security'. While this work – alongside similar encouraging work on emergency politics in philosophy – shows that normative theory regarding security is important, we do not currently have a systematic normative theory of security that applies to all actors and threats across the entire range of security sectors. Taken together, this is the starting basis for JST.

1.2 SECURITY: A TWOFOLD DISTINCTION

A vital yet often overlooked distinction within security studies[3] is that between 'security as a state of being' (i.e. feeling or being secure) and security

---

[3]　Writers in other subfields are generally guilty of the same thing.

as 'a set of social or political practices ' (i.e. specific policies and measures). Jonathan Herington, from whose work I borrow this distinction argues: 'In some instances we [read: scholars of security], use "secure" as an adjective – as in "X is secure from Y", or "Y is secure for X" – to describe a characteristic of X's circumstances. In other instances, we use the word as a verb – as in "X will secure Z from Y" – to describe an action or process undertaken by X' (Herington, 2012: 11). This is a simple but vital observation; if this distinction is observed it renders certain debates and arguments within security studies pointless or groundless. For example, Ken Booth of the Aberystwyth School has repeatedly criticized the Copenhagen School for their rudimentary version of 'security as survival', when true security is 'survival-plus' whereby the plus is 'freedom from life-determining threats, and therefore space to make choices' (Booth, 2007: 102, 164) and security is thus clearly valuable. What Booth fails to see, however, is that the Copenhagen School's claim that 'security is about survival' is not about the circumstances under which a referent object is actually safe from harm (secure), or in other words about the condition of being secure. What the Copenhagen School mean to say when they link security to survival is that to qualify for an emergency response (i.e. securitization), an issue needs to be perceived, and represented, as *existentially* threatening to a referent object by both the securitizing actor and the audience (see Floyd, 2013a: 23–24). In short, they are exclusively concerned with security as – in Herington's terms – a set of social and political practices, not as a state of being.

To take a second example, consider Mark Neocleous' dismissal of the Aberystwyth School's notion that security and emancipation are two sides of the same coin as 'about as mistaken as one can possibility be about security [which] is in fact far closer to classical liberalism . . . security and oppression are the two sides of the same coin' (2008: 5). I would argue, however, that by and large Neocleous fails to adequately differentiate between our two readings of security, his own critique of security as oppression is course primarily concerned with the role security measures play in state power and the political technology of government, not with security as a state of being.

To avoid the same pitfall I separate the literature on the ethics of security into on the one hand those concerned with security as a valuable state of being, and those concerned with the ethics of security as a practice on the other.

1.3 THE ETHICS OF SECURITY AS A STATE OF BEING

The majority of works in critical security studies that are concerned with ethics are likely to focus on security as a valuable state of being. Writers taking this line tend to start from the observation that traditional state-led security measures fail to provide security for individual persons, indeed that 'true' security is about more than the absence of military conflict and pertains also to freedom from want and/or to the presence of valuable functionings. These writers do not tend to spent much time on either teasing out why security is valuable and/or desirable vis-à-vis other concepts (e.g. justice, fairness or equality); instead they readily start from the assumption that security as a state of being is valuable, followed by explications of what security means for individuals and – though usually less well developed – how it can be achieved. This way of thinking and arguing is paradigmatic of works by the extended Aberystwyth School[4] around Ken Booth as well as human security scholars. In a series of articles and books, Booth has repeatedly argued that an interdependent world that is structured by inter alia capitalism, nationalism, statism and patriarchy leads to nothing but inequality, poverty, environmental degradation and religious fundamentalism, and that in such a world *no one* has true security as a state of being (Booth, 2007). The pathway to security is to free people from the belief that these man-made structures are beneficial to them, to lift up the proverbial wool pulled over their eyes. Borrowing from Frankfurt School Critical Theory, which inspires much of his thinking, Booth calls this process emancipation, and declares security and emancipation are 'two sides of the same coin' (Booth, 1991: 319).[5] All the same, one problem with Booth writing is that the relationship between 'world security' as a good, or a value (Booth, 2007) and security as a set of social and political practice is unclear. In particular it is not clear whether the latter could ever be used to render people secure (Peoples, 2011; Browning and McDonald, 2013).

The assumption that individuals are the ultimate referent objects of security is shared also by human security scholars, many of whom believe that security is and should be about more than freedom from fear and also about freedom from want (for a different view see for example MacFarlane and Foong Khong, 2006). Human security emerged in the policymaking world and subsequently transpired into academia, where it proved a popular alternative to mainstream state-centric security policy. The standard definition of human security remains the one put forward in the United Nations Development Report

---

[4] By 'extended', I mean the original Aberystwyth School, namely Ken Booth, Richard Wyn Jones, and their extended circle including Paul Williams, Matt McDonald, Columba Peoples, João Nunes and Ali Bilgic, and perhaps also Anthony Burke.

[5] In his *Theory of World Security* Booth argues that security should be seen as a means and emancipation as an end. '[T]he practice of security (freeing people from the life-determining conditions of insecurity) seeks to promote emancipatory space (freedom from oppression, and so some opportunity to explore being human), while realising emancipation (becoming more fully human) is to practise security (not against other people but with them)' (2007: 256).

from 1994, which defines it as: 'first, safety from such chronic threats as hunger, disease and repression. And second, it means protection from sudden and hurtful disruptions in the patterns of daily lives' (UNDP, 1994: 23).[6]

After almost 20 years of popularity, of late a backlash against human security is becoming apparent. While lamentations over the concept's analytical utility have always been ripe (see *Security Dialogue*, 2004; Paris, 2001), the backlash is about human security as 'an externally imposed attempt to regulate and order the globe on behalf of hegemonic power' (Hynek and Chandler, 2011, 1; Duffield, 2012; Duffield and Waddell, 2006; Owens, 2012; various in Chandler and Hynek, 2011; for a compelling rebuttal, see Newman, 2014). In other words, human security is now subject to the same old criticism of western imperialism that has been levelled at both human needs and human rights.

Human security and Booth's writings have led some authors to distinguish between negative and positive security – variously inspired by Berlin's work on liberty and/or Galtung's work on peace – whereby negative security is simply freedom from threat, whereas positive security is about infusing security with the capacity to enable desired states of affairs (McSweeney, 1999; Hoogensen and Vigeland Rottem, 2004; Roe, 2008a; Hoogensen Gjørv, 2012). Paul Roe, for instance writes that positive security is about 'the maintenance of just, core values' (Roe, 2008a: 793). 'Just' here is understood differently to how I understand it, and refers merely to the fact that core values are intersubjectively understood to matter and be valuable. Interestingly, while positive security is about the values that make individual societies secure, Roe actually aims to bridge the gap between security as a state of being and practice, when he argues that 'positive security of the international order can sometimes be only adequately addressed through the use of force' (ibid.: 794).

This argument is not too dissimilar to that advanced by English School solidarists who are great advocates of humanitarian intervention (Wheeler, 2000). Indeed, because the English School (or international society research)

---

[6] Given the argument advanced in Chapter 4, it is worthwhile pointing out that while the label 'human security' might have emerged in the early 1990s, the ideas behind it date back to the 1960s and 1970s and the development of the Physical Quality of Life Index, which aimed to measure the quality of life in individual countries and was known as Needs Theory (Gasper, 2007: 50). Their initial success was short-lived, with the approach attacked as reminiscent of western imperialism. Following a period of relative silence on human needs, the idea has experienced a revival since the end of the Cold War, if – as Gasper puts it – under the 'more appealing and more ethically charged labels ... "human development" and "human security" ... and then connected to the powerfully focusing and motivating theme of human rights' (Gasper, 2007: 51–52). As a practical example, consider that all eight United Nations Millennium Development Goals give priority to basic needs fulfilment.

is not usually linked to security (for an exception see Buzan, 2015, 2010: 34–44),[7] it is not often acknowledged that at heart, international society research is concerned with security as a state of being. According to Bull 'a *society of states* (or international society) exists when a group of states, conscious of certain common interests and common values, form a society in the sense that they conceive themselves to be bound by a common set of rules in their relations with one another, and share in the working of common institutions' (Bull, 2002: 13). And further, all international societies are informed by three elementary and primary *goals*. A closer look at these goals reveals that at least two of the three are about generating security. Thus,

> first, all societies seek to ensure that life will be in some measure *secure* against violence resulting in death or bodily harm. Second, all societies seek to ensure that promises, once made, will be kept, or that agreements, once undertaken, will be carried out. Third, all societies pursue the goal of ensuring that the possession of things will remain *stable* to some degree, and will not be subject to challenges that are constant and without limit. (Bull, 2002: 4; my emphases)

And while English School scholars do not use the language of positive and negative security, the solidarist pluralist debate so central to this school can be understood in just this way. Thus, while all English School theorists agree that institutions are what has tamed the sovereigns, or in other words, reduced the danger and unpredictability of anarchy (Holsti, 2004: 207, 317–318), a bone of contention for solidarists and pluralists is whether or not the institutions of international society should be such that they give way to either positive or negative security (cf. Bellamy and McDonald, 2004: 311; see also Wheeler, 2000; Jackson, 2000).

Like Roe, Matt McDonald also uses the term 'core values' in his analysis of the meaning of security. He argues that because security is socially constructed, it follows that it means different things for different people in distinct places, and that it therefore makes no sense to reject all conceptions of security as negative as some scholars do (see below). For him, positive security is generated by 'emancipatory security discourse' that is 'radically cosmopolitan, ... oriented to the concerns of the most vulnerable, ... concerned with overturning structures of oppression or exclusion; and that the means envisaged to achieve these goals will not serve to deprive others of them'

---

[7] And also Booth and Wheeler's work on the security dilemma, which recognizes that the English School's 'mitigator logic' of the security paradox is about the possibility and reality of the creation of security as a state of being in international society (cf. Booth and Wheeler, 2013: 144).

(McDonald, 2012: 52). McDonald thus also aims to close the gap between security as state of being and security practice.

More recently, Anthony Burke has advanced the idea of 'security cosmopolitanism'. Like Booth, he is concerned with real insecurity of real people, as well as with the role states and some security measures (e.g. intervention) play in causing widespread insecurity. Echoing the work of Simon Dalby (2009), he argues that states 'will not be able to contain their communities within a prophylactic cocoon of safety in an insecure world; to secure nations, states must ensure the world is secured' (Burke, 2013: 19). In short, his is an argument that stresses interdependence on two levels. First, he diagnoses that insecurity knows no borders, and that no one is truly secure as long as security of self is gained at the inordinate expense of others. Second, interdependence can and must be utilized towards achieving true security, and the worth of states, international organizations and indeed all activities must be assessed in accordance with whether or not they contribute to security as a state of being everywhere. To this end he develops three principles for how security actors ought to behave in order to maximize security as a state of being for everyone. It is important to realize, however, that by security actors he does not mean securitizing actors as defined in this book (i.e. actors who make and implement security policy, or are in a position of power over relevant (governmental) agencies and security professionals who in turn execute security measures), but instead actors 'whose decisions and operations will affect the security of others' (Burke, 2013: 26, fn. 2). With security defined very broadly as the absence of 'serious threats to human survival [and] flourishing' and the presence of 'peace at the global level' (ibid.: 13), this means practically every action is a security action, while almost every political actor is a security actor. While there is nothing necessarily wrong with Burke's assessment, there is the question of value added. What is the advantage of seeing every relationship and dynamic in world politics through the security lens? While security has perhaps more mobilization power than other concepts, it is doubtful that a claim for an equal *right to security* by each and every person (Burke et al., 2014: 131) is likely to mean that states and organizations will behave better, not even if the obligation to do so could be established (cf. Cooper and Turner, 2013: 38).

Moreover security cosmopolitanism runs the risk of oversimplifying very complex relationships and dynamics. It is not clear, for example, how this work compares to that of other cosmopolitan thinkers who do not use the term security in their work but – if one accepts Burke's definition of security – still write about security. I am thinking here in particular about the work by Simon Caney on global distributive justice (2005a) and his more recent work on climate ethics (2005b, 2006, 2010a, 2010b) and also of the work by Thomas Pogge on global poverty (2008), and of Gillian Brock's work on global justice (2009). And while all of these thinkers may agree on the basic cosmopolitan principle that human beings are members of a single global community, how this can be achieved, what matters and exactly what obligations follow diverge widely, making cosmopolitanism not an approach, but its own distinct field of enquiry.

It should be noted here that Burke is not the first to speak of a right to security. In 2007 Oxford law professor Sandra Fredman conceptualized the right to security as a positive right whereby the focus was not only on duties of restraint on the state (which would render it a negative right), but on the duty to protect. Specifically she argued that such a right to security 'includes the duty to provide for basic needs of individuals' (Fredman, 2007: 308). Much of Fredman's argument has been dismissed by Liora Lazarus' contribution to the same edited book that also featured Fredman's piece. In much the same way as I question security cosmopolitanism's value added, Lazerus argues that most things captured as part of a right to security are already part of other, well-established rights. Second-generation human rights, for example, already deal with welfare issues and meeting human needs. Thus 'if "the right to security" means anything at all, it must protect against something not already and explicitly captured by these fundamental and self-standing rights' (Lazarus, 2007: 327). While a narrowly conceived right to security might work, Lazarus worries that a right to security might well be treated as a meta-right, legalizing and legitimizing the sidestepping of other rights (to liberty and privacy for example) in the name of security with a net loss of human dignity. Judging by Edward Snowden's revelations, we can see that Lazarus' worries were very much warranted, in so far as the spy agencies sacrificed a number of established rights in the name of security.

Long before Fredman and Lazarus, there was Henry Shue's work on basic rights. Shue holds that security is a precondition for the enjoyment of human rights: '[n]o one can fully enjoy any right that is supposedly protected by society if someone can credibly threaten him or her with murder, rape, beating, etc.' (Shue, 1980: 21). Lest one should think that his view of security as physical security is rather narrow, he goes on to argue that '[d]eficiencies in the means of subsistence can be just as fatal, incapacitating, or painful as violations of physical security. The resulting damage or death can at least as decisively prevent the enjoyment of any right as can the effects of security violations' (Shue, 1980: 24). In short, Shue's account comes very close to many other versions of human security.

More recently, in the context of the war on terror and resulting impinge-ments on civil liberties, Jeremy Waldron has engaged with the meaning of security. He laments the lack of interest in security by political philosophers, yet he himself displays an astounding lack of interest in decades of scholarship in Security Studies, insofar as he cites almost no one who is known for their work on security (the exception is Arnold Wolfers). Consequently while Waldron's definition is well thought out, his observation that security is more than being merely safe from physical attack (he calls this the 'pure safety conception'), but that being secure pertains to the situation when individuals are at liberty to pursue 'modes of living' (which are similar to Sen's function-ings), which is to say all those things people value doing and being (Waldron, 2010: 116–23), is hardly novel. Thus there seems to be some general consensus that a person is secure not simply when he is free from physical dangers (fear) but when – in addition – some level of freedom from want is achieved. Although this work is valuable in and of itself, unless it is linked to security as a set of social and political practices (for example by providing clues for what we ought to protect, and how we should ideally do that) it does not touch on those things that are uniquely problematic to security practice from a moral point of view, including for example, the legitimacy to go beyond the demo-cratic process or the usage of extraordinary/exceptional measures.

1.4 THE ETHICS OF SECURITY AS A SET OF SOCIAL AND POLITICAL PRACTICES

1.4.1 *Desecuritization*

The vast majority of works that contemplate ethics and security understood as a set of social and political practices in security studies take the form of a rejection of securitization in favour of ordinary politics, by which most people have in mind democratic politics. Ole Wæver is one of the pioneers of this, and his preference for desecuritization over securitization has shaped the ethical thinking of the majority of securitization scholars lastingly. Wæver invented the concept of desecuritization in parallel to securitization. In large part, desecuritization simply describes the process[8] when formerly securitized issues are returned into the realm of ordinary politics (note of course that securitization theory works with the idea that security takes the form of

---

[8] There is some confusion over the meaning of desecuritization in the School's writings. In addition to describing a process, desecuritization can also refer to a (valuable) outcome (cf. Chapter 7).

exceptional politics; see Chapter 2, section 2.2.3) (Huysmans, 2006, 126). From the multitude of remarks by Wæver and other securitization scholars about Wæver's work, it is clear that besides offering an analytical tool, desecuritization has a second function in securitization theory – an explicit normative one (Hansen, 2012).[9] Specifically it designates that the right action for practitioners of security to take is to resist the pull of security framing as simply social and political constructions, while at the same time postulating democratic politics (according to the Copenhagen School, the antonym of security politics) as the good (see Roe, 2012: 260). In addition desecuritization serves as a normative outlet for securitization scholars, who are simultaneously bound to securitization theory's functional distinction, which separates security scholars from actors during securitization analysis (Buzan et al., 1998: 33–34), but also (because of the performative power of language) involuntarily complicit in securitization simply by conducting written or spoken securitization analysis (Huysmans, 2006; Taureck, 2006; Wæver, 1999). Indeed, Wæver recognized very early on that he has no influence over the usage and abuse of the theory of securitization; and desecuritization in its normative guise became his way to take responsibility for having unleashed securitization theory, and thus is intended to curtail the amount of securitizations and their expected negative consequences in the world (Floyd, 2010: 27).

Despite Wæver's commitment to desecuritization, however, both as an analytical category as well as a normative one, desecuritization remains under-developed in his and the wider Copenhagen School's writings. The person who has done the most work on desecuritization as a normative strategy is probably Jef Huysmans, whose interest in desecuritization started from a deep-seated unease with both the securitization of migration in the European Union and the securitization scholar's involuntary co-constitution of security framing simply by writing about an issue (Huysmans, 2006). Very much in the tradition of the Copenhagen School, Huysmans starts from the assumption that there are no objective existential threats (or perhaps rather that we have no means to identify them), and like many within Foucault-inspired International Political Sociology, he views securitization as the production of existential insecurity (Floyd and Croft, 2011: 159). In the absence of objective existential threats, securitization becomes an ineffective strategy, or in other words, a dangerous technology of the powerful. Huysmans argues that the

---

[9]   The only person I am aware of who rejects this claim is Jaap de Wilde, who in his review (2012) of my book *Security and the Environment*, fervently denied that the Copenhagen School has a normative commitment to desecuritization, suggesting perhaps that not all of its members are comfortable with this normative aspect of the theory.

securitization of migration results in an increase of illegal immigrants, as the bar for legality is set too high. Instead of reiterating the security framing of security professionals, security scholars perform desecuritization by 'ignoring or denying the security significance of the problem at hand, or, at least of asserting that security policy should not have priority and that security language should be played down. For security studies this implies that one gives up producing security knowledge in the area of migration and asylum' (Huysmans, 2006: 142). Desecuritization so conceived seeks to do more than to delegitimize security knowledge in the area of migration; it also seeks to unmake security policy as constitutive of political community in the way Carl Schmitt envisaged. The aim is that '[s]ecurity questions should only appear as problems similar to all problems a political community has to deal with. This means that fear of the enemy and of other objectifications of existential insecurity cannot define the essence of political practice. Political community and identity cannot be defined ultimately through the way it handles security questions.' (Huysmans, 2006: 143). While I agree with Huysmans' last point here, I also think that he, like other poststructuralists, over-interprets the role security plays in the formation of identity and the political (e.g. Campbell, 1998; Behnke, 2006, 1999: 13). Thus while distinct political communities might only be able to identify themselves through comparison with others; these others need not be understood in antagonistic terms (Berenskötter, 2007; Hansen, 2006; Floyd, 2010: 69). Indeed, this extreme way of thinking is perhaps only appropriate for security professionals.

Besides Huysmans, Claudia Aradau's work on the ethics of desecuritization has been influential. Like Huysmans, she is concerned with the exclusionary logic inherent to security, whereby one person's security always and necessarily comes at the expense of someone else's security, and the perceived impossibility of chosing which group of people should be protected from another group (Aradau, 2004: 399; see also den Boer and Kolthoff, 2010: 31–33). In more detail, she argues: 'Individual or human security cannot be the answer of emancipatory politics as this would trigger the question of whose individual security is supposed to be sacrificed. Who is to be made dangerous so that others be made secure? On which grounds can one privilege such a construction of security, the security of migrants over the security of racists, the security of HIV-positive people over those at risk of being infected' (Aradau, 2004: 399)? Her solution is an appeal to emancipation; however, her notion of emancipation bears little or no resemblance to that advanced by the Aberystwyth School. Indeed, Aradau argues that 'CSS [Critical Security Studies, i.e. the Aberystwyth School] have got their equation wrong as it is security that needs to be struggled against by appealing to the concept of emancipation, a concept informed by a logic *opposed* to the logic of security' (Aradau, 2004: 401, my emphasis). Instead, her idea of emancipation is drawn from the work of Étienne Balibar and Jacques Rancière and refers to 'democratic politics', and thus to equality, fairness, participation and accountability, and so is remarkably close to Wæver's idea of the outcome of desecuritization. Desecuritization as emancipation plays out similarly to Huysmans' strategy of desecuritization, however, unlike asking security scholars to deny and ignore security framing; the onus is placed on members of existing political communities to unmake the identification of, for example, migrants as dangerous people (Aradau calls this 'dis-identification') and to see them simply as workers and thus challenge state-led security practices (ibid.: 407).

The idea of desecuritization as a normative strategy has been influential in part because it can deal with the securitization theorist's normative dilemma of speaking and writing security (Huysmans, 2006), but also because it does not require proponents to spell out commitment to particular values in great detail. Few scholars influenced by continental political theory are happy to spell out what values should ideally inform political community in the way Huysmans and Aradau do, and many see virtue in simply resisting forms of power. Regardless of the level of commitment to one or other value, however, as an ethical strategy, desecuritization remains problematic. For one thing, it works only when the existence of objective existential threats is ignored. Securitization analysis deprives securitizing actors of the ability to 'hide behind the claim that anything in itself constitutes a security issue' (Buzan et al., 1998: 34). Consequently, if there is no security threat, then nothing needs to be securitized, making desecuritization the logical course of action. While I can accept that threats become security threats by virtue of social and political construction, some threats are real (i.e. objectively present) and existential regardless of whether or not anyone has even taken note of them (cf. Chapter 3, section 3.2.2). In Wæver, I appear to have an unlikely ally in this claim. He argues: 'Lots of real threats exist, but they do not come with the security label attached' (Wæver, 2011: 472). I will argue in more detail in the Chapter 3, not only that the justness of securitization rests in part on whether or not a security threat refers back to a real threat, but also that there are ways to ascertain whether a threat is real or merely perceived as real by the relevant securitizing actors. Taken together, this goes some way towards solving Aradau's perceived inability to decide who may, from a moral point of view, be secured from whom. Thus I argue that securitization is morally permissible only in the presence of an objective existential threat. I also argue – and this is developed in much detail in Chapter 4 – that not all possible referent objects of security are morally equal, but that the eligibility to self-defence or to defensive assistance rests with the moral value of the referent object (i.e. its justifiability). In short, I will demonstrate that it is possible to argue who is eligible to securitize against whom, and why. If I am correct, then desecuritization as a normative strategy simply does not deliver.

Despite these criticisms a commitment to desecuritization as emancipation is still laudable; after all it is a rejection of nihilism and portrays some recognition of the fact that certain things – human rights, democratic governance, equality and fairness – are universally valuable. As such, it is ultimately a more courageous endeavour than either the denial of universality coupled with the equation of emancipation as dangerous Western technique – which are themselves universalist truth claims – or adhering to the Nietzschean call to celebrate insecurity (Behnke, 1999: 24–25, see also Rengger, 2013: 27). It is possible to view this sort of deconstructive resistance as a normative standpoint in itself (see Browning and McDonald, 2013: 10), but in reality they offer very little that merits serious discussion. In the first instance, as the philosopher Thomas Nagel so lucidly shows, it is always easier to argue that universal principles do not exist than to painstakingly flesh-out what they are (Nagel, 1997: 27). Second, a call for the celebration of insecurity shows almost complete disregard for what Booth calls 'real people in real places' (2007: xii), or what Wheeler and Dunne call the 'security have-nots' (2004: 20), and demonstrates just how safe and secure those enjoying the privilege of Western-based academe really are.

This said, however, Neocleous' 'critique of security' and (with Rigakos) idea of 'anti-security' are especially insightful as regards the observation that equating emergency politics with a Schmittian state of exception ignores that the judiciary and the legislative are involved in these kinds of politics just as much as the executive (Neocleous, 2008: 71). Although Neocleous is right to point out that the portrayal of the law as 'an unqualified human good' (ibid.: 73) is questionable once we understand that the exception resides within the law, to me this simply does not add up to capitalist liberal states themselves being morally unjustifiable and/or to the law being beyond redemption. Instead, and although liberal states don't always get it right, on the whole it is a good thing that their security and emergency politics do not exclude the judiciary and the legislator in favour of an all-powerful executive. Consider, for example, that the United States Supreme Court ruled unlawful the part of the Military Commissions Act of 2006 § 7 that had stripped detainees of Guantanamo Bay of the constitutional habeas corpus (Dyzenhaus, 2010: 33). In my view, however, a more productive critique of security is one that is more constructive than resistance alone (see also Loader and Walker, 2007: 92). One way to do this is to think about the moral limitations on what securitizing actors and executors of securitization can do as part of securitization.

To summarize, I have argued in this subsection that many normative engagements with security as a set of social and political practices take the form of desecuritization. This can take many different forms, including a-security, emancipation, anti-security and resistance. Some of this work has been influential and on the whole Security Studies scholars writing about the ethics of security as a set of social and political practices are against securitization. Of late, however, there has been a small but important development within Security Studies and beyond, insofar as a number of constructive works on ethical/moral conduct regards security is emerging. These works come closest to what is attempted in this book; I will examine them in section 1.4.2.

1.4.2 *Positive Securitization, Positive Security and Civilized Security*

Stefan Elbe's 2006 article on 'Should HIV/AIDS be securitized?' was one of the first Security Studies papers to argue that the ethics of securitization are not as clear-cut as the Copenhagen School and other proponents of desecuritization maintain, suggesting instead that policymakers find themselves in an ethical dilemma over whether to securitize or not to securitize, while scholars are in the dilemma of whether or not to advocate securitization. The securitization of HIV/AIDS, for example, may generate 'vital economic, social, and political benefits for millions of affected people by raising awareness of the pandemic's debilitating global consequences and by bolstering resources for international AIDS initiatives' (Elbe, 2006: 120). At the same time, however, it may also 'push national and international responses to the disease away from civil society toward state institutions such as the military and the intelligence community with the power to override human rights and civil liberties'. This not only would work against the aim of many grass-root operations to normalize the HIV/AIDS threat, but also under the military the securitization of HIV/AIDS might mean nothing more than prioritized funding for AIDS for the armed forces (Elbe, 2006: 120). Elbe does not aim to pose a solution to this dilemma; indeed he does not think that whether or not any given securitization is right or wrong can be made *for* scholars and his aim is merely to show that security (securitization) scholars must face the ethical question whether or not to securitize (ibid.: 138). In his own words: 'In the end this choice about whether to endorse or reject securitization processes cannot be made *for* analysts and scholars; it must be made *by* them – independently and with respect to each particular securitization they encounter, as well as with the particular audiences they engage' (ibid.: 138 emphases in original). Yet none of this stops Elbe from telling scholars what they should bear in mind in order to minimize the risks of securitization of HIV/AIDs while keeping all the positives. After all, it appears that it is quite possible to say what positive securitization of HIV/AIDS should ideally look like.

In section 1.4.1, by highlighting some of the conclusions of Roe and McDonald's work I have already suggested that strict divisions between works on security as a state of being and security as a set of social practices can disappear. Roe, for example, argues that even forceful defence of positive security may sometimes be necessary. Gunhild Hoogensen Gjørv's (2012) work on multi-actor security goes further than this. Like Roe, she taps into the negative and positive security distinction loosely borrowed from Berlin, but her aim is not to specify what values make for positive security, but to focus on the actors that can bring about positive security. 'Security is both about identifying the threats to those things we value, and the practices we use to protect them' (Hoogensen Gjørv, 2012: 844). Because traditional providers of security (e.g. the state and the military) are largely concerned with negative security, she argues for an opening-up of security to include, besides the state, non-governmental organizations, humanitarian actors, epistemic communities and even individuals, which all tend to address insecurity by non-violent means, demonstrating that security can be provided by other means. Unlike Booth, however, she does not dismiss the role of the state or even the military as providers of security, her point is rather that a multitude of actors is required to provide comprehensive security which includes both positive and negative security.

A more recent contribution to the positive/negative debate in critical security studies comes from Jonna Nyman. Informed by the belief that objective truth claims are both unattainable and undesirable, Nyman argues for a turn towards pragmatism in ethical thinking about security. She suggests that

> rather than imposing universal notions of 'positive', 'good' security or emancipation, we can look at how security works in practice and when *humans experience* it as a 'good' (and vice versa). As a result, rather than being crippled by divisive perspectives about the abstract potential of security to be 'good' or 'bad', we can move on to conduct empirical research and analyse how it works in practice, gaining practically useful knowledge about the value of security. (Nyman 2016a: 142 emphasis added)

There are at least two problems with this. First, it runs the risk of rendering the value of security an entirely subjective process, and as such can produce objectively unethical forms of security. Without doubt, many German neo-Nazis would 'feel' that the use of firearms at Germany's borders in order to keep at bay the flow of migrants[10] would increase their security. Second, Nyman's suggestions for how we need to judge the value of security reintroduces objectivism. Thus, from where else but an objective standpoint can we assess whether or not security produces 'sensible results' (ibid.: 141)?

As already mentioned, IR and security scholars are not the only ones interested in the ethics of security as a set of social and political practices. Criminologists and academics in public policy research interested in policing and/or intelligence are increasingly considering ethical conduct of security professionals in these professions. Noteworthy here in particular is Monica den Boer and Emile Kolthoff's edited book *Ethics and Security* (2010) that describes in some detail the ever-increasing ethical challenges for security professionals due to the expansion of security thinking into all areas. In the context of just securitization, it is further important to mention that some scholars of intelligence have discussed the implication of just war thinking for intelligence-gathering, and notably the permissibility of torture (see Posner, 2003; Mertens and Goodwin, 2007). Ross Bellaby (2012) has advanced a compelling initial attempt at formulating a set of principles for ethical intelligence-gathering all derived from the just war tradition, focusing on just cause, authority, intention, proportion, last resort and discrimination. Likewise, George M. Clifford (2017: 67) suggests a 'Just Counterterrorism Model for shaping and assessing counterterrorism strategy and tactics that are comprehensive, effective and ethical'.

Although philosophers tend to eschew, even dislike, the term securitization in favour of 'emergency politics', in my view it is here where some of the best work on morality and security can be found. Noteworthy in particular is Tom Sorell's 'sober Hobbesian' approach to emergencies. True to Hobbes, Sorell sees the provision of security as the primary objective of state formation. This means that in the event of grave public emergencies, states are not only permitted to use extraordinary measures, they may even be required to do so (Sorell, 2013: 88, 195). For Sorell, emergency measures amount to states

> being abnormally empowered ... so that they can concentrate decision-making in an executive body, bypass Parliamentary debate and criticism for at least short periods, and suspend or limit civil rights. It means also that some actions done to protect life can be dirty-handed, sometimes by infringing (non-basic) rights. (Sorell, 2013: 88)

---

[10] While this would have been an outlandish example only a few years ago, the suggestion to use firearms against migrants (including women and children) was made (in early 2016) by, inter alia, Dr Frauke Petry, then party chief of the Alternative for Germany (AfD).

State power is, however, not boundless, and Sorell reasons that states have to pass Hobbes' test of the good law and demonstrate that invocation of emergency measures in any given situation is 'necessary for the sake of preventing loss of life or other significant harm' (ibid.: 156). Moreover, in a sober Hobbesian approach, security policy has to be consented to by the general public in normal times (ibid.: 51), yet at the same time – in making those policies – individuals are asked to focus on the common denominator of an interest in avoiding premature death and injury and thus detach themselves from less important values (those associated with cultural identity) that could give way to fundamentalism and conflict (ibid.: 53).

While Sorell does not mention the just war tradition anywhere, it is clear that he endorses a number of ideas that are compatible with that tradition. For example, he holds that only legitimate governments have a right to self-defence, whereby legitimacy is tied to the actual provision of security for its citizens (ibid.: 146); he insists that 'nothing less than a threat to the lives and limbs of the many' constitutes an adequate threshold for a public emergency (later on he uses the term security threat) (ibid.: 147) (together these could be called the just cause for the use of emergency measures). And he also evokes the idea of legitimate authority by arguing that 'extraordinary measures can meet these conditions by being time-limited and by needing authorization when they are used from those who are familiar with the legal norms for normal times and capable of judging the relative claims of security and liberty in particular cases' (ibid.: 156). Lest there be any doubt, Sorell does not aim to devise a list of universal principles in the style of just war theory for emergencies (and consequently the principles he puts forward remain underdeveloped), their creeping presence in a book that is essentially a comment on the right balance between liberty and security (ibid.: 88) suggest that the development of such principles is the way forward for moral thinking on security as a set of social and politics practices.

Sorrel's approach shares some insights with Nomi Claire Lazar's *States of Emergency in Liberal Democracy* (2009), at least in so far as Lazar is also keen to tell the reader that only some kinds of states are morally justifiable and may utilize emergency politics. In particular Lazar seeks to defend liberal democracies as 'justly ordered', which in turn is the basis 'for existential ethics'. Although I am sympathetic to Lazar's argument as a whole, and mature liberal democracies qualify as just referent objects of securitization in accordance with the terms set out in Chapter 4 of this book, Lazar's own argument for why liberal democracies are just is not entirely convincing. Instead of arguing the case, she merely asserts that 'the values and principles embodied . . . by liberal democratic states are ones we hold desirable. Many of these core values are related to rights and their enforcement ... All of this enables the individual and collective pursuit of arts, sciences, commerce, and the protection and development of culture, environment, heritage and so on' (Lazar, 2013: 93–94) without any further examination of how rights contribute to well-being or indeed why any of the pursuits/things mentioned are valuable.

Although Lazar is keen to stress complexity, context and the importance of deliberation in emergency politics, it is interesting that she too ends by suggesting that her analysis gives way to at least the idea that principles could make emergency politics safer (for example, by developing principles for seeking to guide the actions of particular security institutions (ibid.: 157)).

The development of principles governing emergency politics is of course at the heart idea of a theory of just securitization, and closer to my way of thinking still than either Sorell or Lazar is the work of law scholar Lucia Zedner,[11] who argues that: 'In order to delve beneath the rhetoric [of security] a profitable test is to ask whether a proposal made in the name of security addresses a real threat; whether it does so effectively; whether it is right to take the measures proposed; and whether those who resort to the rhetoric of security do so honestly or in order to achieve some other end entirely' (Zedner, 2009: 47). Although she expands on this test somewhat towards the end of the same book when she argues how principles inherent to criminal justice – e.g. minimalism, social defence, equality before the law – could serve to developing principles for 'just security' in this work, these principles remain tentative (ibid.: 167–174). And while she later develops aspects of this thinking more fully,[12] she starts from the premise that 'security threats' are to be reduced to 'crime prevention' (ibid.: 167) and as such only tackles one aspect of the complex subject of security, and certainly not security in international relations.

[11] Security is now increasingly popular in criminology. This is so for two reasons: 1) crime is often regarded as a security threat, and 2) counter-terrorism and other security measures (above all else the Control Order) often undermine due process and other stables of Western criminal justice systems (Zedner, 2009: 132; Sarat, 2009; Ericson, 2007: 24).

[12] Indeed, more recently – together with Andrew Ashworth – Zedner has critically examined the law in England and Wales on preventive criminal law, which they claim is increasingly used in order to provide public protection and security in emergency and non-emergency situations. In particular they focus on the prevention of physical harm to individuals by depriving others (including criminals, the mentally ill and terrorists) of liberty. In *Preventive Justice* (Ashworth and Zedner, 2014) the two law scholars concern themselves with the justification and proper limits of crime prevention, and set out principles that should govern the use of coercive criminal justice in specific situations (they also call this criminalization). Important for the justifiability of principles of preventive justice is that they – as much as possible – correspond to due process and other staples of the English criminal justice system.

Finally, some of Zedner's thinking appears to build on Ian Loader and Neil Walker's attempt to civilize security practice. In a 2007 book called *Civilizing Security*, they advance the refreshing argument that 'security is a valuable public good, a constitutive ingredient of the good society, and that the democratic state has a necessary and virtuous role to play in the production of this good' (Loader and Walker, 2007: 7). Loader and Walker do recognize, however, that security is often abused, that states unnecessarily meddle and are prone to paternalistic and even idiotic behaviour. In order to civilize often uncivil security practice, they propose that four elements are crucial: resource, recognition, rights and reasons. Much simplified, all of these effectively aim at democratizing security practice in the sense of allowing for widespread deliberation on the methods used in, for example, policing, enabling greater levels of scrutiny and legitimacy. Although this approach is quite different from what I am about to propose, I share completely their belief in the possibility of, and commitment to, civilizing security practice.

1.5 CONCLUSION

In this chapter I have sought to examine established connections between ethics and security. I have demonstrated that although some work on ethics and security is being done, as yet we do not have a systematic normative theory of security. Following Jonathan Herington (2015) I argued that 'security' is best understood as either 'a state of being' or as 'a set of social and political practices'. Contributions to the first strand include the wider Aberystwyth School's work on security and emancipation as well as the human security approach. While this work has been important, 'security as a state of being' is not always easily distinguishable from many other definitions of human well-being. Moreover, given that well-being is mostly a question of social policy and/or development economics, and not of security provision, some of the key ethical controversies associated with addressing an issue in security mode simply do not arise. It is not surprising then that although the majority of works on ethics and security pertain to the understanding of security as a valuable state of being, in Security Studies, works on ethics and security understood as a set of social and political practices have been disproportionally influential. In particular, normatively motivated calls for desecuritization (i.e. the unmaking of security rhetoric and measures because of their anticipated negative consequences and the return to valued democracy/normal politics) have set the agenda for much of critical security studies, which tends to be sceptical of securitization.

Latterly the joint observations that 1) securitization has more varied consequences than scholars of the Copenhagen School, who are in favour of desecuritization, have suggested, and 2) that securitization is a powerful concept that gets things done in world politics, has led some scholars to advance tentative arguments in favour of (some forms of) securitization. For the most part, work on this issue in Security Studies is in its infancy, and some of the most promising work on the issue is done in philosophy instead. Sorell's sober Hobbesian approach, for example, takes emergency politics right back to basics, by arguing – true to Hobbes – that states are duty-bound to protect their citizens from grave emergencies, thus reopening the debate – almost closed, in critical security studies – on real/objective existential threats. While Sorell advances a number of valid observations of what constitutes morally right security policy and practice, his observations do not serve as a systematic normative framework for analysis of security understood as political practice in international relations. More generally, his book rather points to some of the issues that ought to be considered by state actors in charge of security policies. By contrast, JST offers a systematic normative theory of security that, inter alia, enables scholars from all relevant disciplines to evaluate any given securitization, past and present.

Unlike some of the normative theories examined in this chapter, JST is not state-centric in its outlook, or else tied to specific security threats. Instead – informed by original securitization theory – it covers the entire spectrum of securitizations possible, including state and non-state actors, traditional and non-traditional threats, as well as all possible referent objects of security. In a word: 'the securitization perspective has the advantage of looking at issue specific exceptionalism' (Wæver, 2004: 109 fn. 11).

Moreover, its simple and straightforward format (i.e. a list of principles) should mean that that it can be easily operationalized, which is to say that it has the potential to guide practitioners of security in decision-making. What is more, JST is the only normative security theory in existence that simultaneously combines the idea that security is a social and political construction, with objective criteria (including the requirement of an objective existential threat as the just cause for securitization). As such, it enables scholars to make meaningful interventions into the ethics of security, while simultaneously recognizing that it is ultimately actors other than the scholar, who orchestrate successful security policy.

Framework: the Meaning of Securitization and the Method of JST

2.1 INTRODUCTION

As we shall see throughout this book, Just Securitization Theory (JST) has a number of distinctive features – inter alia, a focus on objective existential threats, a focus on human needs for determining the referent object's moral value as a precondition for the right to self-defence or for moral eligibility to being defended (i.e. its justifiability), and a concern with moral permissibility of securitization only. Before I can turn to the substantive features of the theory, it will be necessary to examine the precise meaning of securitization I use, in part because the meaning of securitization influences the nature of the criteria of just securitization. This chapter serves this purpose.

As the name suggests, Just Securitization Theory is intellectually indebted to the Copenhagen School's securitization theory. According to the Copenhagen School, 'successful'[1] securitization breaks down into three steps: 1) a securitizing move, which sees a suitably powerful actor identifying a point of no return (i.e. unless we deal with this problem now, it will be too late); 2) audience acceptance (even if, as might sometimes be the case, that acceptance is effectively coerced); and 3) use of extraordinary measures to deal with the problem (Buzan et al., 1998: 26). A lack of clarity as well as a number of contradictions in the early writings by the Copenhagen School and/or Wæver, who is the originator of the theory, coupled with the intuitive appeal of securitization theory (given its ability to seemingly explain any incident of security policy (implemented or otherwise)) have resulted in a veritable cottage industry of 'securitization studies' in which nearly every aspect of the theory has been overturned, revised, simplified and made more complex (see,

---

[1] Unless otherwise stated, by successful securitization I do not mean a securitization which succeeds in averting a (perceived) threat, but rather a securitization that involves a number of steps referring to a complete process of securitization.

for example, Balzacq, 2011c). Much of the discussion has focused on three areas: 1) what decides the success of securitization, or put differently, what satisfies the condition of securitization and thus distinguishes it from politicization, 2) the role and nature of the audience, and 3) the definition and significance of the exception for securitization. In this chapter I take a position on all three of these areas, in the process putting forward my own interpretation of securitization.

The second part of the chapter explains the method used in deriving principles of just securitization. I begin by discussing the possibility of deriving principles in line with discourse ethics. I argue that while this approach would be more in line with the Copenhagen School's manner, I dismiss it in favour of an approach to method following wide reflective equilibrium, the predominant method in political, analytical and moral philosophy.

I conclude the analysis offered in this chapter by considering some of the most prominent objections against the combination of ethics and exceptional politics, notably the pacifist and the realist objections, respectively.

2.2 THE MEANING OF SECURITIZATION IN JUST SECURITIZATION THEORY

2.2.1 *Speech Act or Policy Change?*

One contentious issue among securitization scholars is whether audience acceptance or policy change (e.g. emergency measures) should be the measure of securitization's success. Scholars for whom the main attraction of securitization theory is that security problems are established intersubjectively hold that audience acceptance is decisive of the success of securitization. Juha Vuori (2011b), for example, differentiates between the securitization speech act and security policy action, whereby the former is the intersubjective understanding about a security threat achieved between the securitizing actor and a relevant audience, while policy change is the measure adopted to deal with that threat. For Vuori, the two can, but need not coexist. In his words: 'security measures and their public securitization are theoretically and at times even practically separate from each other, and thereby the application of security practices cannot be a sufficient criterion for the success of securitization' (2011b: 132–133 FN98). By contrast many – to use Vuori's term – 'empirical appliers' of securitization theory insist that unless successful securitization includes (extraordinary) countermeasures, the concept is too vague and non-specific to be useful (ibid.: 165). Nicole Jackson, for example, argues that: 'Once an issue is rhetorically adopted, it must affect the development of policy for it to be effective in practice. Otherwise, the activities have only been rhetorically securitized with no practical result' (2006: 313; see also Mely Cabrella et al., 2006). In a sense, however, these disagreements are unnecessary, as the Copenhagen School accounts for both types of securitization. They argue:

> Securitization is not fulfilled only by the breaking of rules (which can take many forms) nor solely by existential threats (which can lead to nothing) but by cases of existential threats that legitimize the breaking of rules. *Still*, we have a problem of size and significance. Many actions can take this form on a small scale … [a] *successful* securitization thus has three components (or steps): existential threats, emergency action, and effects on interunit relations by breaking free of rules. (Buzan et al., 1998: 25–26; emphases added)

In other words, the Copenhagen School accepts that many issues are in language elevated to security threats and as such 'accepted' by relevant audiences (we may say securitization is present), but that only those securitizations that result in emergency action and the breaking free of rules (at this point, we may say securitization succeeds/is satisfied) are distinct from politicization and consequently of interest for security scholars (see also Wæver, 2011: 473; Collins, 2005; Corry, 2012: 5).[2] Although the distinction between securitization 'existing' and 'succeeding' is not generally recognized in securitization studies (a notable exception is Collins, 2005), many securitization scholars appear to agree with it. Tellingly many of those who have sought to refine what precisely constitutes emergency action/security measures and, to that effect, put forward their own definitions also hold steadfast to the idea of the audience (e.g. Léonard and Kaunert, 2011; Salter, 2008). The influential 'sociological strand' of securitization research which emphasizes 'symbolic interactionism [and] Bourdieu's contribution to the symbolic uses of language' (Balzacq, 2010: 63), and which posits itself as an alternative to the Copenhagen School's 'philosophical approach', for example, insists that while a focus on the intersubjective threat construction in securitization must be retained: '[the] audience can only be one element of a larger theoretical pattern in securitization studies, one which draws its importance in relation to others' (Balzacq, 2011b: 8).

---

[2]   This is of course a crude measure, as clearly simply framing issues in the language of security can have harmful consequences. For example, they can 'insecuritize' or alienate groups of people; they can even create suspect communities (see Floyd, 2017).

2.2.2 *The Audience*

The audience is one of the biggest areas for theoretical innovation in securitization studies. This is the case because in the Copenhagen School's writings, the audience is left largely under-theorized, yet at the same time fulfils a pivotal role, serving to legitimize securitization through acceptance of the securitizing move (Olesker, 2018). Interestingly many scholars identify more than one relevant audience in securitization. Paul Roe, for example, has argued that different audiences provide distinct support in one and the same process of securitization. Thus with reference to the British government's decision to invade Iraq in 2003, he argues that the general public (one audience) provided moral support for this decision, while Parliament (a second audience) provided formal support by passing relevant legislation (Roe, 2008b). Similarly, following Kingdon's 'three streams model' of public policy change, Léonard and Kaunert (2011, 75) configure 'the audience as actually comprising different audiences, which are characterised by different logics of persuasion'. While Salter (2008), in the context of Canadian airport security after 9/11, identifies at least four distinct audiences situated within popular, elite, technocratic and scientific settings, respectively. Balzacq (2011b) does not settle on a specific number of audiences, but instead speaks of an 'empowering audience', which depending on circumstances and context, can be different entities. Regardless of the differences in interpretation of the audience, the vast majority of securitization scholars agree that the audience matters indeed is instrumental to securitization (Côté, 2016).

Importantly, this widespread consensus must also mean that the majority of securitization scholars reject the Copenhagen School's suggestion that securitization operates like an illocutionary speech act whereby saying security is doing security, because the logic of illocution denies the audience a meaningful role (Balzacq, 2005; Stritzel, 2007). And indeed many 'second-generation' securitization scholars seem to concur with Balzacq's (2011b: 5) suggestion that the Copenhagen School confuses the illocutionary speech act (in Habermas's terms, 'to act *in* saying something') with the perlocutionary one (in Habermas's terms, 'to bring about something *through* acting in saying something'), because only the logic of perlocution takes account of an audience to the degree stressed by the Copenhagen School. In Balzacq's (2011b: 5–6) terms: 'in any *intersubjective* process such as securitization, the purpose is to prompt a significant response from the other (perlocutionary effect); unless this happens there is no securitization.'

Bringing together what I have said so far, we can say that there is widespread consensus among securitization scholars that securitization is not an illocutionary speech act, but that there is no consensus on whether the success of securitization is decided by the intersubjective threat construction between a securitizing actor and a relevant audience or by policy change. This means that if one wishes to advance a variant of securitization in line with the suggestion that the success of securitization is determined by policy change as I do here, one needs to explain why the audience should not be seen as pivotal to the success of securitization. This is precisely what I set out to do in the following. We shall see that doing this also affirms the view that the speech act element in securitization is indeed illocutionary.

I share the Copenhagen School's assumption that all manner of actors can utilize the language of security (Buzan et al., 1998: 25), most likely because they would like to see an issue at the top of the policymaking agenda, often with the intention that something is done about it. While there is logically no limit on the number and nature of actors who can utter security speech acts, I hold that only those actors who utter a speech act and either act on it, or are powerful enough to instruct[3] others to act on it, are meaningfully called *securitizing actors*. This is important because, as we will see, this conceptual definition limits what securitizing actors do with securitizing language while it also pinpoints the audience as a clearly defined category. Importantly, when our concern is with bona fide securitizing actors only, we can ignore those 'securitizing actors' who aim to convince audiences to take action on the threat.[4] Instead, by using securitizing language (i.e. in uttering securitizing moves) bona fide securitizing actors – as once elaborated by Wæver – do one of the following: they issue a warning to whoever is at the source of the threat and/ or they promise protection to a given referent object (Wæver, 1989: 42–43).[5] Conceived as such, we can see that the widely held view that would-be

---

[3]   By 'instruct', here I seek to capture the fact that securitizing actors have power over agents I call here executors of securitization (for example, the executive branch of government over the police and border guards).

[4]   This has been suggested, for example by Vuori (2011b: 198) who opens up a wealth of possible types of securitizing moves. As I have argued elsewhere (Floyd, 2017), it does not make sense to call all persons speaking about security securitizing actors, especially when securitization is defined by security action. Neither does it make sense to refer to all forms of speaking security as securitizing moves. Instead, I have suggested that when people speak security with a view to getting others (usually more powerful entities/actors) to securitize, we should speak instead of *securitizing requests*. Securitizing moves in turn are speech acts uttered by would-be securitizing actors and constitute an advance towards securitization proper.

[5]   In more detail, Wæver argued: 'What is the illocutionary act in relation to security? It is to define the particular case as one belonging to a specific category ("security") where the state tends to use all available means to combat it. It is partly a *threat* but also a kind of *promise* since more is staked on the particular issue' (1989: 42; my emphases). The question here is who are the threat (we may say warning) and promise levelled against, or better addressed to?

securitizing actors utter securitizing moves because they seek legitimation for subsequent action from putative audiences makes little sense. Instead, securitizing speech acts are self-executing statements[6] that serve to highlight the would-be securitizing actors' position on, or recognition of, a threat; to be valid they do not *require* acceptance by relevant audiences.

In my variant of securitization theory the speech act element is then clearly illocutionary. As indeed it is and remains for Wæver, who recently argued:

> [...] Searle waters out Austin's speech act theory when he (as most other mainstream philosophers and linguists) re-creates a divide within speech act theory between language and action. The radical potential of Austin's theory is lost when these traditionalists separate everything social from the illocutionary, and de facto reduces the illocutionary act to *communication*, and thus – against Austin's original intent – removes the possibility that speech can really be action. (Wæver, 2015: 123 emphasis in original)

With the securitizing speech act defined as either a warning or a promise, it also becomes clear who the audience actually is. Thus, in line with the philosophy of language, we can say that the audience of speech acts, securitizing or otherwise, is simply the *addressee of the speech act*.[7] If then the securitizing move is understood as: 1) a warning, and/or 2) a promise for protection, and if we accept that the audience of the securitizing move is none other than those who the speech act is directed to, then we get up to two distinct audiences as addressees for securitizing moves by securitizing actors in one instance of securitization: 1) the agent(s) at the source of the threat[8] where warnings are concerned, and/or 2) the referent object in need of protection.[9]

---

[6] I am indebted to Jonathan Herington for this formulation.

[7] Indeed to my mind those securitization scholars who envisage proactive roles for the audience confuse the audience with the completely underdeveloped category of functional actors, which the Copenhagen School describes as 'actors who affect the dynamics of a sector. Without being the referent object or the actor calling for security on behalf of a referent object, this is an actor who significantly influences decisions in the field' (Buzan et al., 1998: 36).

[8] The agent at the source of the threat is either 1) the 'aggressor' for agent-intended threats, or 2) the agent or agents causing a threat in agent-caused but intent lacking threats. See Chapter 3 sections 3.3–3.6 for these distinctions.

[9] I concede that, in addition to agents at the source of the threat (see below), warnings uttered by executives of liberal democratic states could also be addressed to the legislative branch and the judiciary in order for them to grant the use of extraordinary measures, thus generating a possible third audience as addressees of securitizing moves (see, for example, Roe, 2008b). This seems to chime with Wæver's later assertion that 'the audience is those who have to be convinced in order for the securitising move to be successful' (2003: 11). And sure enough, this is how the relationship between securitizing move and audience has been interpreted by many scholars (Roe, 2008b). Three things can be said against this. First, theorizing securitization with

With a notable exception (see below, n. 46) both of these audiences can, at least in theory, co-produce the illocutionary effect.

Following the philosopher of language, Marina Sbisá, Wæver holds that: '[…] Austin's theory of speech acts entails that the illocutionary effect ("done in saying") is co-produced by the audience in a more extensive sense than pure uptake, and the status transformation entailed in, for example, securitization is a redefinition of the rights and responsibilities of actors, not just a form of communication […]' (ibid., 122). However, while the audience may influence securitization, it is incorrect to hold that 'status transformation' *depends* on audience acceptance. To demonstrate why this is the case, I will now discuss a range of scenarios that show the relationship between the securitizing move, audience acceptance and the success of securitization (summarized in Figure 2.1).

As far as securitizing moves as warnings (that is, 'I/we are warning you that unless you stop what you are doing there will be serious consequences') are concerned, the first scenario shows that the relationship between audience acceptance and the 'success' of securitization is the inverse of what is generally assumed in securitization studies. Thus here, if the agent at the source of the threat accepts the speech act and acts or changes his or her behaviour in response to the speech act (the perlocutionary effect), then there is no need for the would-be securitizing actor to act on the warning, because the problem has gone away already. At this point the securitizing move was successful in the general sense of the word, but because nothing further needs to be done to

---

a view to the specifics of liberal democratic states detracts from the aim of having a general theory of securitization. Given, however, that some have tried to theorize this logic of an active audience more generally (Côté, 2016), this refutation has its challengers. My second riposte is this. Splitting the liberal state as securitizing actor into the various branches of government is not entirely convincing, because research has shown that in times of emergency, all branches of government tend to pull together and everyone – at the point of the emergence of the threat – is already on the side of securitization (see Evangelista, 2008; de Londras, 2011; Neal, 2013; Jarvis and Legrad, 2016). In other words, no one needs to be convinced of the need for securitization. In times of emergency – differences of opinion – between the different branches of government will – if at all – pertain to the nature the security measures used (recall the above-cited example of the United States Supreme Court's ruling as unlawful § 7 of the Military Commissions Act of 2006), not to securitization as such. While this might suggest that securitization is just only when consensus between Balzacq's (2011b) 'empowering audience' and the securitizing actor on the nature of security measures has been achieved, this would amount simply to right procedure; by itself it does not tell us anything about whether the measures used are really justified (cf. Chapter 2, section 2.3). Third, Theresa May's decision not to allow parliament to vote on airstrikes in Syria in April 2018 confirms that even in liberal democracies, putative audiences may well be ignored, thus in the given case their consent was not sought in the legitimization of securitization.

The Morality of Security

1) WARNING → AGENT AT SOURCE OF THREAT → ACCEPT → PROBLEM SOLVED, NO
NEED TO ACT= SECURITIZATION FAILS

2) WARNING → AGENT AT SOURCE OF THREAT → REJECT → ACT ON WARNING =
SECURITIZATION

                                         ↘ DON'T/CAN'T ACT = SECURITIZATION FAILS

3) WARNING + ACTION = SECURITIZATION → AGENT AT SOURCE OF THREAT

                      ↗ ACT TO FULFIL PROMISE = SECURITIZATION
4) PROMISE → REFERENT → ACCEPT → ACT DOESN'T FULFIL PROMISE = SECURITIZATION
                      ↘DON'T ACT, BREAK PROMISE = SECURITIZATION FAILS

5) PROMISE → REFERENT → REJECT → DON'T ACT = SECURITIZATION FAILS
                      ↘ ACT, PATERNALISM = SECURITIZATION

                      ↗ ACT TO FULFIL PROMISE = SECURITIZATION
6) PROMISE → REFERENT → CAN'T RESPOND → ACT DOESN'T FULFIL PROMISE =
SECURITIZATION
                      ↘DON'T ACT, BREAK PROMISE = SECURITIZATION FAILS

FIGURE 2.1 Different Scenarios Depicting the Relationship Between Audience
Acceptance and Non-Acceptance and the 'Success' of Securitization

avert the threat, the security policy will not have to be implemented. In other words, securitization fails. Conversely, the second scenario shows that if the agent at the source of the threat rejects the warning, then securitization becomes likely, unless, that is, the would-be securitizing actor does not have the necessary capabilities to act, in which case securitization fails.

Scenario three captures the fact that more often than not, securitizing actors do substantiate warnings by actions. That is, the issue is already 'successfully' securitized *before* the agent at the source of the threat is approached. Actions may include the withdrawal of all diplomatic personnel, trade embargoes, sanctions, raising the issue with the UN Security Council, military drills, and similar activities.

Scenarios four and five depict the relationship between audience acceptance/rejection of the securitizing move as a promise for protection. Scenario four shows that audience acceptance, which would take the form of the relevant referent object accepting both (a) we are threatened and (b) we agree that you, meaning the would-be securitizing actor, are the right 'person' for the job, can have three different outcomes. First – straightforwardly – the securitizing actor true to his or her word keeps his or her promise and acts in order to safeguard the referent object. Second, the securitizing actor acts, but the action taken ends up benefiting the securitizing actor significantly more than the referent object. In this case securitization is 'successful', but the promise is not kept. Third, the actor decides not to act after all. Non-action is not necessarily driven by malign reasons. For example, in securitizations of agent-intended threats the would-be securitizing actor does not need to act on the promise for protection of the referent object if the aggressor has accepted the warning and stopped the behaviour that occasioned the warning. Either way, in this case securitization fails.

Scenario five shows what can happen if the referent object rejects the promise of protection, which could take one of two forms: either (a) we are perfectly safe and not threatened at all, or (b) we might be threatened but we don't think that you, the would-be securitizing actor, are the right 'person' to protect us. There are two possible outcomes. First, the would-be securitizing actor accepts the rejection and drops the issue. This might happen, for example, if the would-be securitizing actor is a democratically elected government that seeks re-election. Second, the securitizing actor ignores the referent object's rejection and acts anyway. The latter is commonly described by the label 'paternalism'. With the American invasion of Iraq in 2003 in mind, Jeff McMahan offers an example. He argues that 'there was no evidence that ordinary Iraqis wanted to be freed from the Ba'athist dictatorship by *the United States* – a country that a little more than a decade earlier, and under the leadership of the current president's father, had bombed their capital [and] decimated their civilian infrastructure [etc.]' (McMahan, 2005: 13).

Finally scenario six captures what happens when the referent object of securitization is a non-human (made) entity and thus incapable of accepting or rejecting the promise for protection.[10] This scenario is interesting because it shows that the inability of the audience to respond does not automatically lead to the failure of securitization instead the number of possible outcomes mirrors those displayed in scenario 4.

---

[10] It is to be expected that this kind of a securitization is largely hypothetical. This is so because most non-human entities are (by humans) valued in instrumental terms, for example, for the eco-system services it offers human beings. In other words, a securitization that seemingly seeks to preserve the biosphere does so for the benefit it has for human beings, not for the biosphere itself. It follows that there is a human referent object at the heart of most such securitizations. Nevertheless, for the sake of completeness, we need to list this possibility here.

These scenarios show that there simply is no *conclusive* relationship between audience acceptance and the 'success' of securitization; sometimes the audience's response to the securitizing move matters, sometimes it does not. This inconclusiveness means that a sanctioning audience *cannot* and thus *ought not* to play a decisive role in the 'existence' and consequently the 'success' of securitization, and a corresponding securitization theory. While this might seem to be against the spirit of securitization theory as an intersubjective process, it is to be remembered that intersubjectivity has come to the forefront in securitization theory only with SANFFA, with the audience not mentioned in any previous publications (Stritzel, 2007: 363).

In my judgement the rise of the audience has to be understood in light of the fact that the majority of securitization scholars – led by Wæver – object to securitization and advocate desecuritization as the preferred long-term option on normative grounds (cf. Chapter 1, section 1.4.1). Hence by insisting on audience acceptance, securitization scholars are seemingly able to further reduce the number of securitizations we can recognize in the world.[11] In other words, the idea of a sanctioning audience is stipulated by the Copenhagen School; it does not adequately capture how securitization actually plays out. It should be clear that JST reduces the need for the audience as a normative bulwark against securitization, precisely because it offers a theory whose main purpose is to reduce the number of securitizations in the world.

2.2.3 The Exception

With this we have arrived at the third contested issue in securitization studies I wish to discuss here, namely the question whether policy change (as argued above, the decisive component of successful securitization) needs to be exceptional and, if so, how the exception ought to be defined. The idea that securitization involves exceptional measures goes back to the Copenhagen School, whose understanding of the exception has been likened to Carl Schmitt's decisionist theory of sovereignty, whereby the sovereign decides not only on the exception, but also on what to do about it (Williams, 2003). Within securitization studies, a number of studies challenge these

---

[11] My assertion that the audience is for the Copenhagen School a normative-political category is actually confirmed by Wæver, when he criticizes the sociological strand of securitization theory made famous by Balzacq for finding that empirically, the audience may not matter in the success of securitization (Wæver, 2015: 124).

assumptions. For example, scholars sometimes labelled the 'Paris School' who focus on security professionals (e.g. police and border guards) have argued that securitization often consists of routine procedures (Bigo, 2002). Jef Huysmans (2011), as well as Louise Amoore and Marieke de Goede (2008), go further still and argue that securitization does not involve one specific speech act, but rather a multitude of small, almost automated events that in isolation 'look unspectacular, unexceptional, continuous and repetitive' (Huysmans, 2011: 376). Taken together, 'these little security nothings' (ibid.) add up to securitization.

Others have attacked the Copenhagen School's notion of the exception through work on specific security sectors. Julia Trombetta, for example, argues that in the environmental sector security practices are not defined by 'the logic of emergency and exception', but often by 'prevention, risk management and resilience' (2011: 143). Without the exception, however, serious questions arise about what separates securitization from politicization. It is also the case, however, that from the point of view of radical constructivism, which supposedly informs the logic of security in securitization theory (Buzan et al., 1998: 204), the meaning of securitization ought to lie not in a particular course of conduct, but rather in its usage (Ciută, 2009). Or to be more explicit, we can say that the meaning of securitization depends on whether securitizing actors consider what they are doing in response to a securitizing move as securitization (Floyd, 2016d, 2010). However, because practitioners will do different things as part of securitization, we are left with a very wide definition of securitization, i.e. securitization is ultimately 'what actors make of it' (Ciută, 2009: 302). A wide definition of securitization is advantageous for security studies, as it allows scholars to capture widely different dynamics, while securitization theory can then be used to explain lots of different phenomena in world politics. A wide definition is, however, a problem for a normative theory of security, as is Just Securitization Theory, because in order to say when something is right (morally justifiable), we need to know what that something is, and for that it has to be more concrete than simply what actors make of it.

While securitization takes many forms, it is also the case that not all of them throw up moral questions in quite the same way. For one thing, not all securitizations have the same degree of impact on the world and people around them. The Copenhagen School has long been aware of this; another reason, perhaps, why they have been interested only in securitizations that involve the breaking of established rules (Buzan et al., 1998: 26), or in other words, in securitizing moves that lead to the adoption of security measures, that are properly labelled as such only when they are exceptional. JST too is concerned *only* with securitization in its exceptional form;[12] however, it works with a different definition of the exception to the Schmittian logic of executive unilateralism (see Neal, 2010; Williams, 2003) advanced by the Copenhagen School, and instead takes inspiration from the work of a number of legal scholars as well as security scholars who in the context of the war on terror have done much research into the nature of what they refer to as emergency politics. Among other things these scholars contest the notion of the executive being above the law in emergency politics and argue instead that 'in order to overrule common law in a period of emergency, Parliament must pass new laws explicitly stating what the government can do. In this way, the rule of law is preserved, rather than suspended' (Sarat, 2010: 7; see also Feldman, 2010; Dyzenhaus, 2010; Zedner, 2009: 132; De Londras, 2011: 34 and chapter 4; Neal, 2013; Gearty, 2013; Honig, 2009: 67; Huysmans, 2014: 43). This certainly fits well with the statement on accountably of MI5 by its Director General, Andrew Parker. In his first interview since the GCHQ spy scandal, he argued:

> We [MI5] operate under law. I am in charge of our operations, but am accountable to the Home Secretary. She in turn is accountable to Parliament and the British People, responsibilities that I know she treats with the utmost seriousness. There is an important double-lock there: Ministers cannot direct MI5 operations, but equally I have to explain and answer for what we do. MI5 initiates operations, but conducting the most intrusive activity requires the signed authority and consent of the Secretary of State in every instance.
>
> Our accountability goes much further. MI5 is overseen independently by Parliament through the ISC, inspected by two independent Commissioners (usually senior Judges), held to account on any complaints from the public by a senior and independent Tribunal of judges and lawyers, and audited by the National Audit Office. We give evidence in court.
>
> Rightly, these arrangements are tough and testing. They have just been strengthened further by the passage of the Justice and Security Act. This has

---

[12]   This is not to suggest, however, that securitizations that do not involve security measures are by definition morally justified. My past work on environmental security in the United States under the two Clinton administrations shows as much. Here security action, although non-exceptional, was at the same time unjustifiable because the securitizing actor was insincere in its intentions and opted for securitization not with a view to protecting the American people (the stated referent object) but because it needed to ensure its own continued existence. Moreover, to argue that all securitizations that do not involve exceptional security action (i.e. security measures) are morally justified would be to assume that all policies are morally justified. Clearly this is not the case. Ordinary or everyday policies come with their own set of ethical challenges concerning the fair distribution of resources and taxes, the role and extent of minority rights, obligations to others, and so on. These issues require their own moral theories and are addressed expertly in much of analytical political philosophy.

expanded the powers and the resources of the ISC by a significant degree, allowing them for the first time to investigate operational matters of significant national importance. (Parker, 2013)

Consequently, we might say that – as far as liberal democratic states are concerned – the exception refers not to the suspension of law altogether, but rather to the situation when (new) emergency laws are passed/put into action and/or (new) emergency powers are granted that seek to govern the insecurity/crisis situation,[13] or when a state's existing security apparatus is employed to deal with issues that are either new, or that it has not dealt with previously. A prominent example of state-led securitization is the securitization of terrorism. In the United States under President Trump this securitization consists of numerous disparate security measures, including the banning of Muslims from six countries from entering the United States, restrictions on immigration, better vetting of people coming into the United States, and de-radicalization programmes mainly targeting Muslim communities (US Government, 2018).

Depending on threat type, however, securitization can be very different to this. Consider the case of the 2017/18 severe draught in South Africa, affecting especially Cape Town. Here securitization involved the following security measures: the turning off of the water supply in many public places; severe restriction of individual water usage (down to 50 litres a day), enforced by raising exponentially the cost for any use of additional water; the criminalization of many everyday water usages, including washing cars, watering gardens etc.; introduction of water theft patrols; restrictions on how many bottles of water individuals were allowed to buy from shops; protection of the few remaining public water taps by security services; award of special police powers to enter farms and seize equipment used to illegally pump water; the creation of a water police enforcing the new laws; and also plans foreseeing the deployment of the military and epidemiologists, should the water be turned off completely (Mahr, 2018).

Moving on from state-led securitization, as the Copenhagen School has shown, sufficiently organized societal groupings united by a strong enough '"we" identity' (Wæver 1997, 257) also can revert to a course of conduct that can only be described as securitization;[14] not to mention the proliferation of

---

[13]   Jef Huysmans (2014: 43) describes the emergency laws/powers I have in mind here as 'transgressions of the rule of law beyond what would be normally acceptable within the constitutional framework'.

[14]   For Wæver and the Copenhagen School this used to pertain to nations, religion and racial groups because only these were large enough to rival the state (Wæver, 1997: 263). The latter was considered important because societal (identity) security became a distinct concept only

private security companies, all of which are non-state securitizing actors. Unlike in the context of liberal democratic states where we have a good understanding of what counts as the procedure of normal politics, and consequently what counts as emergency politics, outside of concrete empirical examples it is difficult to say what counts as the exception where autocracies and non-state actors are concerned. Here 'the exception' might just be whatever most reasonable persons would agree constitutes exceptional means and actions, most notably perhaps, in terms of the amount of harm, risked/caused or intended, and/or the level of violence employed. While this definition might be a bit vague, what matters is that in reality, securitization is not solely the domain of states, because non state-actors too can do things as part of self- or other defence from existential threats most people involved in and/or affected by it would otherwise not tolerate, but might consider permissible in the context of the given threat. Non-state securitization can take the form of secession, civil disobedience, acts of sabotage and resistance. As an empirical example, consider the securitization of whales and other marine animals by the Sea Shepherd Conservation Society. 'Our mission is to end the destruction of habitat and slaughter of wildlife in the world's oceans in order to conserve and protect ecosystems and species ... By safeguarding the biodiversity of our delicately balanced ocean ecosystems, Sea Shepherd works to ensure their survival for future generations' (Sea Shepherd, 2018). Securitization involves a series of direct action tactics, including sabotaging and sinking fishing vessels and equipment (e.g. destruction of drift nets); the ramming of whaling vessels in the open seas in an attempt to sink these; attacks on crews of whaling boats, including with harmful (to eyes and skin) corrosive butyric acid; and the boarding of whaling vessels (New Zealand Herald, 2010).

Another example of securitization by a non-state actor is that of Arizona Border Recon (AZBR), a vigilante organization consisting of ex-military personnel intent on securing the US border with Mexico from drug cartels, traffickers and illegal immigrants. Securitization by AZBR involves the following security measures: intelligence-gathering by collecting data from dozens of

---

in juxtaposition with national security (Buzan et al., 1998: 120ff.). Given, however, that non-state actors have become widely accepted as securitizing actors, and given further that securitization theory suffers from a 'constructivist deficit', whereby the Copenhagen School claims to be constructivist all the way down regarding security, but ends up stipulating who can do security, how effectively and on what threats (Floyd, 2016d) other – smaller – non-state securitizing actors than those who can cement a large enough we-feeling are now a possibility. This said, we must acknowledge that within states, non-state actors are morally permitted to securitize only under certain conditions (cf. Chapter 5, section 5.5.1).

cameras installed by the group tracking the movement of illegal migrants; armed patrols; longer expeditions into the desert by armed volunteers searching for illegal migrants with the purpose of detaining 'persons suspected of illegal activity (i.e. illegal immigration, smuggling)' and to hand them over to state law enforcement (ABR, 2018: 2).

To summarize, whilst inspired by the Copenhagen School's work on securitization, JST works with a distinct notion of securitization; one that simultaneously brackets the ideas of the sanctioning audience, the securitizing power of language and the idea of the exception as executive unilateralism. Instead, securitization is understood as the process whereby an issue is moved from normal politics into the realm of security politics. This process tends to involve: (a) a securitizing move (an existential threat articulation)[15] and (b) security action (a change of behaviour by a relevant agent (the securitizing actor or someone instructed by the same) that is justified by the securitizing actor (and sometimes by the executor of securitization) with reference to the declared threat).[16] Securitization is possible in the absence of (a) but not without (b);[17] however, in most cases (a) will feature even if it is not always traceable for security scholars.[18] Moreover, although securitization can be

[15] Note that the speech act part itself is likely to have multiple iterations. As Guzzini has put it 'Only in its most legal sense can security be empirically conceived as a "speech act" in terms of a single event ... Hence, the idea of a speech act refers here to a process, not a kind of single bombshell event' (Guzzini 2011: 335).

[16] Securitization studies is home to a number of people who have criticized the Copenhagen School for the simplicity of their model of securitization, arguing that it presents an ideal-type and is not representative of how securitization plays out in practice and translates into different contexts (see, in particular, Stritzel, 2014). It is possible that these critics would have a similar view of my depiction of securitization. Two things can be said in response; first by bracketing the audience as a decisive analytical category and instead focusing on exceptional security action (i.e. security measures) my definition of securitization is actually quite permissive; after all, I allow for a large number of exceptional activities to be cast as securitization. Second, I do not deny that securitization can pan out differently to how I view it (note above my acknowledgement of securitizations involving non-exceptional security action); I simply hold that for the construction of a normative theory of security as is JST, we need to have fairly specific ideas of what we are dealing with, because otherwise it becomes a non-feasible theory of everything.

[17] Moreover, and as I have argued elsewhere, unlike security action, the securitizing move is not a necessary condition for securitization to succeed. This much is clear from evidence gathered from formerly secret archival materials (see Floyd, 2010: 54, fn. 36) Compare also with Vuori (2011b: 136), who argues that 'securitisation [which he takes to be the speech act plus audience acceptance, cf. above] is neither necessary, nor sufficient, to achieve "security" (as means to repel an existential threat): there can be activities that can bring about a security logic, or set of practices without explicit securitisation (Huysmans 2006a, 4), and a referent object may remain insecure even after its successful securitisation (if there are no actual means to repel the threat).'

[18] Some scholars are bound to be unhappy with just how narrowly defined the concept of securitization is in this book, including the fact that securitizing moves do not feature

either non-exceptional or exceptional in nature, JST is interested only in securitization as the exception.[19] Throughout this book I refer to exceptional security action as security measures.

While my variant of securitization, including my understanding of the exception is removed from the Copenhagen School's version, like them, I understand securitization as a process involving decisive actors that can be pinpointed, while I also identify a critical point in time when securitization ensues. Together, these factors also show why my interpretation of securitization is comparable to war. The same is not true for all variants of securitization currently in existence. Some writers view securitization as a multifaceted concept involving a multitude of actors and events. Notwithstanding the point that some of these scholars achieve great accuracy when it comes to mapping how precisely securitization occurs in specific cases, they do so at the expense of advancing a general theory of securitization understood as: 'a coherent system in relation to which it is possible to both compare instances and formulate specific hypotheses' (Wæver, 2015: 124–125). My understanding of securitization, in turn, is very much a general theory of securitization akin to the original variant advanced by the Copenhagen School.

2.3 METHOD

JST sets forth a list of criteria that enable scholars, practitioners and even the general public to differentiate between just and unjust securitization and desecuritization. There are two possible ways in which criteria of just securitization can be derived. First, via a communicative process 'taking place under ideal *conditions*' (Mautner, 2000: 146 emphasis in original), in other words discourse ethics. Or second, by taking inspiration from moral, analytical and political philosophy's preferred method: wide reflective equilibrium.[20] I shall begin by explaining why discourse ethics is rejected, in favour of an approach inspired by wide reflective equilibrium. I will continue by outlining the meta-theoretical assumptions and specifics of my approach to method.

Deriving criteria for the justness of securitization via discourse ethics was suggested by Wæver in the context of my 2011 *Security Dialogue* article,

---

separately as part of the analysis. I am not suggesting that securitizing moves and securitizing requests should not be subject of moral evaluation. For a first attempt, see Floyd (2017).

[19] One criticism of my approach will be that in the absence of an audience securitization cannot fail. Inability to fail, however, does not mean that we cannot distinguish between more and less significant – in their impact and outcome – securitizations. Notably, only successful securitizations involve extraordinary emergency measures.

[20] I am grateful to Jonathan Floyd for his help with and useful discussions on this section.

'Can securitization theory be used in normative analysis? Towards a Just Securitization Theory', in which I set out some preliminary thoughts on this topic. His suggestion can only be understood in the context of the parameters set by original securitization theory. Thus Wæver rejects the idea that normative analysis can and should take the form whereby what is valid, legitimate and just is universal and decided irrespective and outside of any given political situation (Wæver, 2011: 473). Wæver's thinking is longstanding and was influenced by his belief in Hannah Arendt's view 'that any position has to be judged by the effects it gains in interaction with others, and therefore 'cannot be "good" all on its own' (Floyd, 2010: 26). Notably, however, Wæver does not reject the idea that securitization can be more or less valuable, and he even argues that criteria for when securitization is valuable would have to be developed with recourse to Habermasian 'discourse ethics' (Wæver, 2011: 473). There can be little doubt that such an approach would be more in line with the premises of original securitization theory. Already some years ago Williams likened the fact that because securitization is decided between the securitizing actor and a sanctioning audience, and never by an all-powerful securitizing actor, to discursive legitimation (Williams, 2003: 523). Notably some authors, with a clear interest in ethics and securitization, have argued that ideally the audience ought to accept – in addition to the securitizing move – also the proposed emergency measures (Salter, 2011; Roe, 2008b). But how viable is such an approach for the formulation of criteria of just securitization? To answer this question it is necessary to understand that Jürgen Habermas's theory of discourse ethics aims at replacing the standard a priori justifications of moral principles (i.e. they abide the categorical imperative, or, they bring about the best consequences) with an actual process of deliberation. One upshot of this is that a deliberative democracy is the preferred way of organising polities. All deliberate democrats subscribe to the following two principles:

> First, they want politics to be more open to democratic forces than has often been the case in liberal theory. For example, they want the constitution, if there is one, to be more open to amendment, and public debate to be more open to radically different viewpoints than was the case in, say, Rawls' political liberalism. Second, they want politics, thus expanded, to be less guided by any one particular conception of justice, and more guided by ideals of fair compromise and respectful negotiation. (J. Floyd, 2017a: 55)

Deliberative democrats' claim is simple; these theories are justified on the grounds that they provide widespread intersubjective agreement on relevant issues. The fact is, however, this justification rests on a prior claim about why intersubjective agreement is valuable. It is here where deliberative democrats diverge. This is problematic because in the absence of agreement on the justification for such approaches, the claims generated by the ideal hypothetical process are not as authoritative as these theorists suggest (ibid.: 55–63). 'The deliberative dilemma, as we might call it, is that deliberation cannot go all the way down. At some point, this political model for resolving value-conflict has to be justified [...]' (ibid.: 61).

The deliberative dilemma is readily observable from Wæver's comments about the value of the democratic process. Roe has argued that 'securitization is predominately conceived as a negative inasmuch as it is bad for democracy' (Roe, 2012: 260), while desecuritization is considered a positive development because it refers to politicization defined as openness, choice and collective decision-making (Wæver, 2003: 10–12), or in other words, to the political struggle. This raises a certain question: on what grounds is the political struggle valuable? Clearly its claim to value is logically based on another claim or set claims, for example, because it is fair, or because it outcomes are likely to be better and so on. Whatever Wæver's reasons for valuing the political struggle, what matters is that he values it for non-discursive reasons.

An equally crippling problem is that all theories of deliberate democracy stipulate presuppositions about what constitutes the 'rhetorically adequate process'. Habermas, for instance,

> understands the idea of rhetorically adequate process as a set of unavoidable yet counterfactual 'pragmatic presuppositions' that participants must make if they are to regard the actual execution of dialectical procedures as a sufficiently severe critical test. [He] identifies four such presuppositions as the most important: (i) no one capable of making a relevant contribution has been excluded, (ii) participants have equal voice, (iii) they are internally free to speak their honest opinion without deception or self-deception, and (iv) there are no sources of coercion built into the process and procedures of discourse. (Bohman and Rehg, 2011)

Any so-motivated theory of just securitization would have to include a number of such pragmatic presuppositions. Pertaining, for example, to participants not knowing what role they occupy in the process of securitization (notably, whether they are the object or the subject of securitization), their nationality, gender or cultural identity. Never mind the exact nature of these rules, my point is that they are not generated by the intersubjective process. In other words, intersubjective argument works only it if is directed by objective rules, which in turn question the validity and contribution intersubjectivity really makes.

Finally, it must be remembered that discourse ethics is a theory about how to deliberate or argue, or in other words: it is thus one kind of theory of how we ought to identify what we ought to do. As such discourse ethics could play a role in ascertaining the morality of securitization in terms of how actors should engage in decision-making, but it tells us nothing concrete as regards what the decision ought to be.

My proposed alternative to discourse ethics for deriving principles of just securitization is to develop a reflective approach inspired by wide reflective equilibrium[21] – the dominant method in analytical, moral and political philosophy (Daniels, 2013). Wide reflective equilibrium has been described as 'a deliberate process' which sees the researcher reflect upon and revise assumptions about a moral problem, more often than not by drawing on insights gained from either rival moral theories or practical ethics (Daniels, 2013). But more accurately, it refers to a state of affairs achieved when one has tested 'theories against judgements about particular cases, but also [...] judgements about particular cases against theories, until equilibrium is achieved' (Blackburn, 2005: 312). Given a lack of alternative established theories of just securitization, it is not possible to derive criteria of just securitization in strict accordance with wide reflective equilibrium.[22] However, given that war and securitization (as I understand it) are comparable concepts, and given further that my aim of curtailing securitization is shared by many just war scholars who – contrary to how they are portrayed – are not pro-war, it is possible to approach the issue of just securitization by *reflecting* on which considerations of the just war tradition are relevant for a systematic theory of the morality of security. Though the number of variants of just war theory is formidable each just war theorist engages – in order to achieve equilibrium – with a set of standard and long-standing ideas in order to put forward their own theory. These standard ideas have been usefully summarized by the BBC's online guide to ethics[23] as follows:

---

[21]   Wide reflective equilibrium takes account of rival moral and political theories; narrow equilibrium does not. Jonathan Floyd argues: '[when] you have rendered coherent the "confused sense of justice" that lies beneath the judgements with which you started ... by aligning both your judgements with each other and the principles to which they (mostly) tend, at which point you have achieved narrow reflective equilibrium ... [E]xamine as many leading moral and political theories as possible, in order to see if any further refinement can be achieved, and by doing so achieve wide reflective equilibrium' (J. Floyd, 2017b: 5).

[22]   This would be an option for anyone wishing to develop a rival just securitization theory.

[23]   I deliberately choose the BBC's guide here because it is impartial, whereas most other lists of criteria are influenced by whatever the respective philosopher author takes to be most important for the justice of war.

What is a Just War?

Six conditions must be satisfied for a war to be considered just:

- The war must be for a just cause.
- The war must be lawfully declared by a lawful authority.
- The intention behind the war must be good.
- All other ways of resolving the problem should have been tried first.
- There must be a reasonable chance of success.
- The means used must be in proportion to the end that the war seeks to achieve.

How should a Just War be fought?

A war that starts as a Just War may stop being a Just War if the means used to wage it are inappropriate.

- Innocent people and non-combatants should not be harmed.
- Only appropriate force should be used.
- This applies to both the sort of force, and how much force is used.
- Internationally agreed conventions regulating war must be obeyed.

It should be immediately apparent that not all of these conditions are relevant to just securitization. Notably, there are no internationally agreed conventions regulating securitization, neither are there combatants. It is also the case that the just war tradition has undergone such significant development that it is possible to identify a traditional (sometimes referred to as legalist) and a revisionist school of thought within the tradition (see, for example, O'Driscoll, 2008a). In part, this development is a result of the changing nature of war,[24] with asymmetric conflicts, for example between states and terrorist organizations, becoming ever more common. Whereas for traditionalists the morality of war is pretty much tantamount to the law of armed conflict which governs warfare between states, revisionists, among other things, 'question the moral standing of states and the permissibility of national defence' (Lazar, 2017: 2). Given that JST includes other securitizing actors than states, revisionist just war theory is often more applicable for thinking about principles of just securitization than its legalist precursor. This said, however, given that this is not a book on just war that perhaps must declare allegiance to one or other school, I feel at liberty to utilize insights from both strands.

---

[24] McMahan (2018a: x) holds that the changes of just war theory are due not to the changed nature of war, but 'arose more in response to development internal to philosophy'.

In developing a theory of just securitization we must be mindful of the fact that adherence to the ideas of the just war tradition should not exhaust our thinking about the morality of security. In other words, ethical considerations not listed as part of the just war tradition may still be relevant to theories of just securitization. Despite these reservations, just war theory serves as a useful point of reference throughout this book. Above all else it offers an entry point into the uncharted territory of the justness of securitization, by specifying what ideas *might* be relevant to a systematic normative theory of security. Like most recent books on just wars this book is divided into criteria specifying three areas: these are just initiation of securitization, just conduct in securitization, as well as just termination of securitization, drawing on *jus ad bellum*, *jus in bello* and *jus terminatio/jus post bellum* respectively.[25]

I specify a total of five criteria for just initiation of securitization, three for just conduct during securitization and a further three for just termination of securitization. For clarity and ease of understanding I proceed by stating the respective criterion early on and use the relevant sections/chapter to defend the principle advanced.

The development of each separate criterion tends to begin by reflecting and establishing why any given basic assumption informing the justice of war (for example: that there has to be a just cause) is relevant also for the justice of securitization. In some cases, as with the just reason, the case is relatively straightforward (i.e. securitization can only be justified if there are valid reasons for such exceptional conduct), and the bulk of the corresponding sections is spent on outlining the specifics of the criterion; this often involves drawing out conceptual distinctions and developing key ideas. In other cases, for example, regards criteria relating to micro-proportionality (6, 7 and 8), things are less self-evident and the bulk of the sections developing these criteria are needed to make the case for the requirements.

Two types of argument thus feature prominently in this book: normative arguments concerned with why inclusion of a particular criterion is required and why it ought to take a particular form, and analytical arguments outlining and explaining key concepts and ideas. Normative arguments are advanced drawing on a 'plurality of sources of normativity' (Rodin, 2002: 9), or in other words, they involve both deontological (i.e. rule-based) and consequentialist (i.e. consequence-based) moral reasoning. Accordingly the list of criteria

---

[25]   Criteria for a just peace are not listed as part of the BBC's ethics guide above, presumably because thinking along these lines is still fairly new.

advanced features both ethical positions. Given that the criteria are – for the most part – informed by the just war tradition, many normative arguments advanced reflect the theory's proximity to the just war tradition.

The analytical arguments I advance do not exist in a vacuum; rather, I draw on a variety of literature (including, for example, strategic studies, the philosophy of science, analytical philosophy, critical security studies) to develop concepts such as objective existential threats, different threat categories and desecuritization.

Finally, it is important to realize that I do not advance an in-depth case study in order to demonstrate the (in-)justice of securitization. Instead, I utilize multiple illustrations (both empirical and hypothetical ones) to exemplify and refine my criteria of just securitization. This approach is not only necessary because I need to illustrate so many different things (i.e. different threat types and distinct types of just referent objects), but due to the nature of the theory advanced. Thus instead of either testing an explanatory theory on one or more empirical case studies, or developing an explanatory theory by inductive reasoning from empirical observation, the job of authors of normative theories of the kind developed here – to echo Dale Jamieson (1993: 477) – is to make their theory explicit, to describe its universality and to demonstrate its persuasiveness. Given that the bar for the moral permissibility of securitization is set high (after all, the goal of JST is to reduce the number of securitizations in the world), it is possible that a real-world example of such a securitization does not exist.[26] Yet its absence does nothing to devalue the theory advanced, because moral theories are concerned with specifying the right thing to do, not with finding evidence that the right thing is already being done somewhere by someone.

---

[26] Some people might object that the absence of an empirical case of just securitization suggests that the criteria advanced are too stringent. In my view, however, stringency is not dependent on whether one or more case constitutes a just securitization, but rather whether the criteria offered are feasible in terms of the changes required of securitizing actors under realistic circumstances. In my view, a normative theory of this type is too stringent only when the criteria are not achievable within the contemporary make-up of international society; for example, because they commence from the requirement of the existence of a world state, or from every actor's adherence to a new global norm of cosmopolitanism, and suchlike. JST requires nothing of the sort; instead all criteria – somewhat conservatively – map out well-known boundaries in terms of the limitations on actual and probable harm caused, on the circumstances when security measures might be taken; while the sort of thing that may be defended or is eligible to self-defence is not some normative ideal but already exists. In short, the criteria are not too stringent.

2.4 CONCLUSION

It was the aim of this chapter to explain and defend the meaning of securitization used in JST and to explain the method by which principles of just securitization are derived. The chapter showed that the meaning of securitization in JST differs with regard to the three cornerstones of original securitization theory: 1) the performative force of language; 2) the significance attributed to the audience in the success of securitization; and 3) the definition of the exception. Securitization was defined as the process whereby an issue is moved from normal politics into the realm of security politics, where it is addressed by security measures.

Before we can turn to the specifics of JST with the next chapter, I want to end by considering two likely objections against what is proposed here, namely the pacifist and the realist objections. JST is a theory that justifies the use of extraordinary measures under certain specific circumstances and with a view to a particular end. The use of extraordinary measures may involve the use of lethal force. Despite the long history of the analogous just war tradition, the justification of organized violence remains controversial. As we have seen in Chapter 1 (section 1.4.1) the majority of critical security scholars are against securitization in part because of a concern with those at the receiving end of security measures.[27] It is worth noting that the normative ideal of many securitization scholars was (even before it bore the name desecuritization) developed in the spirit of peace research and peace activism (Hansen, 2012: 537). The Aberystwyth School too has a strong preference for pacifism, even though Booth realizes that pacifism is not always realistic and 'some things – literally – have to be fought for' (Booth, 2012: 72). Nevertheless, Booth is a forceful critic of the just war tradition. Among other things he believes that the idea of a just war justifies escalation, encourages bad strategy, feeds self-righteousness, promotes militarization, distracts from human security and other things besides (Booth, 2007: 312–314).

The just war tradition has time and again been attacked by pacifists for irresponsibly sanctioning violence, with many objectors commencing from the deontological conviction that killing can never be justified. Just war theorists usually respond by saying that pacifism is neither a plausible nor a just solution when we witness ethnic cleansing and other atrocities against innocent people. Instead, in such cases intervention might well be morally obligatory (see Walzer, 2002). Given that JST is not concerned with the question when securitization is morally required and thus necessary, how

---

[27] The majority because the Copenhagen School is by far the most popular new approach to security.

else may we convince the pacifist of the validity of this approach? My answer to this question is tied to the observation that while securitization is rarely strictly necessary to deal with a threat, other measures may be too costly and might cause inadvertent harm to innocent people by being too slow or insufficient and as such more costly (in terms of the damage done/ harm caused) than securitization (cf. Aloyo, 2015; Lazar, 2012). In other words, pacifism as a political strategy may be more harmful to people than targeted acts of resistance (as securitization) (see also Peoples, 2011).

What is more, pacifism is out of touch with reality, in so far as we are witnessing an explosion of security policy as more and more issues are viewed through the lens of security (Zedner, 2009: 4; Huysmans, 2014). Put more strongly, JST is built on the premise that although it is a political choice to securitize, securitization in international relations is an inevitable and recurring feature. Thus, even if the condition of insecurity from agent-intended threats can be ameliorated by actors practising just securitization, the possibility of intent-lacking threats will – at times – result in securitization, sometimes even with the unfortunate result of creating real threats to other actors/entities. In order to deal with that situation it is more helpful to examine when securitization is permissible, by whom, to what end and how, instead of figuratively speaking, closing our eyes and recommending pacifism by default.

Another possible objection against the idea of just securitization is that morality does not matter to decision-makers in emergency situations. Before turning to examining the veracity of this claim, I would like to begin by saying that this is not the same as stating that morality should not matter even in such situations. In my view it is part of the responsible scholar's repertoire to point to the relevance of morality in all political situations and to try and lay out a pathway for practitioners on how to act morally.

The claim that morality does not matter to politicians, especially in emergency situations, is associated with realist theory and its constitutive parts of self-help under anarchy, power politics and the national interest. While I recognize that sophisticated versions of realism go beyond this and some clearly address moral questions (see Donnelly, 2008: 150–162), we might ask, to what extent does the typical IR realist's view of the world accurately capture what goes on in the world today? While it is the case that realism has some timeless explanatory value (see Buzan, 1996: 59) it is also the case that whole libraries can be filled with all those things realism has a hard time explaining, including: the role and power of international organizations, non-state conflict, self-binding as a matter of self-restraint, the democratic peace, the role of identity in security relations, the rise of security communities, and so on. Above all else perhaps, realism has trouble explaining the emergence of the international norm human rights and its supplementary humanitarian intervention (see Wheeler, 2000), exercised by the UN Security Council as the responsibility to protect (R2P). R2P is explicitly informed by the just war tradition,[28] the thinking being that: 'the threat to human security should be sufficiently great to justify force; the primary aim of the mission should be to eliminate the threat; the use of force should be a last resort; the force used should be the minimum required and proportionate to the threat; and there should be a reasonable chance of the intervention succeeding' (Robinson, 2008: 178). In other words it would appear that moral thinking and responsibility towards others can be the driving force in emergencies.

Two objections to humanitarian intervention can and have been made by realist sceptics. First, the selective usage of intervention for humanitarian purposes (for example, recently in Libya, but not in Syria) shows that the motive behind such interventions is hardly ever benign, but rather subject to some prior egotistical motive (usually a geopolitical interest such as the prevalence of a globally scarce natural resource). Second, the language of just wars and humanitarian intervention is easily abused, and thus both vacuous and dangerous. The latest example is Putin's invasion of the Crimean peninsula in 2014, which he has verbally defended as a humanitarian intervention, whereas the West (the United States in particular) has described the same event as the annexing of sovereign territory. While the language of morality clearly may be abused, the frequent invocation of various of the principles of just war tradition, the laws of war and humanitarian intervention, by policymakers shows that moral considerations concerning reasons for the employment of force as well as the appropriate means do matter in the high politics of security. Nevertheless, it is crucial to never lose sight of the possibility of abuse. Walzer warns that above all else, we must be wary of generals speaking in the language of the just war (2002). 'Just war theory is not an apology for any particular war, and it is not a renunciation of war itself. It is designed to sustain a constant scrutiny and an immanent critique' (Walzer, 2002: 942). I share this same ambition for JST.

---

[28]   In my view, realism's inability to explain world politics since the end of the Cold War drives ever more realists to telling us how things would be better had we only followed a realist's recommendations (e.g. no mess in Iraq and Libya, successful containment of IS, no unmitigated rise of China etc.). As a consequence realism has moved from being an explanatory to a normative theory. This is nowhere more obvious than in Stephen Walt's 2017 E. H. Carr Memorial lecture (2018). Here, in spite of declaring that normative recommendations are not part of realist scholars' remit, Walt spends several pages outlining how the United States *should* behave, notably after conceding that realism can only partially explain world politics since the end of the Cold War.

3

Just Initiation of Securitization: Just Reason

3.1 INTRODUCTION

The first of three substantive parts of JST – just initiation of securitization – is concerned with the justifiability of the move from politicization to securitization. Chapters 3, 4 and 5 are dedicated to this purpose; the various criteria developed in these chapters pertain to just cause, right intention, macro-proportionality and reasonable prospect of success. While, and as I will show, all of these matter for the just initiation of securitization and for the justice of securitization more generally, as Jeff McMahan has argued in the context of the morality of war, just cause has 'priority over the other valid requirements in this sense: the others cannot be satisfied, even in principle, unless just cause is satisfied' (2005: 5).[1] In just securitization theory the just cause is made up of two components: a) the just reason for securitization, and b) the just referent object of securitization. The present chapter is about the just reason for securitization, i.e. it addresses the all-important question: under what circumstances are securitizing actors permitted to use exceptional measures? Chapter 4, on just referent objects, examines what kind of actor or entity is eligible to defend itself or to defensive assistance by others by using such measures.

In world politics, securitization can be triggered by a number of things, including the existence of objective existential threats, vulnerabilities, fears and perceived threats. I argue that securitization is morally permissible – provided all other criteria are met – only if it seeks to address a current objective existential threat. In line with the just war tradition, which in turn borrows from individual self-defence, a *current* threat refers to both the

---

[1] Note that the heightened relevance of just cause also explains why three chapters of this book are given over to just initiation of securitization, whereas one chapter suffices to specify just conduct during securitization. Just cause alone takes up two chapters.

74

possibility of imminent harm and ongoing harm. As Helen Frowe (2016: 55) explains:

> An individual may use force against an imminent threat – that is, a threat [read: attack] that is anticipated but yet to occur. She need not wait until her attacker lands the first blow before she defends herself, provided she can be reasonably certain that the attack is about to take place. And, once the attack is in progress, she may continue to try to forcefully prevent the infliction of future blows. Likewise, a state may use force to avert imminent harm. It may also use force to prevent future attacks *after* the initial wrong. We can think of this as a state equivalent of an ongoing attack.

This chapter will advance and defend the following principle of just securitization.

Criterion 1: There must be an objective existential threat to a referent object, that is to say a danger that – with a sufficiently high probability – threatens the survival or the essential character/properties of either a political or social order, an ecosystem, a non-human species, or individuals.

With just cause tied to the presence of an objective existential threat, this chapter serves to explain three things. First, there is the issue of magnitude why is it that threats need to be not only real, but of a specified extent to qualify? The second concerns the – in security studies – longstanding epistemological question: how do we know that a threat is real, as opposed to simply perceived? Third is the equally controversial issue of whether in addition to current threats, future threats can be a just reason for securitization?

3.2 THE JUST REASON

3.2.1 *The Magnitude of the Threat*

In International Relations, security has traditionally been about survival,[2] or in other words, about existential threats. The reason for this is quite simply that security/securitization is distinct from ordinary (democratic) politics not only because of the way decisions are made (i.e. quicker and more effectively), but also – and perhaps more importantly – because it involves the use of exceptional (i.e. security) measures to combat threats (Wæver, 2009: 22). Such measures are controversial not only because they may involve a high degree of violence, secrecy and even the use of (lethal) force (indeed, it is possible that

---

[2] There are exceptions, notably Wolfers (1952) and Booth (2007).

innocent people are killed as a result of securitization), but also – where liberal democratic states are concerned – they always mean a reduction of democracy in a sense of public scrutiny. Consequently the threshold for when resort to securitization is morally permissible needs to be suitably high. In Jef Huysmans words: 'Only *exceptional conditions* can legitimise a disproportionate increase of executive power and other transgressions of the rule of law beyond what would normally be acceptable within the constitutional framework' (2014: 43; my emphasis).

I too hold that for securitization to be justified (provided all other criteria are met), threats have to be existential in nature. While this might seem excessively demanding – after all, many acute threats are not lethal to people – in reality, this requirement is less demanding than it first appears. This is because when we are concerned with existential threats we are contemplating much more than straightforward lethal threats, i.e. threats where people's lives are threatened either directly or indirectly.[3] Instead, by existential threats, Wæver and the Copenhagen School mean threats of a magnitude capable of changing the 'essential being' or character of the referent object (Wæver, 2009: 23; see also Buzan et al., 1998: 21–22). In short, their concern is not exclusively with threats to the *survival* of the referent object, but with threats to the referent's essential properties. This means that when, for example, humans are the referent object of security, objective existential threats refer not only to lethal threats but to all those things that threaten basic human needs, which when met, enable humans to live minimally decent lives (cf. Chapter 4, section 4.3). An example of a threat that is non-lethal, but nevertheless existentially threatening to being able to be and function as a human, is a severely disabling infectious diseases (e.g. leprosy), as this leaves individuals potentially unable to fully participate in social life.

This less demanding interpretation of existential threats also makes it much easier to include a large array of non-human referent objects. Thus existential threats to states, international order, group identity, the biosphere or

---

[3]   The terminology of direct lethal threats and indirect lethal threats can be found in Frowe, 2014 who defines an indirect lethal threat as 'a person who contributes to the threat to Victim's life, but who is not going to kill Victim'. Whereas 'a direct lethal threat is a person who is going to kill Victim' (p. 7). In my usage, however, direct lethal threats are not limited to the threats of death intended by agents, instead a threat can be directly lethal to humans even when there is no agent doing the threatening (e.g. a tsunami to the beach dweller), while it can also be caused by agents but not intended by them (e.g. by carriers of infectious diseases). Indirect lethal threats, in turn, are threats to non-human referent objects and social and political orders that will also lead to the death of human beings (e.g. disappearance of or extreme damage to the biosphere for example will kill humans). Just like direct lethal threats, indirect lethal threats can be agent-intended or intent-lacking.

endangered species do not always pose indirect lethal threats to people (e.g. citizens of states), but often simply are threats to the essential character or properties of the referent, which might be harmful to humans within these orders, but not lethal. The European Union, for example, is threatened in its essential character by the reintroduction of internal borders during the migrant/refugee crisis, because freedom of movement is one of the EU's definitive features. Its abolition is likely harmful to businesses and inconvenient for people living within Europe, but no one will die.

In summary, the meaning of 'existential threat' depends on the nature of the object in need of protection (the referent object of security), which can be all manner of things. Wæver puts this as follows: 'An existential threat can only be understood in relation to the particular character of the referent object in question ... *The essential quality of existence will vary greatly across different sectors and levels of analysis, and therefore so will the nature of existential threats*' (2009: 23; emphasis added).

Existential threats that threaten human life can be considered different in kind. Importantly – and as argued later on in this book (Chapter 6, section 6.4) – only lethal threats permit as part of securitization, and with certain caveats attached to it, the use of lethal force.

3.2.2 *Objective Existential Threats*

Just causes for war comprise self-defence from unjust aggression and increasingly other defence as humanitarian intervention. Given then that just wars are reactive to prior aggression[4] there is also practically no discussion on whether threats are real. The issue becomes contentious only in the context of discussions on preventing future attack as a just cause, where there obviously is considerable uncertainty over the long-term intentions of a belligerent actor (Crawford, 2007: 108; and see below). Many scholars agree, however, that in such cases the possibility of military attack is real when an aggressor has the necessary military capabilities to follow through on a threat, when he has malign intentions and – crucially – when there is '*measurable military preparation*' (Orend, 2006: 75; emphasis in original).

In much of critical security studies, the notion of objective existential threats is shunned, sometimes ridiculed, and above all they are deemed

---

[4] '[F]or an international act to count as aggression, it must not merely be objectionable or even damaging to a country's interests. It must, at the same time, involve the infliction of serious, direct physical force' (Orend, 2006: 33).

unknowable.[5] Given that – at least in so far as the subject matter is concerned – there is some overlap between just war theory and security studies, how can this be? One explanation might be that when it comes to war, the threat is less ambiguous and more urgent then it is with other issues. While it may be harder to determine the objective status of threats that are not agent-intended, however, this is not the sole explanation. The Copenhagen School – who reject theorization of objective threats, and study the intersubjective construction of threats only – for example, argue that while hostile tanks crossing the border might be 'unambiguous and immediate ... even here, "hostile" is an attribute not of the vehicle but of the socially constituted relationship. A foreign tank could be part of a peacekeeping force' (Buzan et al., 1998: 30). In short, the difference in opinion is not one of difficulty, but one of epistemology, thus most critical security scholars hold that objective facts concerning the matter of an actor's intentions are epistemologically inaccessible. Yet they do so by erroneously equating intentions (i.e. what an actor aims at in doing something) with an actor's private thoughts and beliefs, in other words his motives. In so doing, however, they ignore that criminal law is built on the knowability of intentions, for otherwise murder, which is often motivated by strong inner feelings such as love and hate, could never be detected. While intentions cannot be known with absolute certainty, detectives can gather lots of evidence about what the murderer intended i.e. the desire to live in a world in which the loved/hated person does not exist, and a willingness to face the consequences of wrongful action (Anscombe, 1957: 18–19; Floyd, 2010: 43–44).

Another explanation is that many scholars commit what Roy Bhaskar calls the '"epistemic fallacy" [of transposing] epistemological arguments into ontological ones', namely when they define what is real either in term of 'our experiences' or in accordance with 'our theories and/or linguistic conventions' (Wight, 2006: 28). Clearly many critical security scholars are so immersed in the social and political construction of security threats that they fail to recognize a crucial difference among different security threats: some security threats refer to objective existential threats and some don't (not so Wæver, see 2011: 472). Real threats are threats to the existence of political or social orders, ecosystems, non-human species, or human beings regardless of whether they have been framed as such, or whether we have experienced them. This is in

---

[5]   Exceptions are the Aberystwyth School of Security Studies, led by Ken Booth and scholars of human security.

line with critical realism's view of ontology which, in Colin Wight's (2006: 29) terms:

> [P]resupposes that there are things, entities, structures and/or mechanism that operate and exist independently of our ability to know or manipulate them. It also presupposes that appearances do not exhaust reality, that there are things going on, as it were, beyond and behind the appearances that are not immediately accessible to our sense. The laws of nature, the entities, structures or mechanisms which are often not empirically 'observable', are what Bhaskar terms the 'intrasitive objects of knowledge' and exist independently of (wo)man and independently of his/her ability to know them.

To give an example of a real threat, imagine I am in a nightclub enjoying myself drinking, and laughing with my friends. What I don't know is that while I am dancing to my favourite tune, unseen by any of my friends or bystanders a stranger spikes my half-drunk drink with an odourless, colourless, illegal, and – though unknown to him – lethal substance.[6] Given that I cannot smell that my drink was spiked, I am unlikely to be aware of there being something wrong when I return thirstily from the dance floor, yet my obliviousness is not going to save my life.[7] In other words, real threats exist regardless of our experience of them and whether we have framed them as such. However, even real threats become matters of security, and therefore 'security threats', only when actors (for example, but not exclusively, states) frame and respond to them as such. Importantly, not all objective existential threats become security issues: some are treated as health issues, others as criminal matters, some are matters for domestic emergency services, some may well be ignored. The reverse also holds, and not everything that is securitized necessarily refers to an objective existential threat; some security threats refer to perceived threats only. Securitization is morally justifiable – *provided that all other criteria are met* – only if it refers to an objective existential threat.

---

[6] This example lends itself to expanding some more on the difference between intentions and motives. The perpetrator's actions suggest that he intended to get me into a more inebriated state than drink alone would have done, yet his motives for this action could be anything, including: a dare with friends, a hate of all women, a hate/love of me personally, revenge for not paying attention to him earlier when he tried to flirt with me, and so on. The point is that while it is possible to see what he aimed at in doing what he did, it is impossible to know for sure what motivated him to do it.

[7] I use this example merely to showcase that there are such things as real threats. As explained in Chapter 5, securitization to safeguard individual persons is not generally considered proportionate.

So far so good, but still this does not quite get at what I mean by an *objective* existential threat. Specifically, objective could be understood in either the fact-relative or in the evidence-relative sense.[8] Fact-relativity refers to the situation 'in which people know all the relevant, reason-giving facts', while evidence-relativity refers to the situation when the available evidence suggests decisive reasons that the beliefs people hold about a given situation are true (Parfit, 2011: 162–163). Among other things, these distinctions give way to different notions of moral wrongness and rightness, in a sense that an action may seem right in the evidence-relative sense, but may, when all the facts have emerged, turn out to have been wrong in the fact-relative sense. In Parfit's terms:

> [W]e can use 'wrong' in several partly different senses. Some of these senses we can define by using the ordinary sense. Some acts of ours would be
>
> a) *wrong* in the *fact-relative* sense just when this act would be wrong in the ordinary sense if we knew all of the morally relevant facts
> b) *wrong* in the *evidence-relative* sense just when this act would be wrong in the ordinary sense if we believed what the available evidence gives us decisive reasons to believe, and these beliefs were true (ibid.: 150–151).

Translated into just securitization theory, we might say that a judgement about the objective presence of an existential threat is correct in the fact-relative sense when *all* the morally relevant *facts* confirm that there is a threat to the relevant referent object. Fact-relativity, in short, equates to what actually is the case (independent of what we know about what is the case). A judgement about the status of a threat in the evidence-relative sense, in turn, is based on all the available evidence about the objective status of a threat. In an effort to avoid errors of judgement, any decision to securitize would ideally be based on fact-relatively and thus certainty. The problem is, however, that no one, not even the best-informed advisor, is likely to be omniscient and have all the relevant facts. As Jonathan Herington points out, even if we could have all the facts about the here and now, the future is possibly 'chancy' and consequently certainty about what will happen if we don't act unattainable (Herington, 2013: 67). Consequently the best we have got is objective knowledge in the evidence-relative sense.

---

[8] I am grateful to Jonathan Herington for pointing me in this direction as well as for his help with this section.

Any judgement made in the evidence-relative sense runs the risk of being wrong. For example, all the available evidence (in this case, mathematical calculations) might suggest that an asteroid is on course to hit planet Earth, when unbeknownst to anyone the asteroid will first collide with another asteroid, diverting its course elsewhere. Errors of judgement may occur for a variety of reasons. From security scholars who have theorized the security dilemma we know that uncertainty, insecurity and fear play major roles in the misperception of security threats (see Jervis, 1976: 58–113). Indeed, Ken Booth and Nicholas Wheeler separate out the dilemma of interpretation as an intrinsic part of the two-stage security dilemma:

> [The dilemma of interpretation is] the predicament facing decision-makers when they are confronted, on matters affecting security, with a choice between two significant and usually (but not always) undesirable alternatives about the military policies and political postures of other entities. [It] is the result of the perceived need to make a decision in the existential condition of unresolvable uncertainty about the motives, intentions and capabilities of others. (Booth and Wheeler, 2008: 4)

Errors of judgement in turn generate different consequences for the blame-worthiness of securitizing actors. In evidence-relative judgements the onus is on the securitizing actor to gather evidence *approximating* the actual facts. The failure to gather evidence that is available renders the securitizing actor '*culpably* ignorant if [s/he] continue[s] to act in ignorance' (Herington, 2013: 70 emphasis in original). However, not making use of evidence that could only be obtained by incurring an 'unacceptable moral cost' (ibid.: 70) can be excused.

The relationship between culpability and evidence-relative judgements is more complex than this still. To appreciate it fully we need to understand that in addition to the fact-relative and evidence-relative sense, rightness/wrongness can be judged in a third way. Thus an act of ours can be wrong in the *belief-relative* sense, namely 'just when this act would be wrong in the ordinary sense if our beliefs about these facts were true' (ibid.: 150). Parfit provides the following hypothetical example to showcase how the belief-relative sense links to the other two distinctions. If 'I give you some treatment that I believe and hope will kill you, but which saves your life, as it was almost certain to do' (Parfit, 2011: 151–152), I have acted wrongly in the belief-relative sense insofar as my intentions were bad, whereas in the fact-relative and in the evidence-relative sense I have done nothing wrong. 'I acted rightly [in these two senses], since my act saved your life, as it was almost certain to do. I did what any fully informed adviser ought to have told me that I ought to do' (ibid.: 152).

The addition of belief-relativity aids our understanding of blameworthiness, or in other words, culpability of securitizing actors for unjust securitization. This is because while a securitizing actor's judgement of a security threat may have been wrong in the fact-relative sense, even if it appeared right in the evidence-relative sense, he/she may be excused for that error of judgement only if he/she acted in accordance with the belief-relative ought (see ibid.: 162). That is to say: the wrongful securitizing act (unjust securitization) can be excused only provided that the securitizing actor acted because he intended to secure the referent object from a threat he had decisive reason to belief was true. Conversely, the securitizing actor's failure to align his belief-relative judgements in line with the evidence cannot be excused and remains blameworthy. I will return to the issue of culpability briefly in Chapter 7, when I discuss just desecuritization.

3.3 THREAT CATEGORIES

So far so good, but how, from here, can we find out whether a securitization refers to an objective existential threat or merely to a perceived threat? For analytical purposes it makes sense to differentiate between three different types of threat: agent-intended threats, agent-lacking threats and agent-caused threats. These threat categories help us to focus on what to look for when trying to establish whether a threat is real, while – as we shall see later on – they also help us to gauge whether or not security measures are proportionate, as well as with determining when threats have been neutralized. It is important to note that these are intended as analytical not absolute categories. Agent-intended threats are, strictly speaking, subsets of agent-caused threats (insofar as they are also caused by agents; however, I take agent-caused threats to refer to threats caused by agents without the intention to do harm); while some threats may change threat category over time. For example, transmitted from human to human, HIV/AIDS is best seen as an agent-caused threat. Yet the first persons ever to contract HIV/AIDS did so not from humans, for the virus is believed to originate in primates, hence it was once – provided we do not attribute agency to animals – an agent-lacking threat. Yet if rumours that HIV/AIDS was invented in a laboratory and spread by humans deliberately are to be believed, it may even have once been an agent-intended threat. It is most certainly still an agent-intended threat in those rare cases when HIV-positive people deliberately infect others through either voluntary or forced unprotected sexual intercourse.

3.4 AGENT-INTENDED THREATS

Agent-intended threats refer to those threats where an aggressor is at the source of the threat intent on harming. To establish whether a securitization refers back to an agent-intended threat, scholars have to concentrate on an actor's intentions and on his or her capabilities to follow through on a threat (Singer, 1958: 94). It goes without saying that both of these conditions will have to be met at the same time; thus, in the absence of any intention to harm A, the capabilities of B pose no danger to A (see also Wendt, 1999).

Following Anscombe (1957), I take intentions to refer to *what an actor aims at in doing something*. This means that we must determine intent from actions as well as from statements of intent. The former is central to criminal law. As David Luban explains: 'Teenagers hanging out at a strip mall, passing a joint or drinking a six-pack, may while away the time with conversations that begin "Hey, why don't we rob the Seven-Eleven? ... " without ever seriously planning to do so. The basic US conspiracy statute requires not only a group plan but also at least one *overt* action taken in furtherance of the plan' (Luban, 2007: 192; my emphasis). Just war theorists argue along similar lines; most theorists include alongside statements of intent, something along the lines of what Orend calls 'measurable military preparation' (2006: 75). The latter is important because in world politics, actors say all sorts of things they don't mean, notably bluffing and hypocrisy are standard practices most states employ at one point or another.

I propose that we can get at the intentions of aggressors by comparing what they say with what they do. And by 'doing', I mean a relevant action taken by the aggressor, or by some entity instructed by the aggressor, to back up the verbal threat. Otherwise inexplicable discrepancies between what aggressors say and the actions they subsequently take to follow through on a verbal threat are vital, as they may suggest insincerity on the part of the aggressor.

In addition to the aggressor's intentions, users of JST will also need to assess their capabilities. This is likely to be a time-consuming and potentially difficult exercise. Some within more traditional security studies, where the possibility of establishing the reality of threats is not rejected outright, have made some great advances on this in a state-centric context that are instructive for our purposes here. Zeev Moaz, for example, assesses capabilities by examining the aggressor's manpower availability for military service, weapons capability, military budget, population size and the political capacity to mobilize for national security (2009). Capability assessment is easier in the context of the state where data is more freely available, including from independent sources. In a non-state context, the scholars and practitioners alike will have to try and figure out things such as the size of the aggressor (how many individuals subscribe to the cause), what has the aggressor done in the past, what kind of states/organizations is the aggressor friendly with, and what do we know about them in general.

3.4.1 *Illustrative Example: Islamic Fundamentalist Terrorism*

To illustrate how we might proceed, let us consider the case of fundamentalist Islamic terrorism (specifically Al-Qaeda, and latterly its splinter group the Islamic State (IS)), and whether such groups pose an objective existential threat to civilians in the West. I pick the West here merely to limit the analysis to one region; I do not wish to suggest that it is the West that is most at risk from these groups.

Like all terrorist organizations, Al-Qaeda has never made a secret of its intentions. A fatwa to all Muslims issued by Al-Qaeda's leadership in 2006 read: 'The ruling to kill the Americans and their allies – civilians and military – is an individual duty for every Muslim who can do it in *any country* in which it is possible to do it, in order to liberate the al-Aqsa Mosque and the holy mosque [Mecca] from their grip, and in order for their armies to move out of all the lands of Islam, defeated and unable to threaten any Muslim' (Bin Laden, 2006b: 296). Although, 'Al-Qaeda's leader, Osama Bin Laden, spoke frequently of restoring the caliphate' (Bunzel, 2015: 9), which would become the central objective of IS, the strategies of the two groups differ somewhat. According to Cole Bunzel, Al-Qaeda's practises what he calls 'defensive jihad' aimed at freeing/defending territories and holy sites, while IS practise 'offensive jihad' (ibid., 10). Utilizing various speeches by IS leaders, Bunzel describes offensive jihadism as follows:

> In the Wahhabi tradition [offensive jihadism] is premised on the uprooting of shirk, idolatry, wherever it is found. For example, in a 2007 speech Abu 'Umar al-Baghdadi quoted a Wahhabi-trained scholar on the purpose of jihad: 'The end to which fighting the unbelievers leads is no idolater (*mushrik*) remaining in the world.' In another speech, Baghdadi explicitly emphasized the importance of 'offensive jihad,' which he defined as 'going after the apostate unbelievers by attacking [them] in their *home territory*, in order to make God's word most high and until there is no persecution.' Consistent

with Wahhabi doctrine, 'persecution' is understood to mean idolatry. (Bunzel, 2015: 10; my emphasis)

A series of terrorist attacks since 9/11 provide conclusive evidence that first Al-Qaeda and now IS are sincere,[9] as their words are matched by actions.

These attacks also give us some idea of their capabilities. Although a vast and seemingly insurmountable imbalance of power in military force exists between Islamic terrorist groups and the West, this has not defeated them. As long ago as 1996 Bin Laden announced that because of this imbalance, 'suitable means of fighting must be adopted i.e. using fast moving light forces that work under complete secrecy' (Bin Laden, 2006a: 283). 9/11 is testimony to this. Not only was it prepared in complete secrecy, it also utilized conventional means (passenger aircraft) as weapons during the attacks of 9/11 in New York. The same is true for the Madrid and London bombings, where Al-Qaeda cells attacked busy commuter trains and buses, while more recently loose IS affiliates have ploughed lorries or vans into people, including in Nice, Berlin, London and Barcelona. For our analysis here this is important, as it suggests that capabilities in any conventional sense (stockpiles of arms) are not the foremost requirement for Al-Qaeda-style terrorism to qualify as an objective existential threat. Where capabilities do matter, however, is with regards to manpower. Unless Al-Qaeda and latterly IS are able to continuously recruit new, willing potential suicide bombers, their lack of stockpiles of conventional weapons will become a problem. In short, it is humans prepared to die for the cause that is these groupings most important capability.

This is also why IS pursues an extensive and very slick campaign on social media, mainly through Twitter, Instagram and Facebook. As James Farwell has argued (2014: 49–50) 'its communication strategy aims to persuade all Muslims that battling to restore a caliphate is a religious duty. The group's narrative portrays ISIS [read:IS] as an agent of change, the true apostle of a sovereign faith, a champion of its own perverse notions of social justice, and a collection of avengers bent on settling accounts for the perceived sufferings of others'. Helped by this media strategy, which includes 'a 13- minute long English-language video "There is No Life Without Jihad", featuring testimonials from self-identified Brits and Australians rejecting the current borders of the Middle East as drawn up by foreign powers after the First World War' (Farwell, 2014: 50), IS has been able to recruit foreign fighters from all

---

9   I mean sincerity of intention here. This said, however, I do believe that sincerity of intention can also tell us something about the more elusive sincerity of motive. Especially in cases where sincerity of intention is broken and the actor is unlikely to have had sincerity of motive (compare with Chapter 5, section 5.2).

over the world. In 2015 it was estimated that 30,000 foreign fighters from 100 countries had joined IS since 2011, with about a quarter of these coming from Europe and Turkey (Norton-Taylor, 2015). For as long as they are able to inspire people to join their cause, IS constitutes an objective existential threat to individuals living in the West. Similarly, provided Al-Qaeda is able to recruit jihadists, they continue to pose an existential threat to individuals in the West until they are either defeated, or Western foreign policy objectives in the Middle East change drastically.

3.5 AGENT-LACKING THREATS

The second type of threat I want to include is agent-lacking threats, referring to threats that occur irrespective of human agency. Some scholars would argue that while some threats exist that are independent of human action (e.g. earthquakes), all are mediated by human action, and danger should be evaluated on those terms.[10] It is true of course that, for instance, earthquakes are more or less dangerous depending on whether infrastructure has been built in an earthquake-proof manner (in Japan, for example, it is law that buildings are earthquake-proof) and whether or not an early warning system exists. Moreover – as we shall see – the ability of societies to mediate threats features in whether threats really are objectively existentially threatening across all three categories, yet none of this changes where the threat originates (in other words, its source). It is the initial source of the threat I seek to capture by dividing into the three categories; while the ability to mediate (i.e. any given society's response/resilience) is a factor relevant for threat status (i.e. its magnitude).

Most agent-lacking threats are located within the environmental sector of security; this includes issues related to health security (see Barnett, 2001: 17; Price-Smith, 2002: 137ff.; Pirages and DeGeest, 2004; McDonald, 2010: 64–67). Prominent examples include floods, earthquakes, and tsunamis. Epistemologically agent-lacking threats are the least controversial, in part because no blame has to be placed, while we also do not face the problem of other minds. This is so because what is actively doing the threatening in any given situation is not humans, but the thing itself (see Sandin, 2009; Rubinstein, 2007; Sorrell, 2003); which is to say the advancing tsunami, the earthquake, the virus on the loose, the asteroid headed for planet Earth, and so on. This, in turn, has the advantage that we can rely on the natural sciences to gauge whether an agent-lacking threat is

---

[10]   I would like to thank one of the anonymous reviewers for this point.

real.[11] Epidemiologists, for example, will be able to tell us what the consequences of the Zika[12] virus are and the possibility of it spreading. However, even the natural sciences will only be able to tell us part of the story, to gauge the magnitude of an objective threat (i.e. whether it is existentially threatening) and to whom, we need research from the social sciences on the ability of different societies to cope with a threat. In the case of the Zika virus, for example, how poor are the affected areas, how many pregnant women live in the affected areas, does adequate health-care and education about the possibilities of contracting the virus exist, how far off is a vaccine, and so on.

While I would expect the inclusion of agent-lacking threats to raise few hairs on the epistemological front, some within security studies will be against the inclusion of agent-lacking and also agent-caused threats in just securitization theory on the grounds that traditionally, intention structures the field of security. The lack of intent in environmental threats used to mean that many academics questioned the logic of referring to environmental threats

---

[11] In the context of climate change in particular some scholars have pointed out that research generated by the natural sciences community ought to be enjoyed with care. The so-called 'climategate' scandal, whereby researchers were alleged to have cherry-picked empirical data strengthening the case for climate change, did much to mar the name of science as objective. Noteworthy in security studies is Villumsen Berling's work on science and securitization. Among other things, she is worried about the mobilization of scientific facts in securitization, because it runs the risk of closing off debate, of objectifying securitization and that it is – due to the proclivity of scientific language – almost immune to being challenged (2011: 393). While these are real possibilities, I still believe that scientific research is an essential element in trying to ascertain whether or not a relevant threat is real. After all we (by which I mean everyone who is not a climate scientist) would have little idea that climate change is actually happening, and even if we did, we could not be sure of its cause and might consider changes in climate, the melting of glaciers and the polar ice caps simply as natural phenomena. In other words, we cannot talk about climate change *without* science, *ergo* science matters. Nevertheless science has to be employed carefully. Ian Hacking, for one, reminds us that science must always be contextualized against a given historical context, and that what is deemed true now, may not be considered thus in the future. I state clearly that science alone cannot tell us what the socio-economic implications of climate change or a particular disease will be – so we will always need a mix of natural and social sciences research, in order to determine the objective presence of a threat. What is more, the objective presence of an existential threat does not mean that securitization is required; the magnitude of a threat merely gives just reason to securitize.

[12] The Zika virus, which is transmitted by *Aedes* mosquitoes, was first discovered in Uganda in 1947, but its epidemic outbreak in the Americas in 2015 as well as the link to microcephaly in newborn babies to mothers who had contracted the viral condition during pregnancy, were unforeseen and previously unheard of (WHO, 2016b). I class this as agent-lacking because I do not attribute agency to insects or animals, while the number of transmission of Zika virus through sexual intercourse was statistically insignificant (0.9%); in continental United States 15 out of 1,657 cases, https://news.nationalgeographic.com/2016/08/zika-florida-travel-sex-cdc/.

as security threats (Deudney, 1990; Wæver, 1995; Buzan in Wæver, 1995; Sweeney, 1999: 89). And to this day, some academics hold that environmental threats amount to imminent risks or urgent vulnerabilities, *not* (security) threats (Corry, 2012). Three objections can be made to this. First, the Oxford dictionary definition of threat does not require human agency. It defines a threat (noun) as: '(1) a stated intention to inflict injury, damage or danger or hostile action on someone. (2) a person or thing likely to cause damage or danger. [and also] 3) the possibility of trouble or danger' (Soanes, 2000: 1199). Second, as I have argued elsewhere, 'labelling threats from environmental change anything other than threats risks downgrading them in importance vis-à-vis other threats, for example, terrorism' (Floyd, 2013b: 285). Third, and probably most importantly, many practitioners of security now speak in terms of climate/environmental/energy security, and consider climate change a security threat on a par with, for example, terrorism. In short, we cannot plausibly ignore environmental and health threats simply because they lack intent.

3.5.1 *Illustrative Example: Volcanic Eruptions*

As an example of how we may proceed in establishing the existence of an agent-lacking objective existential threat, let us consider the example of volcanic eruptions, specifically a comparison between the 2010 eruption of Iceland's Eyjafjallajökull and that of the Tambora volcano in 1815 located in modern day Indonesia. In order to know for certain what volcanic eruptions are as well as their immediate effects, we need to turn to the natural sciences, specifically geology and earth sciences. Volcanologists differentiate between different types of volcanic eruption; these can be 'effusive, where lava flows like a thick, sticky liquid, or explosive, where fragmented lava explodes out of a vent. In explosive eruptions, the fragmented rock may be accompanied by ash and gases; in effusive eruptions, degassing is common but ash is usually not' (Ball, 2016). Eyjafjallajökull and Tambora were both explosive eruptions, but Tambora, which 'expelled around 140 gt of magma (equivalent to »50 km^3 of dense rock) ... propelling plumes up to 43 km altitude' (Oppenheimer, 2003: 230) was significantly bigger than Eyjafjallajökull. There, 'the erupted material was $4.8\pm1.2\cdot10^{11}$ kg (benmoreite and trachyte, dense rock equivalent volume 0.18 ± 0.05 km^3). About 20% was lava and water-transported tephra, 80% was airborne tephra (bulk volume 0.27 km^3) transported by 3–10 km high plumes' (Gudmundsson et al., 2012). While interesting in and of itself, this does not tell us anything about whether or not these eruptions constituted an objective existential threat to individuals or states. To ascertain this, we need to examine the socio-economic consequences of both eruptions. Eyjafjallajökull's most significant consequence was the grounding of much of European air travel (due to the presence of ash particles), which cost airlines $1.8bn in revenue and grounded hundreds of thousands of passengers (Dopgane, 2011). The grounding of all air travel, including cargo planes, had a negative effect on several businesses within and outside of Europe. For example, it had a statistically significant negative effect on horticulture in Kenya which is one of the largest exporters of cut flowers and fresh vegetables to Europe ('<2 million kgs in export, a quantity [last] observed in early 1990s') (Justus, 2015: 1212). While clearly negative, these effects did not pose an existential threat to either the airlines in question, persons unable to travel or the national economies where airlines were based. Even in Kenya, the impacts on horticulture from the grounding of airlines did not amount to an existential threat to people employed in the horticultural industry, neither did it lead to rioting or conflict which could have threatened regime security, considering that the political situation in the country at the time was already volatile following on from the Kenyan crisis in 2007/08 (Justus, 2015).

The story is quite different when it comes to Tambora. In the first instance, this historically largest-scale explosive volcanic eruption led to approximately 71,000 people dying on the surrounding islands (Oppenheimer, 2003). Secondly, it led to short-term global cooling, caused by the levels of sulphur in the atmosphere. Global cooling took the form of frost and snow in the spring and summer months in Western Europe and Northern America, leading to widespread crop failure (ibid.: 250ff.). In popular culture, 1816 – the year after the eruption – is widely known as 'the year without summer', while in German-speaking countries it is known as 'Das Hungerjahr' (the hunger year). Indeed, it is widely accepted that crop failure (down by 75 per cent across Western Europe (Wood, 2014: 61)) and a dramatic increase in the price of grain, led to widespread famine, and that malnutrition in turn contributed to the rise of epidemics such as typhoid and cholera, killing thousands of people (Oppenheimer, 2003). The exact numbers of dead attributable directly to the eruption are hard to gauge, but in landlocked states, for example, in Switzerland, 'deaths exceeded births ... in both 1817 and 1818, suggesting an excess mortality rate in the tens of thousands' (Wood, 2014: 63). Given the number of deaths and the role global cooling played in the rise of epidemics which killed hundreds of thousands of people, the volcanic eruption of Tambora clearly was an objective existential threat to individuals worldwide.

Although the price hike of grain led to riots, including in Britain (notably in East Anglia) and Switzerland, that required dispatch of the army, these riots did not constitute an existential threat to any of the political regimes in power.

This example shows that we can ascertain the objective existence of agent-lacking threats by first trying to understand what actually happens mechanically and physically when – in this case- volcanoes erupt. For example, it was only recently discovered that global cooling following the outbreak at Tambora was not a result of the presence of ash particles, but instead because of the lingering presence of sulphur in the atmosphere (Oppenheimer et al., 2016). Beyond the consequences ascertainable with help of the natural sciences, however, we need to consider what effects such an occurrence has on specific societies. Is the threat mediated because societies have adapted and do not, for example, live in great numbers in the vicinity of active volcanoes? What of the political and economic costs of the eruption? How well equipped are affected societies (companies, businesses and states) to deal with the loss of earning etc? All are relevant questions here.

3.6 AGENT-CAUSED THREATS

Turning now to my third category of threats, agent-caused threats refer to situations where an actor's behaviour leads to a threat to someone else, or even to the self, without the actor intending to do harm. Two sub-types of agent-caused threats[13] can be identified, as such threats can manifest by: a) obliviousness, i.e. when people do not realize that their (combined) actions are potentially threatening to other entities; or b) by harmful neglect i.e. when relevant agents fail to protect against foreseeable harmful consequences/events.[14] It is possible to illustrate these categories using the example of climate change, which is perhaps the most prominent agent-caused threat in the current era.

---

[13] I am indebted to Jonathan Floyd for clarity on this distinction.

[14] We might also say that A is ignorantly caused, while B is culpably caused, whereas agent-intended threats, which are strictly speaking subsets of agent-caused threats, are intentionally caused. To understand B it is useful to determine foreseeability in terms of David Miller's 'standard of reasonable foresight', whereby 'an agent is outcome responsible for those consequences of his action that a reasonable person would have foreseen, given the circumstances' (Miller, 2007: 96). Arguably, however, culpability in origin of threat is relevant primarily in terms of thinking through who – especially in securitizations by collective actors – is required to bear some of the inevitable financial costs of securitization, not so much for the permissibility to securitize (cf. Floyd, 2019a). It might also be important when considering the obligation to securitize.

While for a long time no one was aware that the burning of fossil fuels is the main cause of global warming, and climate change thus was caused through obliviousness, since the publication of the Intergovernmental Panel on Climate Change's (IPCC's) fourth assessment report in 2007 there is near scientific consensus that the recent levels of climatic change are man-made (Solomon et al., 2007). This means that no government, multinational corporation, firm or individual, provided that they have access to the necessary information, can reasonably claim obliviousness, and indeed objections to climate change are usually based not on ignorance but rather on denial/scepticism.

In spite of the general consensus that climate change is man-made, really happening, and that we have a good understanding of its likely consequences, many governments are slow to act on climate change. The United Nations Framework Convention on Climate Change (UNFCCC) negotiations have been protracted and tedious, and even now after the signing of the Paris treaty in December 2015 there is not only a question of how many signatory states will follow the United States, after the latter abandoned the agreement, but also whether it can be effective, given its bottom-up approach to emissions reduction, whereby states set targets themselves. Similarly while multinationals and many firms readily display their climate action, these are often nothing but token efforts, or else greenwashing. In short, the behaviour that causes climate change to worsen is no longer obliviousness, but rather harmful neglect.

While the climate threat has moved from being caused by obliviousness to the failure to respond to its foreseeable and well-documented consequences (i.e. harmful neglect), more often than not, these two sub-types of agent-caused threats coincide. During the financial crisis in Europe, for example, ordinary citizens by withdrawing their savings en masse from struggling banks (so-called bank runs), were able to trigger the collapse of banks (as happened with Northern Rock in the United Kingdom). Yet these bank runs could have been avoided had governments and banks put adequate safeguards into place making bank runs impossible.[15]

Importantly, all agent-caused threats are non-intentional. Some scholars will be uncomfortable with the inclusion of non-intended threats, because such threats may include the much written-about issue of immigration as an objective existential threat. I have argued elsewhere that even high levels of

---

[15] In the Republic of Cyprus, possible bank runs during the financial crisis had the potential to threaten the EU budget (European Commission, 2013) and potentially even the EU's continuous existence. They were successfully curtailed with the help of capital controls that are a form of securitization (Floyd, 2017b).

immigration are unlikely to qualify as a just cause for securitization, because the issue lacks the element of intent (Floyd, 2011: 434). And that with regards to immigration, intentions come into it only when something comparable to the following occurs: one state A, perhaps after failing to provide for its own people, would urge or perhaps even pay for its own people to emigrate en masse to another state B in order to benefit from B's welfare system[16] or economy. Under such circumstances, emigration from A might then become an objective existential threat to the receiving state B. While this logic still holds (immigration would then be an agent-intended threat by state A), I no longer believe it correct to claim that immigration cannot be a just reason for securitization simply because it lacks the element of intent.[17] In short, if there are such things as agent-caused threats then immigration and migration can very well be a just reason for securitization.

3.6.1 *Illustrative Example: The European Migrant/Refugee Crisis*

For an illustrative example of how we might proceed in order to establish the existence of objective existential threats for agent-caused threats and to tackle head on the emotive issue of immigration, let us consider the European refugee/migrant crisis of 2015–18.

In January 2016, at the height of the crisis, the French Prime Minister Manuel Valls criticized German Chancellor Angela Merkel's open-door asylum policy, arguing that Europe could not take all the refugees fleeing the wars in Syria and Iraq, otherwise 'our societies will be totally destabi-lised'. And that: 'If Europe is not capable of protecting its own borders, it's the very idea of Europe that will be questioned' (Valls, 2016). Valls's comments were echoed by the Dutch Prime Minister, Mark Rutte. For Valls and Rutte, the cause of threat lies in a combination of the number of migrants/refugees coming into Europe in a short space of time, but also in the (mis-) management of the migrant crisis, notably Germany's open-door asylum policy. Arguably, Germany failed to account for the foreseeable consequences of such a policy, many of which put the EU as we know it at risk. Among the foreseeable consequences were a worsening of the eco-nomic and political situation in Greece (as a transit country, among the worst affected by the migrant crisis) pushing them towards needing a further

---

[16] This sort of scenario is obviously only possible where bi- or multilateral immigration/asylum benefit agreements exist between countries, as they do for example in the EU.

[17] I had my reasons for initially wanting to exclude immigration; one certainly was that I wanted to try and avoid addressing the issue of the securitization of immigration because it is politically so sensitive.

bail-out,[18] the unwillingness of some Eastern European member states of the EU to take in Muslim migrants, the fact that migration has had destabilising effects on the viability of the Schengen area of free movement since 2007 (Alkopher and Blanc, 2016). But also considering that within modern Germany there are long-term and persisting problems with the integration of immigrants (Collier, 2013: 70), while there remains an east/west divide in terms of living standards and economic productivity, all of which feed the agendas of right-wing parties. Notably, the most successful of these, the Eurosceptic AfD has emerged as a considerable force within German politics against the background of the refugee/migrant crisis (Spiegel Online, 2016).

How then can we establish whether the refugee/migrant crisis is an objective existential threat for Europe? In the absence of an actor intending to do harm, the establishment of causality is pivotal, which is to say, we need to work out whether, first, the sheer number of refugees/migrants and/or, second, Germany's open door policy really existentially threaten the EU. There is much overlap here, but with regard to the first, one would have to look at how many people are actually coming over and where they are going/have gone. For each recipient country, one would have to examine the demographic make-up, in particular it would be necessary to compare the number of pensioners and the level of birth-rates with the number of migrants. Germany, for example, suffers from an ageing population. A study by the Bertelsman Foundation think-tank found that 'the country needs about half a million migrants a year until 2050 to counter that fall in the workforce' (Nasr, 2015). Beyond this, it would be necessary to look at healthcare provision and whether immigrants would be a benefactor (through income tax) or simply a beneficiary on healthcare provision. The same goes for schooling and housing. It might also be useful to examine how well immigrants are integrated in recipient countries. In order to avoid 'evidence' based on public perception, this ought to be done by considering objective indicators charting, among other things, the language spoken at home, unemployment compared with the native population, educational attainment, home ownership and number of endogamous partnerships (see OECD, 2015).

With regards to identifying Merkel's open door policy as the trigger, it would be necessary to establish whether or not the temporary suspension of the Schengen agreement on free movement by among others Sweden, Denmark, Austria, Germany, France and Belgium, resulted primarily from

---

[18] Noteworthy here is that the bail-outs of Greece had been highly controversial, with some member states openly discussing whether or not to leave the eurozone and even the EU.

a) the handling of the refugee crisis, or b) the terrorist attacks in Paris and Brussels in 2015 and 2016, or c) from a deep-seated rejection of the European project and its future. It would also have to be established whether Britain's historic decision to leave the EU – which could lead to further member states leaving the EU – was influenced by the refugee crisis, specifically by the forced allocation of migrants due to the EU's deal with Turkey (the EU-Turkey Statement). Only if direct causal connections between these factors could be established can we say with certainty that Mr Valls is/was (proven to be) correct in his claim.

These examples show that there is no standard formula to establishing the reality of agent-caused threats beyond establishing causality, alongside a detailed analysis of the consequences of the threat to the referent object, in order to establish its magnitude. While many critical scholars might be opposed to the inclusion of agent-caused threats,[19] it is important to remember that even if the presence of an objective threat can be established, securitization might still be, for example, a disproportionate response and as such unjust.

3.7 FUTURE OBJECTIVE EXISTENTIAL THREATS

So far I have talked only in terms of current objective existential threats. In this section I want to consider if, in addition to these, we should also include future objective existential threats as just reasons for securitization. In what follows I want to attempt to answer this question by drawing on insights gained from first security studies, and second from the just war literature.

In security studies, future threats are usually discussed with reference to the concept of risk. Like security, risk is a contested term, but for most risk-security writers, 'risks are generally less immediate than threats, more future-orientated and not based on specific threatening actors' (Corry, 2012: 12). Although in sociology the idea of risk is relatively longstanding (Beck, 1992), the literature on risk-security emerged largely as a consequence of the terrorist attacks of 9/11 and a resulting shift in the governance of security towards anticipating and preventing potential future terrorist attacks (Aradau and van Munster, 2007; Kessler, 2010: 18–19). Some risk-security scholars have gone so far as to declare a complete transformation of security policy. Mikkel V. Rasmussen, for

---

[19] I mean specifically (im)migration. It is a curious fact that practically all critical scholars otherwise sceptical of objective threats have no problem with the view that climate change is a real threat. Indeed securitization theory is becoming increasingly popular in Environmental Security Studies. Note, however, that securitization scholars working on climate change do not necessarily think that the issue should be securitized (cf. Floyd, 2019c).

example, holds that 'the purpose of security policy is no longer to stop threats, but to "filter" the really bad risks away' (2006: 109). While there is little doubt that governments and security services, especially in counter-terrorism, also focus on uncertainty, possibility and prevention, Olaf Corry (2012) convincingly argues that risk and threat are different things that require a different kind of response. He argues that although the risk-security literature is large and 'risks are clearly seen as somehow different to threats … the exact difference between them is not always made clear in risk literature' (ibid.: 10). Instead of suggesting that, for example, threats are big and risks small, or that risks lack immediacy whilst threats don't, he suggests that risks are the *conditions of possibility for harm*, whereas threats are about *direct causes of harm* (ibid.: 12). For example, 'the *risk of terrorism* or even the *risk of nuclear war* relates to factors that make terrorism or nuclear war possible, that is, the vulnerability of societies with political tensions, or the existence of nuclear weapons and weak international regimes. In contrast, the *threat* of terror is connected to particular agents believed to exist and have malicious intent and capability to commit acts of terror' (Corry, 2012: 12). Important for our purposes here is that only threats can be defended against, whereas risks can only be managed. As Corry explains, contra to securitization which 'involves a plan of action to *defend* a valued referent object against a threat, riskification implies a plan of action to *govern* the conditions of possibility for harm. The referent-object itself rather than an enemy becomes the primary target of risk programmes – something to be changed and governed rather than something to be defended as such' (ibid.: 13 emphases in original).[20] In other words, the inability to securitize, as opposed to manage risks or future threats, should mean that these threats are not plausible candidates for the inclusion into JST, which is not to say that the ethics of risk management policies should not be assessed in its own right.

Moving on to the just war literature, here the question of whether the possibility or risk of future attack qualifies as just cause for war is a much-debated topic (see various in Shue and Rodin, 2007). The discussions were very much fuelled by the war on terror in 2006, when the US National Security Strategy, Secretary of State Condoleezza Rice and US President Bush all evoked the right to a pre-emptive strike against terrorist cells. As Rodin explains, however, the use of 'pre-emptive' as opposed to 'preventive' war here was very much a 'rhetorical sleight of hand'. Thus '[a]ccording to well-established

---

[20] As we shall see in Chapter 6, section 6.2, however, while it is possible to separate riskification and securitization in theory, in practice the two may coincide. Elements of riskification were certainly part of the wider securitization of terrorism in the West.

legal usage, pre-emption consists in a first strike against an enemy who has not yet attacked but whose attack is clearly imminent. [...] Prevention, on the other hand, involves a first strike against a potential future aggressor who does not yet pose an imminent threat' (Rodin, 2007b: 144).[21] The reason for this deceit on the part of the Bush administration presumably was that many people accept that there exists a right to pre-emptive defence in international law, even if as Rodin points out, such a right exists really only in customary law and is not supported by Article 51 of the UN Charter (Rodin, 2007b: 145).

Since the justice of securitization does not feature in any kind of international law, these considerations do not necessarily translate into just securitization theory, in the sense of providing the grounds for rejecting prevention as a just cause for securitization. Since, however, the morality and the legality of war are two related but ultimately different things, it is also the case that quite a few just war theorists contemplate the possibility of just preventative wars (see various in Shue and Rodin, 2007). McMahan, for example, has argued that: 'there is a straightforward sense in which all self-defensive action is preventive. When you strike a person who is currently attacking you, your aim, so far as you are acting in self-defence, is to avert any *further* harm the attacker may do you; it is too late to defend yourself against the harm he has already caused' (cited in Buchanan, 2007: 126). However, established moral theories also recognize limitations for when I am allowed to act so as to prevent myself from *further* harm. Simply put, if I am attacked by a vicious aggressor, I am allowed to retaliate to prevent further harm to myself while the fight goes on. In this case, permissibility is tied to what has already occurred and to the fact that more beatings are very likely imminent (indeed I was able to retaliate, only because the attacker took a short breather during beatings). What is not permissible, in turn, is this: say I escape my attacker and encounter him by chance several weeks later in the street. For fear he might attack me again I strike first. The reason why the latter is not permissible is that I cannot know that he intends to do any further harm to me (my attacker, for example, may have mistaken me for someone else and since realized his mistake, etc.). Unlike in the first scenario, my actions here are not in self-defence; instead I have become the aggressor. So yes, strictly speaking, all acts of self-defence aim to prevent further harm, but not all violent acts are self-defence. In the absence of proof of imminent attack (i.e. a threat), my act of preventative defence turns into unjustifiable aggression. This is why for most people, permissibility of anticipatory defensive action (including anticipatory

---

[21] Criminologists interested in security speak of precaution instead of pre-emption (see Zedner, 2009: 85).

offensive defence) is tied to the likelihood of the attack occurring, and certainty as well as the likelihood itself of this occurring decrease over time, in all likelihood to the point that preventative action on future threats is unjustifiable.

Besides this, there is another reason why distant future threats are unlikely to be just reasons for securitization. Unlike most versions of the just war theory, JST does not specify last resort as a criterion for moral permissibility. I argue that if last resort is satisfied when all other viable options have been tried at least once and failed to meet just cause, then last resort specifies the point in time when securitization is morally required (cf. Chapter 5, section 5.5.2; Floyd, 2019b).[22] The latter also means that although it is possible to argue that securitization could prevent future harm, it is unlikely to be the only and last thing that could deliver the desired result in a relevant situation; especially not, considering that time is on our side to try out other things.[23]

Finally, I am inclined to agree with Suzanne Uniacke, who has argued that prevention comes (in time) before the use of harmful force, and as such, preventative measures are considered vastly morally preferable to using harmful force, provided prevention can be achieved by legitimate (i.e. non-exceptional) means and with acceptable risk and cost (Uniacke, 2007: 69). In short, prevention would be what is done before securitization is contemplated.

3.8 CONCLUSION

The just cause is perhaps the most important principle of any just war theory, and it is the same for Just Securitization Theory. I have argued in this chapter that the just cause for securitization consists in part of the just reason for securitization. Securitization is distinct from ordinary politics in the way decisions are made and because of the means used to achieve a desired end. Securitization almost always has some negative consequences, at a minimum because it is tantamount to a reduction of democracy in a sense of public scrutiny. I have argued that because of securitization's adverse consequences/

---

[22] To be clear, last resort is not the only criterion relevant for the moral obligation to securitize, it merely designates the point in time when it ought to be done.

[23] While it is important to consider such preventative securitizations, it should be noted that they are highly unlikely. Andrew Neal has convincingly demonstrated, for example, that in 'parliamentary the debates, however, arguments about hypothetical future risks were not successful: they were too intangible and too difficult to authoritatively assert. They were met with incredulity' (Neal, 2013: 127).

side-effects, the criterion setting the just reason for securitization needs to be sufficiently demanding. Consequently my first criterion specifies that it is not sufficient if a referent object is simply at risk or rendered vulnerable by a threat; instead it needs to be objectively existentially threatened, which is to say threatened in its essential being or character or its survival.

I understand objective in the evidence-relative sense, whereby a judgement about the status of a threat is based on all available evidence about the objective status of the threat. I thus acknowledge the impossibility of fact-relative verdicts concerning the future.

In addition this chapter has sought to demonstrate how scholars and practitioners interested in assessing the status of any given threat need to go about doing just that. To facilitate this analysis the chapter distinguishes between agent-intended, agent-lacking and agent-caused but not intended threats. The chapter concluded and ultimately rejected the viability of including future threats as just causes of securitization.

4

Just Initiation of Securitization: Just Referent Objects

4.1 INTRODUCTION

If magnitude and real presence of a threat were the only things determining a just cause for securitization, then anything so threatened would either be entitled to self-defence or eligible to defensive assistance by others. The result of such a proposition could potentially be devastating, as it would effectively permit even the most vicious dictator to protect himself and his cruel, inhumane regime against rebel forces intent on regime change. In short, such a theory would have little if any potential to improve the world. The world has a hope at being an improved place if only morally valuable entities are entitled to defend themselves, or are eligible for defensive assistance by others. In the context of just war, Orend puts it as follows: 'it seems paradoxical to suggest an *immoral* form of governance has a *moral* right to arm and defend itself' (2006: 36–37 emphases in original; 2007: 583; cf. Rodin, 2002).

In this chapter I set out how the value of potential referent objects as diverse as social and political orders, ecosystems or non-human species ought to be established. I argue that the value of any of these referent objects, and consequently the entitlement to self-defence (i.e. self-securitization), or eligibility to being defended by securitization is tied to the relative satisfaction of basic human needs (specifically physical health and autonomy). In other words, I argue that all of these referent objects are thus – at best – instrumentally valuable. The exception to this rule is human beings, who are themselves intrinsically morally valuable and as such – with one exception – entitled to defend themselves (securitization of self). The exception to this is examined in section 4.7, where I argue that morally wicked people have made themselves targets for defensive emergency action (i.e. securitization).

4.2 THE JUST REFERENT OBJECT

The research question for this chapter might be put in the following terms: what features render a potential referent object of security (which as we have seen could refer to many different things) morally valuable, and thus entitled to self-defence or eligible for being defended by way of securitization? The criterion of just securitization this chapter develops and defends can be summarized as follows.

Criterion 2: Referent objects are entitled to defend themselves or are eligible for defensive assistance if they are morally justifiable. Referent objects are morally justifiable if they meet basic human needs, defined here as necessary components of human well-being. *Political and social orders* need to satisfy a minimum level of basic human needs of people part of or contained within that order and they must respect the human needs of outsiders. *Ecosystems* and *non-human species*, in turn, need to make a contribution to the human needs of a sufficiently large group of people. *Human beings* are justifiable referent objects by virtue of being intrinsically valuable; all other referent objects therefore have instrumental value derived from the needs of human beings.

While moral philosophers establish the value of things in different ways – for example, some focus on consequences, others on the intrinsic value of certain procedures, and others yet again on the character of individual human persons – most, and indeed most humans, agree that a thing is valuable only insofar as it contributes to objective human well-being (in other words, when the thing is instrumentally valuable). To be clear, I do not wish to suggest that all philosophers theorize with explicit reference to human well-being, only that preoccupation with, for example, liberty, desert and fairness are ultimately concerned with how the human condition can be improved.[1]

Objective human well-being does not refer to personal happiness (which philosophers would call subjective well-being), but instead to the conditions that would have to be met so that people can *be* and *do* what they value (Sen, 1999: 75). While so defined, human well-being is an end state, definitions and theories of human well-being usually specify the means or the components needed to achieve it. Many competing formulations and theories of human well-being exist (see Alkire, 2002: 78–84); among the most convincing ones are

---

[1]   Raz speaks of the humanistic principle which holds that 'the explanation and justification of the goodness or badness of anything derives ultimately from its contribution, actual or possible, to human life and its quality' (1986: 194).

theories specifying (basic) human needs. As I will go on to explain in this chapter JST works with a particular theory of human needs in order to establish the moral justifiability of referent objects of security. In the just war tradition, eligibility to self-defence is usually based on rights, not needs, including on the collective right to self-determination (Walzer, 1977)[2] and sometimes also on whether states meet human rights.[3] Considering the conceptual closeness between human rights and human needs, it is first of all necessary to begin by explaining my choice.[4]

In philosophy, rights are generally taken to be a measure of justice or more likely legitimacy, whereas basic human needs chart either the presence of objective human well-being or the absence of harm (Dean, 2010). While they are clearly not identical concepts, many scholars ground human rights in human needs (see Floyd, 2011b), and some human needs are best met through rights legislation (see Simmons, 2009; Gasper, 2007; Gough, 2017; Doyal and Gough, 1991: 224). While there is often a connection between rights and needs, it should be clear that simply having a right does not necessarily increase well-being. Thus merely having a right does not mean that one is necessarily better off than not having that right. Consider the following in support of this argument. Two countries A and B have the same extensive set of rights, as well as the same institutions and policies suggesting that they are just the same. A close look at their respective economies and welfare budgets, however, indicates that A spends vastly more money on healthcare and education leading to consistently higher living standards, higher life expectancy and better levels of education. The lower levels of spending do not necessarily render B (more) unjust (especially not if it spends the same percentage of GDP on the welfare state system as does A); what it shows is rather that in spite of having all of the same rights well-being in A and B still differs, suggesting that well-being cannot be adequately charted by looking for rights alone, we

---

[2] In more detail: 'The moral standing of any particular state depends upon the reality of the common life it protects and the extent to which the sacrifices required by that protection are willingly accepted and thought worthwhile. If no common life exists, or if the state doesn't defend the common life that does exist, its own defence may have no moral justification' (Walzer, 1977: 54).

[3] Orend, for instance, argues that a 'minimally just' or 'legitimate' state is one that 'make[s] every reasonable effort to satisfy the human rights of their own citizens' (2006: 36) and identifies the 'foundational five: physical security; material subsistence; personal freedom; elemental equality and social recognition as a person and rightsholder [as the] things we all need to live minimally decent and tolerable lives in the modern world' (ibid.: 33, see also 2007: 582).

[4] For a view closer to what is suggested here, albeit limited because of its state-centrism, see Deane-Peter Baker's essay on 'Defending the Common Life – National-Defence after Rodin', presenting an account of national defence that is based in human flourishing (2007: 28).

ought to look for needs-satisfaction as well or instead (cf. Doyal and Gough 1991, 223).

There is a second reason why needs are superior in charting the value of a potential referent object of securitization. Unlike scholars of the just war, it must be remembered that my concern is with more than simply uncovering what constitutes minimally just states; instead, referent objects of security can include besides states any form of social and political order but also ecosystems, non-human species and individuals. While it has been suggested that the environment ought to be thought of as a human right (e.g. Thorme, 1990) so doing would enable us – at best – to examine the value of social and political orders in terms of whether they adhere to this right. Other potential referent objects, including ecosystems and non-human species, cannot in any meaningful sense be examined in terms of their human rights record; neither of these can be construed as duty-bearers for such rights. As I will show in this chapter, however, it is possible to examine all possible types of referent objects in terms of their ability to satisfy basic human needs, whereas in cases where the referent object is a human being, our concern is with her human needs.

Not all needs theories are explicitly about human flourishing and human well-being; some define human needs negatively in terms of what is needed to avoid being harmed (see Dean, 2010). When harm is avoided, however, human beings – depending on how harm is defined – attain at least some very basic level of well-being. In short, all human needs theories are implicitly about well-being, if different levels of it. Some specify what we may call 'rudimentary' well-being, avoiding only that which acutely endangers survival; while others put forward elaborate theories of needs necessary for human emancipation or human liberation (see for example, Nussbaum, 2011; Brock, 2009). All human needs theories, however, are informed by the principle of the equal moral worth of all human beings. 'Moral equality can be understood as prescribing treatment of persons as equals, i.e., with equal concern and respect, and not the often implausible principle of treating persons equally' (Gosepath, 2011).

One reason why needs theories are convincing is because they are truly universal; everyone has basic human needs regardless of cultural background and geographical location.[5] The philosopher Tim Mulgan makes this point particularly powerfully when he separates the moral realm into 'the realm of

---

[5] In this context Caney's point that the 'geographical location of the invention of the idea does not determine its later applicability' (2005a: 87) is relevant. See also Ken Booth, who argues: 'It is important to keep in mind that emancipatory politics need not be dominated by what are often loosely called "Western" ideas. Nor should ideas of universal significance be dismissed just because they are identifiable as having origins within the multifaceted Western world. A more benign world politics needs to be free of ethnocentrism and ethnoguilt. *All ideas come*

reciprocity' and 'the realm of necessity', and as such into two separate domains that are concerned with altogether different moral issues. The realm of reciprocity is dominated by *goals*, whereas the realm of necessity is dominated by *needs*. In this distinction, needs refer to 'biologically determined necessities of life, such as food, oxygen, or shelter, [whilst] goals are our chosen pursuits, projects, and endeavours, which give life much of its meaning and purpose' (Mulgan, 2001: 173). In Mulgan's view human needs are quite obviously not tied to cultural boundaries but rather arise by virtue of being human. More interestingly still, Mulgan further addresses the realm of reciprocity in relation to cultural relativism. The realm of reciprocity is defined as the realm where 'we, as active members of the moral community, decide how we will interact' (ibid.: 172). That is to say, it is the state of affairs where we as humans get to choose the goals that make our individual lives meaningful to ourselves. Mulgan argues that goals are only meaningful when certain conditions are met. Much simplified, this is the case only when actors have chosen their own goals autonomously, when there was an adequate and equally good number of goals available (choice and incommensurability), and when said goals are recognized as valuable by fellow human beings (community) (ibid.: 181 ff.). With regards to cultural relativism, Mulgan goes on to argue that whilst the particulars of certain goals may indeed be culturally specific, the *mechanisms* that make goals meaningful (autonomy, choice, incommensurability and community) are not. The reason why some may nonetheless associate these mechanisms with the West *only* is because they are not honoured or indeed promoted equally in all types of cultures/societies, and it is within a 'liberal system of non-interference' where the recognition of these mechanisms (or in other words: needs) is strongest (ibid.: 201).

One of the most compelling – in part because of its operability[6] – theories of human needs is Len Doyal and Ian Gough's *Theory of Human Needs*,

---

from somewhere, and it is foolish and naïve to dismiss something simply because of its geographical or cultural origins' (2005: 181; emphasis added).

[6] There are other reasons why I have chosen to work with this theory, and not one of the many other theories of human needs available. Each of these reasons will hopefully become clearer as I go along; for now, let me state the most important ones in brief. First, the theory is grounded in both ideal theory (philosophy) and social indicators (statistics); as such, it is epistemologically and methodologically convincing and holistic. Second, the theory emphasizes the preconditions for well-being only, and makes no claim on well-being itself. This is important, because even if the preconditions for well-being are met, there can be no guarantee that individuals achieve well-being. Third, as a result of having been developed with a view to charting well-being in the developed world and not in the first instance in the developing world, the theory goes beyond some other human needs theories and includes critical autonomy among its basic needs. Fourth and perhaps most fundamentally, I agree with the

published in 1991.[7] Just Securitization Theory relies on this theory both to identify components of human well-being and to measure its prevalence in any given context; in short, for the formulation of criterion 2. I will elaborate on this theory as well as its ease of operationalization in the next section.

4.3 HUMAN NEEDS AS A MEASURE OF HUMAN WELL-BEING

Doyal and Gough's theory defines human needs as negative concepts, meaning that they encapsulate what is needed in order to avoid serious harm. This definition presupposes that all humans have the potential for being harmed, and that all are harmed by the same things. [8] 'Serious harm itself is explicitly or implicitly understood as the significantly impaired pursuit of goals which are

---

conception of human beings as social animals and with the corresponding list of basic needs identified.

[7] Expanded upon by Ian Gough (1994, 2000 and 2013; Gough et al., 2007) and by Lesley Doyal with Len Doyal (2013).

[8] Given that I write about securitization, some – as Kamilla Stullerova put it to me – may wonder why the referent object's value does not rest in its contribution to security (as a state of being) rather than well-being (see, for example, Herington, 2015: 43). Aesthetically at least it would make good sense to opt for security as opposed to well-being, when we contemplate the value of different referent objects of security. However, it is also the case that human security is somewhat indistinguishable from conceptions of objective human well-being, many of which include physical security as one constituent part, with other components specifying what is needed to be free from want (for an overview, see Alkire, 2002: 78–84). Nevertheless, I am not convinced that (human) security is a more appropriate label than human well-being; especially not given that security for many has strong subjective connotations whereas – as this chapter shows – objective levels of human well-being can readily be charted. Or, put differently, the distinction between objective well-being and subjective happiness is better established than a similar distinction as regards objective or subjective (ontological) security as a state of being. While it seems then that the choice of 'security' or 'well-being' is purely a matter of personal preference, this would not be entirely correct either. Which of the two one settles for in a theory of just securitization also depends on the objectives one foresees for one's own theory of just securitization. JST is about the moral permissibility of securitization. As such, it does not prescribe when a threat should be securitized, it merely identifies the circumstances when securitizing actors may securitize, and what form security policies ought to ideally take including their implementation. In other words, it observes the functional distinction between security scholars and securitizing actors that is so central to the Copenhagen School's original securitization theory, but that is rejected by the critical theorists of the Aberystwyth School (see Floyd and Croft, 2011: 165).

  A theory of just securitization concerned with the moral obligation of securitizing actors to securitize, in turn, might benefit from theorizing the value of the referent object in terms of (its contribution to) human security; indeed this is precisely what we find in Booth's work and also in the newer, but related cosmopolitan security approach spearheaded by Burke (2013, 2014). This is so, because when one is concerned with the question when is securitization morally required, the parameters of analysis are likely to have shifted, in so far as mere scholars have transformed from being simply observers and/or evaluators of security policy and practice, to having become utterers of securitizing speech acts. (Some would go as far as to say that scholars

deemed of value by individuals. *To be seriously harmed is thus to be fundamentally disabled in the pursuit of one's vision of the good'* (Doyal and Gough, 1991: 50; my emphasis). Importantly, however, notions of what are valuable goals in life are not formed by individuals in isolation. Instead, humans are seen as fundamentally social creatures, who become what they are, and recognize what they want to be through the interaction with, and learning from, others only.

> Our entire lives – even when we are alone – are dominated by what we learn from others, how they assess what we think we have learned and how they respond to changes in our actions on the basis of such assessment. In other words, we build a self-conception of who we are through discovering what we are and are not capable of doing, and achievement based on our participation in social life. (Doyal and Gough, 1991: 50–51)

It is possible to identify basic human needs that, if met, would increase people's chances of successfully participating in social life and thus avoid being harmed.[9] Doyal and Gough identify *physical health* and *autonomy* as two such basic human needs.[10]

Physical health, it is important to note, is much stronger than survival, which many have specified as a basic human need. The idea is that simply being alive does not necessarily leave you in a position to participate successfully in social life. If you are crippled by ill-health and disease, the chances are that you will not be able to work or take part in other social activities. Whichever name or cause any given culture attributes to any given disease the effect on the individual is always going to be the same. Therefore 'physical health can be thought of transculturally in a negative way. If you wish to lead an active and successful life in your own terms, it is your objective interest to satisfy your basic need to

are not only utterers of securitizing moves, but in fact securitizing actors. This logic, however, is at odds with the definition of securitizing actor advanced in this book.) As such, they are likely to find the language of (human) security more evocative and powerful than that of well-being. Indeed, as I have argued elsewhere (Floyd, 2007b), human security scholars are not – in the first instance – concerned with security analysis, but their aim is to perform securitizing moves, or as I would now call it securitizing requests (Floyd, 2017).

9   This is what is meant by being and functioning as humans (cf. Introduction and Chapter 3, section 3.2.1). Importantly while their formulation of needs as avoiding serious harm suggests a commitment to a rudimentary idea of human well-being, the inclusion of autonomy, specifically what they refer to as 'critical autonomy', defined as the capacity to critically evaluate the socio-political context of one's place of birth, change it, or – if need be – move to another culture, suggests otherwise (cf. Gasper, 1996). Indeed in addition to avoidance of serious harm, 'critical participation in chosen form of life' constitutes a second universal goal of their theory of basic human needs (Doyal and Gough, 1991: 170).

10   These two are identified as basic human needs by a number of scholars. For a list of other human needs theorists see Alkire (2002: 78–84).

optimise your life expectancy and to avoid serious physical disease and illness conceptualised in biomedical terms' (Doyal and Gough, 1991: 59).

Lack of autonomy, whereby autonomy is in the first instance defined in the minimalist version, as the 'the ability to make informed choices about what should be done and how to go about doing it' (ibid.: 53) also leaves one 'objectively disabled' (ibid.: 68) from partaking fully in social life. Autonomy is impaired 'by severe mental illness, poor cognitive skills, and by blocked opportunities to engage in social participation' (Gough, 2000: 6). We can see from this that the achievement of autonomy is not simply down to the individual, but rather that society plays a role in fostering autonomy in individuals. To elaborate, consider the case of mental illness. Some mental illnesses (anxiety, mild forms of depression and eating disorders) are to a large extent learned forms of behaviour, and as such can be 'unlearned', provided that appropriate therapy and care are available. Given the cognitive element in these mental disorders and their malleability, society can act to improve the mental health of its people, by employing and training health care professionals in the relevant skills and by making this service available freely and widely.

With regards to cognitive skills, the role of society is even more straightforward. Doyal and Gough mean by this 'the level of *understanding* a person has about herself, her culture and what is expected of her as an individual within it' (Doyal and Gough, 1991: 60), and not intelligence, which is at least in part genetically predisposed. Understanding, in turn, depends on 'the availability and quality of teachers' (ibid.: 60) in a given society, not merely in school but in all walks of life.

Finally, by opportunities, Doyal and Gough mean the availability of meaningful work, relationships and other forms of participation in social life.[11] In the same way as physical health refers to more than simply survival, we can thus see that autonomy too refers to more than the minimalist version of autonomy described so far.[12] Holistic[13] autonomy encompasses both

---

[11]   This is also captured powerfully by one of philosophy's foremost writers on autonomy, Joseph Raz: 'To be autonomous and to have an autonomous life, a person must have options which enable him to sustain throughout his life activities which, taken together, exercise all the capacities human beings have an innate drive to exercise, as well as to decline to develop any of them ... Autonomy requires a choice of goods. A choice between good and evil is not enough' (Raz, 1986: 375, 379).

[12]   Doyal and Gough identify six criteria that need to be in place for a person to have minimal autonomy. They are 'a) that actors have the intellectual capacity to formulate aims and beliefs common to a form of life; b) that actors have enough confidence to want to act and thus to participate in a form of life; c) that actors sometimes actually do so through consistently formulating aims and beliefs and communicating with others about them; d) that actors perceive their action as having been done by them and not by someone else; e) that actors are able to understand the empirical constraints on the success of their actions; f) that actors are capable of taking responsibility for what they do' (1991: 63).

[13]   My terminology.

minimalist and critical autonomy, or else freedom of agency and also political freedom. Critical autonomy goes beyond 'the necessary conditions [needed] for participation in *any* form of life, no matter how totalitarian' (ibid.: 67); it is present when agents have the opportunity 'to question and to participate in *agreeing or changing* the rules of a culture' (ibid.: 67). Again, society, or rather the political system of a state (note Doyal and Gough are only concerned with states) plays a crucial role. Specifically *only* democratic forms of government protect political and civil rights and hence grant political freedom. In other words, democracy is a 'societal pre-condition' for basic needs satisfaction (ibid.: 170).

Doyal and Gough operationalize their theory of human needs by drawing on research from within the social sciences (e.g. anthropology, political science, sociology, psychology and economics) and the natural sciences (e.g. medicine, biology). Doyal and Gough are able to generate a list of 'properties of goods, services, activities and relationships which enhance physical health and human autonomy in all cultures' (Doyal and Gough, 1991: 157). The latter they refer to as intermediate needs.

Intermediate needs are second-order goals that must be met if the first-order goals of autonomy and physical health are to be met. There are eleven intermediate needs in total. Five of these correspond to physical health: 1) adequate nutritional food and clean water; 2) adequate protective housing; 3) a non-hazardous work environment; 4) a non-hazardous physical environment; 5) appropriate health care. The remainder: 6) security in childhood; 7) significant primary relationships; 8) physical security; 9) economic security; 10) appropriate education; and 11) safe birth control and child bearing correspond to autonomy.

While the relationship between 'physical health' and its corresponding intermediate needs is plain to see, the same might not be the case for autonomy. In order to understand the connection between autonomy and the specified intermediate needs, consider the point that good mental health is a key factor in being autonomous. The absence of many, if not all of corresponding intermediate needs of autonomy could be a source of mental ill-health, in other words, diminished personal autonomy.

From a practical point of view the most useful aspect of Doyal and Gough's contribution is the operationalization of their theory. Their key idea is that they translate both basic and intermediate needs satisfaction into social indicators.[14] For the most part the latter are well-known and regularly monitored

---

[14] In *A Theory of Human Needs* Doyal and Gough propose two separate lists specifying social indicators for basic human needs and intermediate human needs satisfaction. It seems to me that there is no need for that separation. In personal correspondence 7 August 2013 Gough

by international organizations such as the World Health Organization (WHO), the World Bank, UNESCO and HUMANA. For instance, the indicators that measure needs satisfaction with regards to physical health include the percentage of babies with low birth weight, life expectancy at various ages and age-specific mortality rates, the percentage of people lacking access to adequate safe water; and calorie consumption below WHO requirements.

Social indicators of autonomy include lack of higher education, the lack of primary education, and levels of illiteracy. Importantly, Doyal and Gough recognize both that there might not always be consistent data for all countries for all social indicators, and also that social indicators might change over time (notably the occurrence of HIV/AIDS has only been recorded since the emergence of the disease). As a result of this, the list of social indicators is both extensive and non-binding. This means that anyone applying Doyal and Gough's theory of human needs is not exclusively bound to the indicators they have identified, but can work with those for which sufficient data is available.

4.4 POLITICAL AND SOCIAL ORDERS

So far, I have made the case for human needs as universal values; I have shown what they are and how they can be measured. What remains is to discuss the appropriate scale of needs satisfaction and the implications of this for the value of potential referent objects of security. I want to begin with political and social orders.[15] We shall see that here, scale in terms of needs satisfaction is important because we cannot simply argue that political and social orders are morally justified provided they do not selfishly and wilfully infringe the basic human needs of others, including those outside their boundaries (cf. Fabre, 2012: 47). For example, when a powerful state that in the name of national security forcefully obtains scarce resources (fresh water, food etc.) from a neighbouring country, in total disregard for the basic human needs of the people living within the invaded country. While such a state does not qualify as a just

---

explained: 'yes ... there is no need for two separate lists of indicators of BNs and INs. The two separate chapters were necessary because a) there was still quite a bit of conceptual work needed to arrive at the BN indicators, and b) a combined chapter would have been inordinately long. But I have amalgamated the two lists on several occasions.'

[15] I differentiate between political and social orders, not because the two are always necessarily distinct, but because in addition to organized political communities (i.e. states, the EU, the UN) I wish to be able to include less formal orders held together by a shared identity, values and beliefs (i.e. citizens, religious group, minorities etc.).

referent object, deliberate infringement of basic human needs of insiders or outsiders cannot be the full answer, because it would set the bar for moral justification too low. That is, a theory of just securitization including this principle would hold out little promise for improving the world. In its place, I hold that social and political orders need not merely avoid doing overt wrong/ harm by infringing human needs, but that they qualify as morally justifiable referent objects only if they further the human needs for people within them (i.e. insiders).[16] Yet this raises the difficult question: what amount of basic human needs satisfaction does a political and social order have to meet so that that same order is morally justifiable? Answering that question will be the task of this section.

In order to understand my answer to the question, it is in the first instance important to realize that I do not insist on complete satisfaction of all basic human needs. Such a 'moral maximum' would set a false standard for moral justification, as most orders that could be referent objects of security only contribute to human needs but do not satisfy human needs. For example, all available evidence suggests that welfare states characterized by state inter-ventions in the form of providing 'income maintenance, health care and social services, [as well as] education, housing and employment policies' (Gough, 2000: 181) – are comparatively better at meeting human needs than any other kind of state (Doyal and Gough, 1991; Wilkinson and Pickett, 2010). Yet even in the best-developed welfare states, the basic human needs of some people are not met. Homeless and disenfranchised people are found everywhere, while national bodies like the United Kingdom's National Institute for Health and Care Excellence (NICE) still have to decide how to spend finite healthcare budgets, inevitably leaving some drugs unfunded, consequently not optimally treating some patients. In other words, different states contribute more or less well to meeting human needs, but human needs are unlikely to be completely satisfied by any existing system. Moreover, insisting on very high levels of needs satisfaction, as opposed to referents meeting a minimum amount of human needs, would exclude the vast majority of states in the developing world and unfairly tilt the scale in favour of the developed world, when development, which usually focuses on

---

[16] It is not particularly contentious to focus on insiders. Even some cosmopolitan philosophers emphasize that our duties towards strangers and our nearest and dearest are quite different. Fabre, for example, argues: 'we have some rights and duties *vis-à-vis* fellow citizens which we do not have towards distant strangers' (Fabre, 2012: 39 emphasis in original). In part, this is most certainly so, because even a very wealthy state could not hope to satisfy the basic needs of everyone, at least not at great and disproportionate cost to itself (see Shue, 1988: 695).

investments into literacy, education and health care, is all about meeting human needs.

In addition to the moral maximum, which would see all needs satisfied, two further points on a thinkable scale of needs satisfaction can be identified: optimization and a moral minimum. In *A Theory of Human Needs*, Doyal and Gough focus on optimal needs satisfaction. They are informed not by the observation that full needs satisfaction sets a wrong standard, but by Warr's 'vitamin model', which specifies that intake of vitamins is important up to a certain point, but not beyond it (Doyal and Gough, 1991: 162). They argue that: 'a particular level of satisfaction for each intermediate need is required if human health and autonomy are to be optimised, but beyond that point no further additional inputs will improve need-satisfaction' (ibid.: 162). As a practical measure Doyal and Gough suggest as a threshold 'the most recent standards achieved by the social group with the highest overall standards of basic needs satisfaction' (ibid.: 160). They take account of the vast gap between the developed and developing world by suggesting a 'constrained optimum' for developing countries, in other words the standards of basic human needs satisfaction achieved by the best performing developing country (Gough, 2013). There is no need to go further into Doyal and Gough's threshold for human needs satisfaction here. For our purposes, their threshold is unusable because it is concerned only with states, and it is not clear how optimum needs satisfaction could be established for non-state social and political orders that might become referent objects of security.

By a process of elimination, this leaves us with the moral minimum, or in Gillian Brock's terms, a 'minimum floor' (2009: 73) as the only plausible threshold for the moral justifiability of social and political orders as referent objects of security. So, what has to be the case, in order that we can say that basic human needs are minimally satisfied in any given political or social order? To my mind it would seem absurd to argue, for example, that only states with a life expectancy at birth of 72.0 years (the global average for 2016) and over can be said to meet a minimum of human needs (note that life expectancy at various ages is a suggested indicator for measuring physical health), and thus can justifiably defend themselves or be defended by others with recourse to security measures against objective existential threats. Even if similar thresholds could be found for the suggested indicators of autonomy, as well as for non-state and less formalistic social and political orders, this logic remains absurd because whether or not individual countries meet such thresholds is also subject to external factors, and even the best intended development programmes might result in little improvement in life expectancy at birth, for example, due to the prevalence of infectious diseases. Similarly it would also be wrong to arbitrate between different basic needs, and to claim, for example, that the satisfaction of intermediate needs corresponding to physical health is more important than the satisfaction of the intermediate needs corresponding to autonomy, and on that basis that the satisfaction of the former is enough to constitute a minimum floor of needs-satisfaction. To argue thus would be tantamount to elevating autonomy to a higher need, while only physical health would be a basic need, undermining Doyal and Gough's framework which has been selected here among competing theories of human needs to inform JST. In other words, the moral minimum for needs satisfaction cannot be set too low (see also Doyal and Doyal, 2013: 14–15, fn. 15).

For these reasons, I suggest that what matters is not that a specific and quantifiable minimum level of basic human needs satisfaction is met but that – in cases where the referent object is a political or social order – there is: a) hard evidence of the vital importance of the basic human needs physical health and autonomy; and b) that basic needs are actively promoted and that needs satisfaction remains a target. For state actors and political orders made up of states (e.g. the EU), the former is obvious from investment into development, health-care, and education, the presence of civil and political rights, political freedom and free and fair elections; the latter from political and open public discourse concerning the importance of individual well-being and the inalienability of liberal democratic values. For non-state-based social and political orders, needs satisfaction in line with the moral minimum is harder to locate, however, because such orders are not – unlike individuals (cf. below) intrinsically valuable, it must rest with a more substantial positive contribution than simply not infringing basic human needs, but instead with clear evidence that the human needs of those within such societies are being furthered by them, in terms of the values, norms and principles they hold and that co-constitute them.

4.4.1 *Illustrative Example: Kiribati*

In order to illustrate how we might proceed to establish whether a state meets the moral minimum of basic human needs satisfaction, let us briefly consider the case of Kiribati. I have picked Kiribati for three reasons. First, it is one of the world's lesser-developed countries. Second, it is regularly in the news because of the acute threat it faces from climate change. Third, it is a rare example of an intent-lacking threat to a regime to which Kiribati (given its small size and relative level of development) has contributed less than other states. While the latter might suggest that Kiribati, as a party with low levels of culpability in threat creation, has an intrinsic right to self-securitization, recall that I hold that states – unlike humans – have no automatic right to self-defence; instead, eligibility for self-securitization has to be earned by meeting the moral minimum of needs satisfaction.[17]

The Republic of Kiribati is comprised of thirty-three atolls in the Western Pacific with a population of approximately 100,000 people (Aus DFAT, 2013). About half of the population lives in Tarawa (the capital island) the remainder on the Gilbert Islands (ibid.). Ranked 121 out of a possible 187 countries and territories in the United Nations Development Index of 2012, Kiribati classified as being 'in the medium human development category' (UNDP, 2013). Freedom House scores the country with a 1 (most free for) for civil liberties and political rights respectively, it also has a free press (Freedom House, 2018).

Along with other low-lying Pacific island nations, Kiribati is objectively existentially threatened by rising sea-levels resulting from global climate change. 'Satellite data indicate the sea level has risen across Kiribati by 1–4 mm per year since 1993, compared to the global average of 2.8–3.6 mm per year [the latter attributable to phenomena such as the El Nino-Southern Oscillation]' (Office of the President of the Republic of Kiribati, 2011; cf. McCarthy, 2001: 935). Even such a comparatively low figure of sea-level rise is critical, because Kiribati has an average elevation of just two metres above sea-level and is therefore in danger of disappearing altogether. Although some costly sea defences are being put in place and landfill measures are being considered, the government is now considering migration for entire island populations.

In 2012 Kiribati's government entered talks with Fiji's military government in order to buy up to 5,000 acres of freehold land, with plans to resettle the entire island nation (Chapman, 2012). In the summer of 2014, Kiribati's President Anote Tong bought resettlement land on Vanua Levu, Fiji's second largest island, 'so that his 103,000 people will have some high ground to go to when a rising sea makes his nation of 33 low-lying coral atolls unliveable' (cited in Pala, 2014). The latter is beyond doubt a case of securitization, and from the point of view of JST it is thus interesting to ask whether Kiribati constitutes a morally justifiable referent object. Notably the issue is not whether the international community is morally required to enable or assist Kiribati with relocating; the issue is rather whether Kiribati is eligible to defend itself and to act so as to ensure its continuous existence. To be clear,

---

[17] It should be noted here that in line with JST, unjust regimes are not eligible for self-securitization or to defence assistance by others. However, unjust regimes are permitted to securitize against threats to the people living within their states (cf. Chapter 5, section 5.5.1). I recognize that when applying JST it will sometimes be difficult to ascertain whether a threat is primarily to a regime or to the people within it.

when I am talking of Kiribati, here I mean the state apparatus that exists beyond specific political administrations. Purely for the purposes of argument, let us assume that a) I-Kiribati would be happy to resettle elsewhere; and b) that they would be welcome to resettle elsewhere. In other words, let us frame the semi-hypothetical situation in such a way that there is no specific need for Kiribati (the state) to continue to exist.[18]

In line with the premises of JST, we need to look at whether Kiribati satisfies a minimum of basic human needs, that is to say whether there is evidence that basic human needs are fostered in action and discourse. On the face of it, Kiribati is one of the world's poorest economies, that draws much of its income from the fishing industry, tourism and foreign aid. Unless the new territory is able to sustain the former two industries, Kiribati could become entirely reliant on foreign aid. This might potentially void the case for continuous independent existence, as I-Kiribati might be better off housed in those states from which they already receive foreign aid (i.e. Australia and New Zealand), where they would also enjoy more varied opportunities for employment. If used towards development, however, receipt of foreign aid is not a sufficient argument against continuous independent existence. Recent figures show that in Kiribati since 2002, per capita government expenditure on health at average exchange rate (US$) doubled in the ten years until 2012 (WHO, 2016). Over the same period, general government expenditure on health as a percentage of total government expenditure increased from 8.2 per cent to 10.1 per cent (in 2013) (WHO, 2016). Life expectancy increased from 55.9 years in 1980 to 68.4 years in 2012, while Kiribati's GNI per capita increased by about 7 per cent between 1980 and 2012 (UNDP, 2013: 2). Similar progress has been made on social indicators of autonomy. Combined gross enrolment in education (both sexes) was up from 69 per cent in 2000 to 75 per cent in 2012 (UNESCO, 2013). And since 2008, Kiribati has established a national curriculum and assessment framework, universal primary education has been put in place, and teacher training curricula have been established (Kiribati Government, 2012: 10–11). Importantly, change has been driven by the understanding that human needs matter; indeed, that people are a state's biggest asset. The government's 2008 development plans were as follows: 'The 2008–2011 Kiribati Development Plan set out

---

[18]   I make these choices on the grounds that the situation of small island states is so unique that it would require a much more detailed analysis than I can provide here. I merely want to use this example to showcase how one needs to proceed in order to establish whether any given state meets a moral minimum of needs satisfaction.

a strategy to invest in Kiribati's main assets – its people and to transform the lives of I-Kiribati through further development of the economy and their *capabilities*' (ibid.: 10; my emphasis).

This brief analysis suggests that Kiribati meets the minimum threshold for human needs satisfaction, and as such qualifies as a morally justifiable referent object of securitization. To be absolutely clear, I do not wish to suggest that Kiribati as a country *should* 'relocate' (there might be other good reasons not to, including costs, practicability); all I want to say is that should they chose to act in this way, Kiribati has a moral claim on survival on the grounds that they satisfy a minimum floor of basic human needs.[19]

4.5 ECOSYSTEMS AND NON-HUMAN SPECIES

So far, I have discussed how the value of political and social orders as referent objects of security should be assessed. But what if referents are not man-made entities and we are therefore unable to assess the beliefs and actions of the humans within that order? In other words, what if the referent object of security is a natural entity? Two distinct referents come to mind. First, ecosystems defined as 'a community of living organisms and its physical environment' (Beeby and Brennan, 2008: 359). And, second, non-human species, whereby species is defined as '[a] collection of individuals able to breed with each other and produce viable (fertile) offspring' (ibid.: 366). I propose that the measure of eligibility for being defended by recourse to securitization (obviously the question of self-defence by securitization does not arise in this case) must rest with the ecosystems and/or the non-human species ability to make a contribution to the basic human needs of a sufficiently large group of people. Let us examine this claim in more detail, beginning with ecosystems.

Beyond any doubt, the United Nation's initiated authoritative, multinational working-group Millennium Ecosystem Assessment (MEA) (comparable to the IPCC for climate change) has established links between the following four ecosystem services: supporting services (e.g. soil formation, nutrient cycling, primary production); provisioning services (e.g. fresh water, food, fuel wood, fibre); regulating services (e.g. regulation of climate, disease and water); and cultural services (e.g. recreation and ecotourism, aesthetic, educational) with each of the following four constituents of human well-being: 1) security (defined as the ability to live in an environmentally clean

---

[19] There might be additional moral reasons supporting this, but here I am focusing only on the given reasons to make a specific point.

and safe shelter, and the ability to reduce vulnerability to ecological shocks and stress), 2) basic material for a good life, 3) health, and 4) good social relations (Millennium Ecosystem Assessment, 2003: 78). These links have been further expanded upon by national ecosystem services assessments and by the United Nations' TEEB (*The Economics of Ecosystems and Biodiversity*) studies. In summary, while ecosystems cannot hope to satisfy the same amount of needs as political and social orders can, all ecosystems make contributions to the basic human needs of some people. This said, however, not all ecosystems are eligible to being defended with recourse to securitization; some may well be too insignificant, here in the sense that the number of people whose needs are contributed to by the ecosystem in question is too small. One tree in a city square destined for development by the town-planners might provide some city dwellers with cultural services, but as an ecosystem, its contribution in terms of supporting and regulating services is likely to be too insignificant to warrant protection by securitization (cf. Chapter 5, section 5.3).

While non-human species of plants and animals are of course part of ecosystems and threats to species are often actually threats to wider ecosystems, including through pollution and climate change, species can also be directly threatened, for example through exploitation, habitat loss and the introduction of invasive species. It is also possible that the loss of a single species can cause the collapse of entire ecosystems. In conservation biology, the latter is called 'chains of extinction', whereby the metaphor of 'chains' seeks to capture the fact that ecosystems are interdependent and that the extinction of certain species can trigger further extinctions. An example is dung beetles (*Coleoptera Scarabaeidae*) in the Brazilian rainforest which 'through their role in burying dung and carrion as a food source for their larvae [facilitate] rapid recycling of nutrients and the germination of seeds defecated by fruit eating animals, and reducing vertebrate disease levels by killing parasites that live in the dung' (Middleton, 2008: 303).

The interdependence of ecosystems also means that the loss of one species can reduce the functioning of an ecosystem, thereby reducing the number of ecosystem services available to humans (Beeby et al., 2008: 345). In other words – and this is the argument championed by both the MEA and TEEB – nothing less than human well-being is at stake. The effect of biodiversity loss on human well-being explains why conservation bodies are concerned with maximizing biodiversity. Conserving as many species as possible is considered necessary as an insurance policy because we do not know how many species actually exist, and what kind of ecosystem services they provide (Millennium Ecosystem Assessment, 2003). While all non-human species might be worth saving, not all of the 1.8 million non-human species that have been described

(Vié et al., 2008) are worth saving at the considerable cost which securitization might entail, not to mention the fact that this is entirely unrealistic.

It is fortunate then that conservationists differentiate between species in terms of the benefits they have either for the wider ecosystems they are part of, or for conservation as a whole. In any ecosystem, the most important species are so-called keystone species. Keystone species play 'a critical role in maintaining the structure of an ecological community' (Jepson and Ladle, 2010: 62) or ecosystem through their activities. Examples include the already mentioned *Coleoptera Scarabaeidae*. Umbrella species, in turn, are species which roam a large area of land and whose protection and conservation is thought to benefit a large number of species residing in the same ecosystem (though for some problems with this theory, see Roberge and Angelstam, 2004: 76). Examples include capercaillie (*Tetrao urogallus*) and grizzly bear (*Ursus arctos*). Flagship species is a term introduced by the World Wild Fund for Nature (WWF) and refers to iconic animals that stimulate interest in conservation (West, 2004: 221). Examples of flagship species include polar bears (*Ursus maritimus*), the giant panda (*Ailuropoda melanoleuca*) and tigers (*Panthera tigris*). Fauna & Flora International's Flagship Species Initiative identifies a number of trees as flagship species, including the she cabbage tree (*Lachanodes arborea*) and the lansan tree (*Protium attenuatum*). Finally there are those species which have known medicinal or palliative properties. An example of a medicinal plant species is rosy periwinkle (*Catharanthus roseus*), which is the source of two cancer-fighting medicines, vinblastine and vincristine. 'Vincristine has helped increase the chance of surviving childhood leukaemia from 10% to 95%, while vinblastine is used to treat Hodgkins' Disease' [a type of lymph cancer] (The Living Rainforest, 2013).

It is easy to see why among the 1.8 million or so species defined as keystone, umbrella and medicinal plant species serve as valuable entities eligible to being defended by securitization. Thus the former two contribute to both the functioning and to the protection of whole ecosystems and their services, while the latter provide a service in and of themselves and ecosystem services in turn foster basic human needs. Things are more difficult when it comes to flagship species. Some conservationists have openly argued for letting some endangered species within that category 'go extinct', in order to spend the resources on conservation of other species. The BBC wildlife programme presenter Chris Packham, for instance, has advanced this argument regarding the giant panda (The Telegraph, 2009). This view however is not compatible with the MEA's ecosystem services categorization, which specifies non-material benefits obtained from ecosystems, and within that, recreation and ecotourism. Besides landscapes and natural environments (coastlines, woodlands, mountains etc.) flagship species are among the primary providers of recreational value. Not only are many ecotourism trips centred on viewing one or more flagship species, but also zoos, with news of flagship species' pregnancies and births regularly filling newspapers. In addition, many flagship species are primates, and research has revealed interesting insights, relevant also for human life. Although many flagship species count as the world's most wonderful animals, they do not make a contribution to the satisfaction of basic human needs in the way some other species do and therefore ought not – when objectively existentially threatened – to be protected by securitization.

4.5.1 *Illustrative Example: Ash Die-Back Disease and the Emerald Ash Borer Pest*

Across the European continent[20] common ash (*Fraxinus excelsior*) and other ash trees such as *Fraxinus angustifolia* are subject to the fungus *Hymenoscyphus fraxineus* (previously called *Chalara fraxinea*), which causes these trees to die back once infected. Chalara dieback of ash was first seen in Poland in the early 1990s, and by 2002 it had spread to twenty-two European countries (Timmermann et al., 2011), causing devastation. In Denmark, for example, it wiped out 90 per cent of the ash tree population, and in Britain it is on course to do the same (Thomas, 2016). Here, ash trees are so common that 90 per cent of ash trees (approx. 80 million trees) account for 20 per cent of all trees (Vidal, 2015).

In the United States, Canada and increasingly Russia, ash tree populations are existentially threatened for a different reason: the emerald ash borer pest (*Agrilus planipennis*) a phloem-feeding (i.e. feeding of the sap) beetle native to Asia that was introduced to the United States by accident (Poland and McCullough, 2006). Discovered in North America in 2002, by 2012 it was estimated to have killed 100 million ash trees, with a further 7 billion ash trees under threat. The ash borer pest is expected to arrive in Western Europe in the next few years (Thomas, 2016). While there can be no doubt that both the fungus and the beetle constitute an objective existential threat to ash tree populations in both Europe and North America, do ash trees make just referent objects for securitization? According to JST, ecosystems or individual

---

[20] 'Ash natively reaches its most northern point of 63° 40'N in Norway and 61°N on the Baltic coast. It extends eastwards to the Volga River basin in western Russia … In southern Europe, *F. excelsior* is replaced in the most Mediterranean climates by *F. angustifolia*. In Spain, ash extends into the northern mountains but is absent from central and southern parts of the Iberian Peninsula and N. Africa. It is also absent from Iceland' (Thomas, 2016, 1159).

species may be saved by recourse to securitization only when they make a contribution to the human needs of a sufficiently large group of people.[21]

The link between well-being and the natural environment (green spaces in particular) as suggested by the MEA (see above) has been substantiated by a number of studies which have confirmed the linkage between mental health (a feature of autonomy) and exposure to nature (Mayer et al., 2009; White and Heerwagen, 1998). Ash trees are the most common street and city trees in North America and Western Europe (Thomas, 2016), providing people with green spaces in which to relax and deal with the stresses of modern life. Beyond that, one recent study in the prestigious[22] *American Journal of Preventative Medicine* on the impact on physical health of the loss of 100 million ash trees due to *Agrilus planipennis* found that during the years of 1990–2007 across fifteen states, 'the borer was associated with an additional 6113 deaths related to illness of the lower respiratory system, and 15,080 cardiovascular-related deaths' (Donovan et al., 2013, 139). The authors of the study explain that '[r]esults do not provide any direct insight into how trees might improve mortality rates related to cardiovascular and lower-respiratory-tract illness. However, there are several plausible mechanisms including improving air quality, reducing stress, increasing physical activity, moderating temperature, and buffering stressful life events' (ibid. 144). If the authors are correct, and there is a causal connection between the dying of ash trees and increased human mortality, then the combination of ash die-back and the ash borer constitutes an objective existential threat to physical health of people living in the affected areas, and the issue may be securitized. What this would actually involve (see Duffy, 2015 and Eckersley, 2007 for some suggestions in related contexts) is another thing altogether.

4.6 HUMAN BEINGS

So far so good, but what happens if human beings and not ecosystems or political/social orders (i.e. states) are referent objects of security? We might

---

[21] Some readers will object to this and argue that nature is intrinsically valuable. In environmental ethics this is a hotly contested issue. Arguably, however, once we consider the origin of value, the case seems settled in favour of instrumental evaluations. Thus, what is the value of a pristine, beautiful planet as rich in flora and fauna as we imagine the Garden of Eden, when there is no one there to value it? The question of the value of the natural environment is a perennial issue that cannot be settled here. From the point of view of using emergency measures to save (parts of) the natural environment, tough decisions have to be made, and I simply don't see how we can justify emergency action – including against humans – in order to safeguard flora and fauna for their own sake.

[22] Impact Factor: 4.527 © 2015 Journal Citation Reports ®, Thomson Reuters.

argue, as I have in the past (Floyd, 2011: 438) that the question of eligibility on moral grounds does not arise in the same way as it does for other referent objects, as our concern is simply with the well-being of the threatened individuals, who as human beings are intrinsically valuable. While this formulation still stands, I have since realized that – as we will see – this standpoint, especially for agent-intended threats, is not always sufficiently action-guiding. I will explain this in more detail below, but to come by this problem I propose that a theory of just securitization needs to distinguish between those that are morally wicked and those that are not. In the same way as JST cannot hope to improve the world if it has no means of distinguishing Bashar Al-Assad's Syria from say Angela Merkel's Germany, it also cannot hope to improve the world if it does not distinguish between Adolf Hitler, the Nazis and most ordinary, reasonable and law-abiding people. People who intentionally and without valid excuse deprive innocent others of their basic human needs simply to further their own ends are morally wicked, and not themselves 'deserving subject[s]' (McLeod, 2008). I propose that the basic minimum floor for human beings in order for them not be classed as morally wicked is *not* that they actively promote human needs, but simply that they do not intentionally infringe other people's human needs.[23] Naturally, the morally wicked still have human needs; my point is that certain types of actions (unlawful killing of innocent people, intimidation, terrorism, extortion etc.) mean that they effectively lose the entitlement of either securitization as self-defence or to being made safe and secure by others, at least in situations where their behaviour has made them liable to become the subject of securitization.

While this might seem a bold statement (notably, I include the idea of moral wickedness with some trepidation), some of it is influenced by Rodin's (2002) work on war and self-defence. Rodin argues that the right to self-defence is a defensive right, its defining feature being that it is a 'derivative', not a 'core right', which is to say part of a group of rights that 'derive their normative force from some prior right or normative relation' (Rodin, 2002: 37). This normative relation may concern protection of the self, for example, 'the right to defend one's own life derives from one's right to that life' (ibid.: 38), it can concern right to property, or a defensive right to protect third parties established through a 'duty of care' (ibid.: 37–38). For the purposes of the argument advanced in this section I am interested in the right to self-defence, and specifically in the possibility of losing that right. To be clear, all just war theorists need to engage with the conditions

[23] Fabre (2012: 30) makes some similar observations but does not use the phrase morally wicked.

when this right is forfeited by aggressors, as otherwise the right to life by the aggressor would stand in direct opposition to the right of self-defence by the defended, making the just war theory an impossible proposition (see ibid.: 50). For Rodin the forfeiture of a right to self-defence and the related right to killing are intimately connected and ultimately tied to fault: 'the feature which provides the required explanation for why a victim has the right to kill his aggressor is the fault of the aggressor for the aggressive attack' (ibid.: 77). McMahan argues along similar lines, when he states that in war, soldiers are justified in killing a person, when that person 'has acted in a way that has made him liable to be killed' (2009b: 157). Soldiers are most clearly liable to be killed when they commit *jus in bello* violations. But where does this liability to being killed come from? McMahan explains this in terms of what he calls 'culpable threats'. He argues:

> *Culpable Threats* ... are people who pose a threat of wrongful harm to others and have neither justification, permission, nor excuse. They may intend the harm they threaten, or the risk they impose, or the threat may arise from action that is reckless or negligent. But because they have neither justification nor excuse, they are fully culpable for their threatening action. As such, they are fully *liable to necessary and proportionate defensive action*. (McMahan, 2009b: 159; first emphasis in original, second one added)

For JST this means that morally wicked people make themselves targets to defensive emergency measures, whilst at the same time losing the moral right to counter these defensive measures with their very own security measures. For example, a state may securitize an extremist group spouting hatred and taking offensive action against minorities (e. g. killing and maiming asylum-seekers, burning down places of worship during prayer time) by banning them, but that same group has no moral right to defend itself against this ban, even though it clearly constitutes a real threat to their existence as a group (cf. Fabre, 2012: 59). A similar logic informs Orend's requirement that states need to be minimally just to have the moral right to resist aggression. He explains the difference between legal and moral rights as follows: 'Legally, any UN member state has the right to go to war to resist aggression directed either against itself or another UN member. But morally, only those states which are minimally just have rights to sovereignty, territory and to resist aggression' (Orend, 2006: 37).

It remains to discuss what happens to the moral right to self-defence if the morally wicked are objectively existentially threatened not by a defender of those intentionally and deliberately harmed, but by another threat. To put this differently: do the morally wicked have a moral right to defend themselves against a meteor hurtling towards them from outer space and threatening to wipe them out? At first sight it seems logical to say that because the morally wicked had already (i.e. prior to the meteor approaching) lost the right to defend themselves, they are not morally permitted to do so now, even though the source of the threat is different. Thus it is not clear at what point they would regain the right to defend themselves. This said, however, there are problems with this line of thinking. First, what does it achieve to say that the morally wicked are not morally permitted to defend themselves, when individuals will always – as a matter of human nature – do just that? Second, and more importantly, in the case of the meteor strike, the morally wicked are not at fault for *causing* the threat, they have not, in other words, rendered themselves liable to being killed by meteor strike and thus may take appropriate securitizing measures to protect themselves. Third, if we were to suggest that the morally wicked do not have a right to defend themselves against an unrelated threat (i.e. one they did not bring about through their own actions), we would go one step further than anyone who believes in culpable threats, and arguably where no just war theorist would venture. Thus, what we would be saying is that the morally wicked have not only lost the right to defend themselves, but the right to life also. Translated into the just war theory, it would mean that wars would only be just at the point when unjust warriors and aggressors are killed. It goes without saying that acting thus would be wholly disproportionate (cf. Rodin, 2002). In short, we can conclude that where unrelated threats are concerned even the morally wicked – in virtue of being human – are just referent objects of securitization, and as such eligible to be defended by third parties or entitled to self-defence.

4.7 CONCLUSION

This chapter was about the just referent object for securitization, which together with the just reason for securitization forms the just cause for securitization. I argued that unless a theory of just securitization specifies a criterion of moral justifiability of referent objects, it cannot hope to improve the world, as it would bestow immoral and moral agents with the same entitlement to self-securitization when in fact such a moral right to self-defence is derivative of some prior normative relation. I further argued that the moral justifiability depends on the referent object's ability to meet basic human needs which are necessary components of objective human well-being, insofar as they allow a person to meaningfully partici-pate in the society of which he is part.

Just cause is an important, but ultimately only one part of the just initiation of securitization. The next chapter discusses further substantive criteria within this category. Among other things, we shall see that the novel and explicit category of just referent object which does not as such feature in just war theories, reduces the need for one of just war's staples: legitimate authority.

5

Just Initiation of Securitization: Right Intention, Macro-Proportionality and Reasonable Chance of Success

5.1 INTRODUCTION

This chapter identifies three further criteria that besides just cause, govern the just initiation of securitization. Criterion 3 is concerned with sincerity of intention; it holds that resort to securitization is morally permissible only if, by securitizing, the securitizing actor aims at protecting the designated just referent object informed by a just reason. Criterion 4 is concerned with what just war theorists refer to as *ad bellum* proportionality, or macro-proportionality, which is to say the idea that the expected good gained from securitization must be greater than the expected harm from securitization. Criterion 5 is concerned with probable consequences of securitization, in so far as it requires that securitization stands a reasonable chance of achieving the just cause, whereby reasonable chance is to be established comparatively to alternatives to securitizing. In addition to this, this chapter also discusses why some criteria prominent in the just war tradition – notably legitimate authority and last resort – are omitted from JST.

5.2 SINCERITY OF INTENTION

In addition to the just cause, just war theorists also generally require that wars are informed by the right intention. Orend (2006: 46) explains that this requirement stems from the idea that morality requires not only 'proper external behaviour' (for example, a child returning a bike they stole to its rightful owner) but also 'internal reflection and right attitude' (a return of the bike – to run with Orend's example, because the child is sincerely sorry, not because she was coerced to return the bike by her parents).[1]

---

[1] McMahan writes: 'I think the theoretical case for the relevance of intention to permissibility is a matter of reflective equilibrium, a matter of integrity and coherence of our core moral

Underlying the requirement of sincerity is the observation that wars can and do happen without right intention. Orend uses the Iraq war to make this point, whereas many questioned the integrity of NATO's intentions in Operation Unified Protector in Libya.[2] In other words, we can say that right intention is supposed to ensure that the 'entity intends to achieve the just cause, rather than using it as an excuse to achieve some wrongful end' (Lazar, 2017: 5). Partially informed by this thinking, but as we shall see also by the view that right intention allows agent evaluation, this section develops the following principle.

Criterion 3: The right intention for securitization is the just cause. Securitizing actors must be sincere in their intention to protect the referent object they themselves identified and declared.

The requirement that just securitizing actors have to be sincere in their intentions to address the just cause, makes sense only if we can accept that securitization can be satisfied even in the absence of sincerity of intention on the part of the securitizing actor. This is certainly the case when one emphasizes the speech act part of securitization only. The peculiar fact that speech acts can be insincere but nonetheless successful has been observed by Austin and Searle. Austin, for example, held that the non-observance of the felicity condition specifying sincerity (one of a total of six felicity conditions) leads not to the misfiring of the speech act, or in other words its voidance, but merely to its unhappiness (Austin, 1965: 16). Elsewhere I have used the following example to illustrate this point: suppose 'a person gets married without the needed thoughts and feelings required, and once married behaves in discordance with the marriage vows, then the speech act is unhappy, but the marriage still is valid and can only be fully dismantled by lawful divorce' (Floyd, 2010: 13). Building on Austin's work, Searle argued: 'An insincere speech act is one in which the speaker performs a speech act and thereby expresses a *psychological state* even though he does not have that state ... An insincere speech act is defective but not necessarily unsuccessful. A lie, for example, can be a successful assertion' (Searle and Vanderveken, 1985: 18; emphasis added).

beliefs ... many of our firmly held moral beliefs – such as that there is a significant moral difference between just war and terrorism ... are explained in a simple and seemingly plausible way by the principle that one's intention can affect the permissibility of one's action' (2009a: 369–370).

[2] Towards the end of this section I argue that there is likely to be a connection between right intention and referent object benefiting securitization. In the Libya case, we can see the connection between intention and outcome quite clearly; thus we can assume that had the intention of the West been to avert humanitarian catastrophe, as opposed to regime change, the intervention would have been done better, and with greater thought given to the aftermath.

Searle's argument raises the following question: if sincerity is a psychological state internal to the actor, then how can one have a hope of gauging sincerity?

I suggest that we have to differentiate between on the one hand, sincerity of motive, and sincerity of intention on the other.[3] Recall that – following Anscombe – I hold that motives correspond to an actor's private beliefs and thoughts, while intentions are what an *actor aims at* in doing something. Sincerity of motive is hard, often impossible to ascertain from any given situation, because even if actors act in accordance with what they said (for example, employ security measures following a warning to an aggressor) and thus display sincerity of intention, we cannot know for sure whether they were sincere in their motives for giving a warning or for making a promise.[4] Luckily their inner psychological status need not concern us here; all that matters for our purposes is whether actors are/were sincere in their intention to act on the just cause. I follow the philosopher Nick Fotion here, who argues that: 'With promising the sincerity condition [of speech acts] has nothing to do with what the speaker believes or is supposed to believe. Rather, it has to do with intent. The person who made the promise is supposed to have the intent to carry out what he promised' (Fotion, 2000: 29). If they do not have this intention, then they are insincere.

If Fotion is correct, then sincerity of intention in securitizations featuring promises as securitizing moves can be read off from an actor's behaviour, compared with the security language they use (cf. Pattison, 2010: 163–164). As far as securitization is concerned we need to compare what securitizing actors say in terms of who is threatened and by what, with what they subsequently do to avert the threat they themselves identified. If there is an otherwise inexplicable disconnect; securitization may still be considered successful/complete (provided there is an observable change of relevant behaviour on part of the securitizing actor, or in other words that security measures are taken) but nevertheless the promise is broken.

If our concern is with securitization where the securitizing move was a warning only, we again proceed by comparing what an actor says with

---

[3] Some of this comes very close to James Pattison's discussion in Chapter 6 of his book on humanitarian intervention (2010). However, I only read this later and did not draw on him to elaborate on the difference between motive and intention.

[4] Recall that I take all securitizing speech acts (securitizing moves) by securitizing actors to be one of three things: 1) a promise for protection to a referent object (for agent-lacking and agent-caused threats), 2) a warning to the aggressor (for agent-intended threats where the referent object is the self), or 3) a combination of the two (for agent-intended and agent-caused threats). Securitizing speech acts by other actors are securitizing requests.

what he does.[5] Yet here we have the added difficulty of bluffing. That is to say, situations when the warning itself amounts to nothing more than a bluff and actors do not intend to act on the warning, for example, because they do not have the capability to do so. How are we to treat those situations? It seems to me that while here everything points to insincerity of intention, it might be more accurate to say that the securitizing move was not credible. In such situations, the securitizing move – even in the absence of exceptional security measures – can still have the desired effect, provided the latter is the same as that stated in the securitizing move. Thus it is possible, for example, that an aggressor stops whatever they are doing as a result of a warning (perlocutionary effect) and no further action on part of the securitizing actor is necessary (cf. Figure 2.1).

An empirical example of an insincere securitizing actor is that of the Clinton administration's environmental security policy.[6] Led by President Clinton and since turned green campaigner Vice President Al Gore, the administration identified the American people as existentially threatened by global environmental change and degradation, and promised to protect them. What was done as part of the administration's environmental security policy, however, did little to address global environmental change and the actual beneficiary of this policy was not the American people, but rather the US national security establishment (Floyd, 2010: 116–120). This instance of an 'agent-benefiting securitization' provides clues to *why* actors would securitize without being sincere. Security is a powerful concept that attracts money and status, and quite frankly awards a state's often vast security establishment with a raison d'être; in the same way as attaching the security label to political problems generates money for the research community. It is thus not surprising that state actors have deliberately overstated and manufactured threats, a phenomenon described by David Campbell as 'discourses of danger' (Campbell, 1998). So the abuse of securitization is not only possible, but very plausible. Any normative evaluation of the justice of securitization must test for the sincerity of intention.

---

[5] Although I am not concerned with the sincerity of motive, it seems to me that sincerity of intention can also sometimes tell us something about sincerity of motive. For example, it does not make sense for states, which delicately balance their affairs through a whole host of peaceful international practices, to risk 'picking a fight' (which is what a warning potentially does) without good reasons for doing so. As far as warnings are concerned we can be fairly sure, but not certain, that securitizing actors sincerely believe that there is an aggressor intent on harming them.

[6] While in this case securitization did not take the form of the exception, this does not deflect from the general point I want to make.

Importantly, sincerity does not trump the just cause, which is logically prior to other principles making up the just initiation of securitization. We might therefore say that the right intention is the just cause. It is important to note, however, that not every securitization that satisfies just cause automatically satisfies sincerity of intention. Just cause can be met *without* the securitizing actor having the right intention, but accidently as a side-effect. James Pattison exemplifies this on the following example:

> Suppose, in the middle of the night, the electrics in house No. 1 short-circuit, causing a small fire. The battery in their fire alarm has run out and so it does not sound. Soon after, a burglar breaks into the neighbouring house, No. 2, setting off their intruder alarm. It is so loud that it awakens the residents of house No. 1 before the fire in their house has time to spread and put their lives at risk. Indirectly, then, the burglar has saved the lives of inhabitants of No. 1. But we would not call the burglar's action humanitarian because, despite it yielding a humanitarian outcome, the *intention* was not to save the lives of the inhabitants of No. 1. (Pattison, 2010: 162)

This example allows us to recognize that right outcome is not solely dependent on intention (though we must expect that right intention is more likely to generate right outcome than wrong intention, partly because guided by the wrong intention the actor is less likely to focus and work hard on achieving right outcome than they would be guided by right intention). Indeed, as Pattison explains, the intention of the actor (in his case as intervenor, for his concern is with humanitarian intervention) allows us to characterize an act as humanitarian in the first place (Pattison, 2010: 162). Paraphrasing Pattison (ibid.: 168) we can say that securitizing actors who do not have right intention are simply not engaged in just securitization, and any unjust use of emergency measures is, of course, morally impermissible. While right intention then influences the overall justice of securitization, we must recognize then that right intention is primarily about the securitizing actor. Right intention not only enables us to categorize a securitization as just, it is also definitive of the moral standing and hence the 'legitimacy' of the securitizing actor.[7] That is to say: an actor who intends to do the right thing has the 'morally justifiable power' to do it (Pattison, 2010: 32).[8]

---

[7] Pattison (2010: 165) argues that this is the view of Tesón and Bellamy, but – in my view – the quotes he uses to substantiate that claim do not fully support it, as both write about the overall legitimacy of the intervention, and not specifically the intervenor.

[8] Note that in line with Pattison, legitimacy here refers to qualities of the actor only (Pattison, 2010: 31).

One final point is relevant in the context of sincerity of intentions. An actor who acts on the basis of wrong intentions is morally culpable for doing so. Moreover, situations where securitizing actors are sincere and act in good faith to secure a referent object they have erroneously identified as objectively existentially threatened, do not count towards just securitization. Securitizations, lacking a just cause, but which are made on the basis of good intentions are no less permissible than those informed by wrong intentions (i.e. agent-benefiting ones). The difference between good and wrong intentions in unjust securitizations comes into play in particular with regard to the blameworthiness of actors in desecuritization. Thus those acting with good intentions are less blameworthy than those who acted on the basis of wrong intentions (Parfit, 2011: 150), an observation that will become relevant in Chapter 7 in the context of just desecuritization.

5.3 MACRO-PROPORTIONALITY

Most formulations of just war theory include in the list of criteria specifying *jus ad bellum* a proportionality requirement concerning the ends of war. This is sometimes known as macro-proportionality, and it tends to hold something along the lines here formulated by Orend: 'a state considering a just war must weigh the expected *universal* (not just selfish national) benefits of doing so against the expected *universal* costs. Only if the projected benefits, in terms of securing the just cause, are at least equal to, and preferably greater than, such costs as casualties may the war action proceed' (Orend, 2006: 59; emphasis in original). Or, as Kateri Carmola (2005: 98) puts it, the question is: 'Will the good of the war [securitization] outweigh the evil of the harm inflicted'? In this section I develop and defend the following criterion:

Criterion 4: The expected good gained from securitization must be greater than the expected harm from securitization; where the only relevant good is the good specified in the just cause.

In order to develop this criterion it is first of all important to understand that proportionality considerations feature in both the just initiation of securitization and also again in just conduct in securitization. In the former, proportionality is concerned with whether the harm securitization inevitably causes is a proportionate response to a given threat; in the latter, proportionality considerations concern whether the specific security measures used exceed the threat and adversely affect innocent bystanders as well as the harm one may justly inflict on aggressors, or else those who have rendered themselves liable to being harmed. From this we can see that the entity harmed relevant for establishing securitization's proportionality can be two different things. McMahan explains that narrow proportionally (henceforth proportionality$_n$) is concerned 'with the harm inflicted on the person or persons who are liable to be harmed because of their moral responsibility for a threat of wrongful harm'. Wide proportionality (henceforth proportionality$_w$) in turn is concerned with 'risks or harms imposed on innocent bystanders, usually but not necessarily as a side effect of the defensive action taken against those who are liable to attack' (McMahan: 2009–10: 4).

Having thus introduced the different dimensions of proportionality recognized by just war scholars, the question is whether wide and narrow proportionality considerations ought to inform macro-proportionality in JST? In traditional just war theory, McMahan explains *jus ad bellum* proportionality has ignored proportionality$_n$ in part because 'it conceives of war as a relation between states, not as a complex set of relations among individual persons. The aggressor is the enemy state. *Ad bellum* proportionality is therefore assessed in terms of harm *to the aggressor state*, and it is difficult to measure and compare harms to states' (ibid.: 5; emphases in original).

One advantage of McMahan's view is that it allows us to recognize that some just causes 'would be too trivial for war to be proportionate' (McMahan, 2005: 4). On the example of the Falklands War, McMahan demonstrates the implications of this logic. He suggests that this war was unjust for proportionality$_n$ reasons, because threatening the sovereignty of a small patch of land (and not the basic human rights of its inhabitants) is not a wrong of a sufficient magnitude to render the threateners liable to be killed.[9] What does all this mean for securitization? It seems intuitively right to hold that some just causes may well be too trivial for securitization to be proportionate,[10] and therefore that the agents at the source of the threat are not liable for the harm securitization is going to cause them. For example, fragmentation of the EU due to member states leaving the union is an objective existential threat to the essential properties of the EU, especially if fragmentation leads to disintegration, the abolition of the Schengen area, as well as the euro currency. Arguably, however, a securitization that would target the architects of Brexit or other comparable national movements orchestrating the departure of member states would be disproportionate$_n$.

---

[9] I am indebted to Jonathan Parry for this formulation as well as helpful discussions on the issue of macro-proportionality.

[10] Some proportionality considerations can be rolled into just cause to exclude just causes that are too trivial to be proportionate (McMahan, 2005). I do this with ecosystems and non-human referents that do not benefit a sufficiently large group of people with a view to reducing the number of possible referent objects.

Thus here, the just cause is insufficiently harmful to justify the harms securitization is going to cause agents at the source of the threat (including detaining them, penalizing them, monitoring them, excluding them from positions of power/influence, not only in political life but in the media etc.) because – as in the Falklands case – 'the conditions of ordinary life' will be 'little different' outside of or without the EU (McMahan, 2009–10: 5). In short we can see that proportionality$_n$ considerations ought to factor in an assessment of the permissibly to initiate securitization. This being said, unlike with war, in securitization proportionality$_n$ does not always matter. Where agent-lacking threats are concerned, the issue of proportionality$_n$ does not arise, because here we are not dealing with threats caused – intentionally or otherwise – by agents.

Besides proportionality$_n$ macro-proportionality is concerned with proportionality$_w$ considerations. Vital for proportionality$_w$ is that 'the expected harm to innocent bystanders caused as a side effect may not exceed the expected harm one prevents' (McMahan, 2009–10: 11). In short, just securitization cannot produce more harm to innocent bystanders than it seeks to prevent.[11]

So far so good, but what do we mean by harm, anyway? Recall, first of all that we have said in Chapter 2 that securitization is tantamount to the exception; as such, it allows state actors to temporarily (i.e. for the duration of the threat) suspend ordinary political measures and to ensure the continued existence of the referent object with recourse to exceptional measures, including – depending on threat – surveillance, curfews and greater police powers, often at the expense of civil liberties. Recall further that we have said in Chapter 4 that harm is the inverse of human well-being, and that well-being can be established by measuring the relative

---

[11] 'There are many kinds of bystanders' (Tesón, 2017: 114). In securitization we can – at a minimum – differentiate between the beneficiaries of securitization (the referent object) and neutral bystanders. Differentiating between non-combatant bystanders (neutrals) and non-combatant *beneficiaries*, McMahan has argued 'that in some cases [namely: where innocent non-combatants are beneficiaries] it is permissible for just combatants to fight in a way that will foreseeably harm innocent non-combatants as a side effect rather than fight in a different way that would involve greater risks to themselves' (2010a: 359), thus going back on the obligation – inherent to JWT – to always fight in the least harmful way. Importantly, however, this does not change the logic that war/securitization cannot produce more harm than it seeks to prevent, because 'a noncombatant is an expected beneficiary of a war only if the war would diminish her expected risk of harm' (McMahan, 2010a: 360). While McMahan suggests that idea seems relevant for *in bello* proportionality or else requires formation of a new criterion for the just war (McMahan, 2010a: 378–379), there are reasons to believe that a full theory of macro-proportionality of securitization needs to take account of the fact that very often, innocent bystanders are actually the beneficiaries of securitization, and consequently that harms caused to them may be partially discounted.

satisfaction of basic human needs. Human beings are very obviously harmed when the intermediate need of physical security is compromised; however, human beings are also harmed when their autonomy is restrained. Securitization can compromise the physical security of innocent bystanders (think again of de Menezes), but it can also curtail their autonomy, including by rolling back civil liberties. Considering that securitization is only ever justified during a specified time period restricted to the presence of the just reason (cf. Chapter 3), the difference in magnitude of harm caused matters. Physical harm that can have longer-term consequences (for example, if a person is maimed) and is of a greater magnitude than the harm caused by short-term rights derogations (for example, to be disallowed entry to the United States because of your religious beliefs as a Muslim). I therefore think that macro-proportionality calculations need to account – on this side of the equation – not only for the *number* of innocent bystanders expected to be harmed (i.e. the scale of the threat), but also for *how* they are expected to be harmed (i.e. the magnitude), differentiating between severe and minor harm. Together, in order to establish whether securitization is proportionate$_w$, these considerations need to be weighed up against the harm that is prevented by securitization. On this side of the equation we already know that the harm prevented is of a similar magnitude for all cases. In Chapter 3 we established that only existential threats count as just reasons for just securitization. And above we learned that unless such threats are sufficiently harmful they are too trivial for securitization to be proportionate. Existential threats are sufficiently harmful when they undermine objective human well-being. This, in turn, is the case when humans are existentially threatened, and it can be the case when other just referent objects are existentially threatened. In other words,the severity of the harm to be prevented by just securitization is comparable in all valid cases; what differs is the entity threatened (i.e. the referent object) and with that crucially the number of people (scale) that would be adversely affected should the entity cease to exist in its current form. We can now put this in the following terms. There are four variations on the scale and magnitude of the harm caused by securitization. These are:

A. Number of innocent bystanders severely harmed is expected to be smaller.[12]
B. Number of innocent bystanders severely harmed is expected to be larger.
C. Number of innocent bystanders harmed in a minor way is expected to be smaller.

[12] Smaller/larger in comparison between A, B, C or D with E or F.

D. Number of innocent bystanders harmed in a minor way is expected to be larger.

Likewise, there are two variations on the scale and magnitude of the harm prevented by securitization:

E. Number of people not suffering severe harm because referent object is secured is smaller.[13]
F. Number of people not suffering severe harm because referent object is secured is larger.

Starting from established reasoning that – where proportionality$_w$ is concerned – the harm caused by securitization cannot exceed the harm prevented, we need to first compare like with like in terms of the magnitude of harm (i.e. is it minor or severe) and focus on A, B and E, F. We can say that securitization is not proportionate$_w$ if the number of innocent bystanders severely harmed by securitization is expected to be larger (B), when either the number of beneficiaries (in terms of harm prevented) is smaller (E) or when it is roughly equal (F). The same would be true when comparing A and E, while securitization would be proportionate$_w$ if the number of innocent bystanders severely harmed is expected to be smaller (A), provided that F is on the other side of the calculation.

Things are different when we contemplate situations where the harm expected to innocent bystanders is minor (C and D). Here securitization is proportionate$_w$ when the number of innocent bystanders harmed in a minor way is smaller (C) because here the scale of the harm (number of people affected) and/or the magnitude of the harm outweigh C in cases F and E respectively. In line with this it is also possible that E outweighs D. Importantly although the latter appears to suggest that it is proportionate$_w$ even when securitization is expected to cause greater harm than it seeks to prevent this is not so. We need to recognize that key to the level of harm expected is not only its scale (i.e. number of people) but also its *magnitude*. It may be proportionate$_w$ to harm a larger number of people in a minor way to prevent major harm to the few. However, this is not categorically the case, and minor harm to the many can outweigh the prevention of major harm to the few. We can see this when we consider whether it is proportionate$_w$ to protect, when objectively existentially threatened individual persons (presidents, royalty and religious figures come to mind) through state-led securitization. It seems that here, even if securitization is expected to cause

---

[13] A less cumbersome way of putting this is to say beneficiaries of securitization.

only minor harm to bystanders, this is likely to outweigh the severe harm caused to one person. This is because proportionality$_w$ relies on a proportionality calculation that requires us to multiply the magnitude of the harm caused by securitization with scale (i.e. the number of people affected) and to weigh this up against the scale and magnitude of the harm prevented. In the given case, let's demonstrate this by giving magnitude of the harm prevented a score of 1, considering that there is only one person affected, the score remains 1 (in the given example it would be 2 if there where two people, 100 if there where 100 people, and so on). Let us then attribute the minor harm inflicted on each of four million innocent bystanders a score of 0.1, generating an overall score of 400,000. It is easy to see that the minor harm that is expected to be caused to the many outweighs the severe harm to the one significantly. While my example suggests that things are straightforward, we must recognize that this case is complicated by the problem of how harms should be aggregated. It seems intuitive that minor harms to the many only outweigh major harm to the few when the minor harm is 'sufficiently close' in magnitude to the major harm to be prevented. But below these thresholds, small harms don't seem to aggregate so as to outweigh big harms (for example, no number of people suffering headaches seems to outweigh the harm of one person being tortured).[14] It seems then that a full theory of macro-proportionally of securitization would have to factor in aggregation. Overall, we can say that what matters for proportionality$_w$ is 'whether inflicting . . . harm is the *lesser evil*, all things considered' (Tesón, 2017: 109 emphasis in original).

So far, we have seen that proportionality considerations pertain to the effects of securitization on agents at the source of a threat as well as to innocent bystanders vis-à-vis doing nothing. In all of this, however, we have primarily focused on the harm securitization is expected to cause, and little on the nature of the 'good' gained from securitization. As a result, it is not yet clear whether the good refers to ensuring simply the essential properties of the referent object, or to all the good consequences of securitization. This question can be answered by engaging with Thomas Hurka's work on proportionality.

He argues that some account of the goods produced by war is necessary to an assessment of the proportionality of war. Notably, it is important to understand that unless goods are specified, one might end up counting goods that are not contained in the just cause. Hurka points out that war might produce incidental goods such as economic boom or scientific/technological research (Hurka, 2005: 40). The point is that regardless of the value of incidental

---

[14] I am indebted to Jonathan Parry for the formulation and helping me to see this clearly.

goods, they cannot be used to justify war, and by extension securitization, as they are not constitutive of the just cause. In Hurka's words: '[T]he goods that count toward proportionality ... are only those contained in the just causes' (ibid.: 40).

While it seems logical to hold that the only relevant goods to be counted are those specified in the just cause, complications arise when one considers that it is possible to distinguish between sufficient and contributing just causes. Following McMahan and McKim (1993), Hurka argues: 'Sufficient just causes suffice by themselves to fulfil the just cause condition ... contributing just causes do not suffice to satisfy the just cause condition; given only these causes, one is not permitted to fight. But once there is a sufficient just cause, contributing just causes can further legitimate aims in war and can contribute to its justification' (ibid.: 41). In other words, contributing just causes refer to the right kind of incidental goods war/securitization may produce; as far as war is concerned, these might be disarming the enemy, or showing others that aggression does not pay. As far as securitization is concerned, these may be freedom from want as opposed to simply freedom from fear, achievement of security in an area other than that specified in the just cause. These are qualitatively different incidental goods than boosting the economy through war, or, to give a prominent example from security studies, boosting the security establishment through 'discourses of danger' (Campbell, 1998). Given that securitization can generate incidental goods that are not part of the just cause, two questions emerge: 1) Does the extra good mean that it would be permissible to cause more harm than just cause would allow? And second, are securitizing actors required to aim for the additional good contained in the contributory just cause? McMahan and McKim answer this first question when they argue: 'Contributing JA's [just aims] add to the case for war and constitute goals that can justify belligerent action in war that is not justified by reference to a sufficient JA' (McMahan and McKim, 1993: 503). Notably, however, the pursuit of a contributory just cause is permissible only in the presence of a prior sufficient just cause.

The second question is harder to answer, and potentially requires much work; ultimately I think this depends on both the costs the securitizing actor is going to incur in doing the additional good, as well as on the nature of the additional good. It seems to me that if a major additional good can be achieved at little or no additional cost to the securitizing actor, then such actors are indeed required to do it. For example, one security measure of a wider securitization of climate change could involve the mandatory planting of millions of trees. Here an additional good, at acceptable cost to the securitizing actor, is achieved when such trees contain many different native species (in the respective states), as this will have the additional benefit of increasing biodiversity.[15]

In the context of the size of the just referent object and incidental goods, a further point needs to be made. I argue over the course of this book that a securitization is just in a sense of morally permissible provided that all principles are met; however, this does not mean that just securitizations do not differ in terms of the good they do in the world. Clearly, some securitizations avoid harm to a greater number of people than others. The same is true of just wars. Notably – and all other things being equal – a war fought justly on the grounds of humanitarian intervention that saves 100,000 lives does more good than one that saves 50,000. My point is that securitizations and wars that save more people than others are not more just than those that save a fewer people. To understand this, we can compare the idea of just securitization to being married;[16] thus in the same way as one cannot be more or less married, a securitization corresponding to the principles of JST is no more or less just. However, in the same way as a marriage can be better or worse, just securitizations can prevent more or less harm, and as such, one just securitization be better or worse than another just securitization.

5.4 REASONABLE CHANCE OF SUCCESS

One reason why securitization has such a bad name in many quarters of the academic study of security is that it is expected to lead to what Booth and Wheeler (2008) have called the 'security paradox' which but most people think of as the security dilemma: the situation whereby one state's search for security leads to insecurity in other states (Robinson, 2008: 191). Even within the remit of JST it is hard to stop this from occurring, because even an otherwise just and well-intended securitization might trigger a sense of insecurity in other actors, and subsequent counter-securitization (cf. Watson, 2013; Olesker, 2018; Stritzel and Chang, 2015). Gunhild Hoogensen Gjørv, for example, argues: 'When the state invokes security-producing measures to protect the state, these same measures may or do have a deleterious affect on *other* actors, like individuals and communities, who may feel inclined to respond to ensure their own security' (2012: 841; my emphasis). For securitizing actors this means

---

[15] It is also possible that contributing just causes could reduce the level of culpability of securitizing actors of unjust securitizations, and it would ultimately have to be discussed how this affects what desecuritizing actors (in cases where they are the same as the securitizing actors) need to do in the way of restorative measures to bring about lasting security (as a state of being), which I consider an important part of just desecuritization (cf. Chapter 7).

[16] I am grateful to Jonathan Floyd for this example.

that the successful securitization of one problem can open up another bigger problem elsewhere, leaving the referent object more insecure than they would have been, had they not acted at all, or had they responded with politicization.[17] As a case in point, consider the 2012 Israeli rocket attack purposely killing the Hamas military leader Ahmed al-Jabari, by pinpointing his car driving down a Gaza street. We might – purely for the sake of argument – say that Israel satisfied all the applicable principles of just initiation of securitization – just cause, right intention, macro-proportionality – the problem is, however, that the use of lethal force triggered another uprising, leaving both Israelis and Palestinians more insecure than they were prior to this action. Given the volatile relations between Israel and Palestine as well as their history, we might argue that Israel could have foreseen this response, and should have acted differently and either not re-securitized the conflict or – at the very least – by using different means.

A similar argument has been advanced by many in the context of the war on terrorism. Karin Fierke, in her immanent critique of the war on terror, for example, argues that war and securitization have 'increased the threat and contributed to the *construction* and deepening of conflict' (Fierke, 2007: 173). Instead of a military response, which in Fierke's view is part of the problem not of the solution, she recommends that the US should have embraced its moment of vulnerability and asked some hard questions about its conduct and the consequences of years of domineering foreign and security policy, with the expectation that this would have generated a new understanding of security as a state of being that does not rest in hegemony, but the realization that America no longer is 'the shining city on the hill' (ibid.: 201).

All of these are arguments caution against using the harm securitization inevitably involves without a reasonable chance of securitization succeeding in rendering the referent object secure.[18] Just war theorists are attuned to the possibility of futile violence. Most renditions of the theory include a reasonable chance of success requirement. 'The traditional aim of this criterion [. . .] is to bar lethal violence which is known in advance to be

---

[17] McMahan differentiates between conditional and unconditional threats, whereby the former designate what aggressors 'will do . . . if they are unopposed', while the latter refers to what they will do if opposed (2009–10: 2).

[18] Noteworthy in this context is Booth and Wheeler's notion of security dilemma sensibility, by which they mean 'an actor's intention and capacity to perceive the motives behind, and to show responsiveness towards, the potential complexity of the military intentions of others. In particular, it refers to the ability to understand the role that fear might play in their attitudes and behaviour, including, crucially, the role that one's own actions may play in provoking that fear' (2008: 7).

futile' (Orend, 2006: 58).[19] In line with this thinking, this section aims to develop and defend the following principle for JST.

Criterion 5: Securitization must have a reasonable chance of success, whereby the chances of achieving the just cause must be judged greater than those of alternatives to securitizing.

This criterion requires that it is necessary to anticipate securitization's prospect of achieving the just cause. Empirical evidence shows that even when states have the right intention, this is not always the case. In their analysis of the securitization of migration in Greece, for instance, Georgios Karyotis and Dimitris Skleparis (2013: 696) observed not only that securitization led to an 'increased ... possibility of physical threats to public order' (in part because migrants felt disenfranchised, and reverted to anger and criminal behaviour, and because of an increase in anti-migrant violence), but also that 'securitisation ... failed spectacularly to reduce migrant flows or curtail irregular migration' (ibid.).

Important in the context of assessing the likelihood of success is to acknowledge, that while securitization might be reasonably able to deal with one problem, it might create a related bigger problem in the process. For example, the securitization of terrorism managed to temporarily reduce the threat from Al-Qaeda cells, but in the process contributed to the radicalization of European-born Muslims (cf. Croft, 2006: 277–278), and thus did not manage to achieve the just cause.

While the importance of a criterion specifying a reasonable prospect for success is plain to see, difficulties arise from the fact that it does not offer 'a precise standard' specifying when the condition is met (Uniacke, 2014: 70). Rather, it appears to be met when 'a [legitimate] political authority ... believes on *reasonable grounds* that success is significantly more than an outside chance' (ibid.: 70; my emphasis). Not only does this interpretation problematically delimit the use of force to legitimate political authority,[20] but it also provides no suggestions for how such beliefs are arrived at. Reasonable grounds for the belief that securitization will succeed in securing the referent object cannot depend simply on the right kind of people (e.g. securitizing actor and putative audiences) believing it will succeed (cf. Chapter 2, section 2.3); such agreement merely absolves the securitizing actor from blame when

---

[19] In war, futility refers to the impossibility of winning the war, and is as such narrower than for securitization, where futility refers to both not succeeding in making the referent secure from a given threat, as well as creating a new threat.
[20] See section 5.5.1 below on why this is problematic.

things go wrong and securitization fails to secure the referent object (cf. section 5.5.1). The question remains, when does a securitizing actor have reasonable grounds for believing securitization has a good prospect of success? I wish to suggest that we can find an answer in Hurka's revision of the macro-proportionality criterion already utilized above. Leaving aside whether Hurka is correct,[21] it is noteworthy that he advocates for an *ad bellum* proportionality criterion that incorporates both the last resort and reasonable chance of success criteria. Important for our purposes here is that as part of his argument, he suggests a method for establishing when these conditions have been met:

> For war and each of its alternatives [one must conduct] a proportionality calculation, identifying the relevant goods and evils it will produce compared to a baseline of doing nothing, or continuing to act as one would have had there not been a just cause. This yields the net good or bad effects of each, and it then says war is permitted only if its net outcome is better than those of all alternatives. (Hurka, 2005: 38)

In line with this I propose that securitization's prospect for succeeding in securing the referent object must be established comparatively against the alternatives to securitizing.[22] That is to say, I hold that a securitizing actor has *reasonable grounds* for believing that securitization meets the prospect of success criterion, when securitization is expected to have a better chance of achieving the just cause than other relevant less harmful alternatives.[23]

As with so many other issues concerning just war, alternatives to war are easier to ascertain than alternatives to securitization. When it comes to war, we are talking of a well-established, concrete and finite list of alternatives, consisting of arms embargoes, punitive sanctions, diplomacy etc.[24] Alternatives to securitization, in turn, seem fuzzier; they include the potentially very broad category of politicization as well as inaction. Starting with the latter, inaction refers to the issue not being securitized or politicized, but ignored by would-be securitizing actors. Given that inaction has a chance of addressing a just cause best only where agent-caused and agent-intended threats are concerned (notably ignoring intent-lacking threats would simply make them worse), this is

---

21   For a critique of his idea to run proportionality and chances of success together, see Frowe (2014: 151–152).

22   Throughout the course of this book I have acknowledged that alternatives to securitization are always an option, yet thus far no criterion guards against securitization being launched *without* at least also considering the chances of the success alternatives to securitization have in averting the threat. The criterion developed in this section remedies this oversight.

23   To be sure war is excluded as such an alternative because it is more harmful.

24   Some analysts class these as tools of soft war, but note that in this book, war pertains to kinetic use of force only (cf. Introduction).

rarely a viable option. Indeed, the only possible example I can think where inaction *might* work best – and has been suggested – is terrorism (Mueller, 2006), because inaction would starve terrorism of its lifeforce – fear.

Unlike inaction, politicization is hard to grasp. Depending on whom one considers to be meaningful political actors, it involves potentially every kind of action, making the generation of a finite list of alternatives difficult. This said, however, it is also the case that politicization occupies a special place in securitization theory, because we can only really grasp the meaning of securitization when the concept is juxtaposed with politicization (Hansen, 2012). This means that we can say that the meaning of politicization is necessarily tied to the meaning of securitization found within any given theory of securitization. I have argued in Chapter 2 that in JST, decisive of securitization are exceptional security measures, and I have defined the exception as – in liberal democratic states – the situation when (new) emergency laws are passed/put into action, and/or (new) emergency powers are granted that seek to govern the insecurity/crisis situation, or when a state's existing security apparatus is employed to deal with issues that are either new, or that it has not dealt with previously. Politicization must then mean that three things are in place: first, that the issue is on the political agenda of powerholders within liberal democratic states; secondly, that the issue is addressed using either existing, or new 'ordinary' powers and laws, and thirdly, that the solution does not involve the existing security apparatus taking on new issues, or issues that are new to them. I have also argued that for non-state actors and autocracies the exception refers to what most reasonable persons would agree constitutes exceptional means and actions, most notably perhaps, in terms of the amount of harm, risked/caused or intended, and/or the level of violence employed. It follows that politicization here means that the would-be securitizing actor addresses the issue using commonly accepted political means not generally considered harmful, and exceptional in terms of the violence employed and the harm risked or caused.

In order to ascertain which of these three – securitization, politicization and inaction – has the best chance of succeeding in addressing the just cause, it will be necessary to anticipate, in the evidence-relative sense, the likelihood of the success of each one.[25] For the reasons already mentioned, the 'battleground' will be between securitization and politicization. Concretely, and in

---

[25] In the abstract, the answer is far from obvious. We can consider securitization also as a form of punishment (for example, Britain expelling Russian diplomats after the Salisbury poisoning case in March 2018), whereas politicization in response to a threat is a form of appeasement. Captured by the 'spiral model' Robert Jervis has shown that 'conflicts arise from punishment applied in the false expectation that it will elicit better behaviour from the other side, when in fact it elicits worse behaviour' (Van Evera, 1997: 1). His 'deterrence model' holds that 'conflicts

the absence of a finite list of alternative political solutions that we can tick off (as one might do with war), this means that anyone using JST must ascertain whether new emergency laws and powers and/or involving the security services have – on all available evidence – a better chance of achieving the just cause than existing laws and powers, and possible new, non-exceptional laws. This is not always the case. Critics of the securitization of terrorism have argued, for example, that criminalization of terrorism using existing procedures is a plausible alternative to securitization. In more detail, Matthew Evangelista reports that before 9/11, the United States 'dealt with Islamist terrorists through the criminal justice system'. In order to capture the Islamist ringleaders behind the 1993 World Trade Center bombings, for example, 'US authorities used [existing] legal methods to infiltrate their organization, for instance informants wearing listening devices to record incriminating evidence. To convict them, US courts relied on domestic law, with all its protections in favour of the defendants' (Evangelista, 2008: 57).

With this, I have come to the end of the criteria designating just initiation of securitization. In the remainder of this chapter I will elaborate on why some key *ad bellum* criteria do not feature as part of JST.

5.5 OMISSIONS: LEGITIMATE AUTHORITY AND LAST RESORT

5.5.1 *Legitimate Authority*

Many contemporary just war theories include a criterion specifying that a war can only be fought by a legitimate authority in accordance with their *jus ad bellum* criteria. Traditionally, legitimate authority rested with the body or actor who had *authority to speak for the state* (e.g. parliament, a monarch, a prime minister); however, as wars are increasingly fought by sub-state groups (including terrorists), the question is not only who – in those situations – has the legitimate authority to publically declare a war,[26] but also what counts as a war.[27] After all, as Frowe points out, 'the

---

arise from acts of appeasement made in the false expectation that appeasement will elicit better behaviour from the other side, when in fact it elicits worse behaviour' (ibid.).

[26] Public declaration of war is a requirement of just war theorists bound up with legitimate authority. I do not include public declaration in JST because while most securitizations are announced by virtue of the securitizing move, it is also possible that some threats are best dealt with covertly.

[27] There are very good reasons for delimiting the concept of war. As Finlay points out: 'A presumption of legitimate authority for *all* politically motivated non-state entities would

requirement of legitimate authority is not only a constraint on whether a war is *just*. It is, for many a constraint on whether a use of force counts as a war *at all*' (2011: 59 emphases in original; see also 2014: 158). It is the aim of JST to reduce the occurrence of securitization, yet my theory excludes the requirement of legitimate authority. Given this, it stands to reason that I miss a trick by not specifying a legitimate authority criterion; because surely the latter would make just securitization harder to achieve? My reasons for not including legitimate authority are three-fold. First, while JST imports ideas liberally from the just war tradition, the compatibility between the two has its limitations. As far as I am aware, the question whether or not a morally illegitimate actor can do a good deed – which is what this boils down to – is not often asked by just war scholars.[28] When it comes to the just cause, most of them list something along the lines by Orend (2006: 40): '[A] state has a just cause for resorting to war if and only if: 1) it is the victim of aggression, or is coming to the aid of a victim of aggression; 2) it is a minimally just or legitimate state; and 3) its resort to armed force fulfils all aspects of the principle CPA [core principle on aggression]'. Orend's second point here is key: he effectively argues that only minimally just/legitimate states have a right to resort to war. The asymmetry between legitimate and illegitimate states is motivated by the fact that war, including humanitarian war, necessarily involves at least two parties in opposition to one another, and it cannot be the case that both are fighting justly. As such, the legitimate authority criterion serves to ensure that unjust states are not permitted to wage wars against states involved in humanitarian intervention on their own territory.[29] When it comes to securitization, however, it is not necessarily the case that it will result in an opposing securitization by another party. Many securitizations are 'one-sided', in the sense that they target agent-lacking threats or the non-agential effects of agent-caused threats (e.g. sea-level rise from climate change). Moreover, there is no logical reason why a morally dubious state/actor cannot secure a morally justifiable referent object in accordance with the criteria

---

thus efface the distinction we need to make, between groups whose killing of military personal or police belongs in the criminal category of "murder", and those which can justifiably describe otherwise similar actions as the discriminate targeting of "combatants"' (Finlay, 2015: 176 and 177; emphasis in the original).

[28] One exception here is James Pattison's scalar approach to legitimacy in humanitarian intervention (2010).

[29] The question of whether unjust states are permitted to intervene on humanitarian grounds does not arise because it is unlikely that a morally unjustifiable state (bearing in mind that for Orend and other just war scholars, injustice stems from a disregard for human rights) will wage war in the name of human rights elsewhere.

specified by JST.[30] An unjust securitizing actor[31] can in principle do even a praiseworthy thing and say secure climate change for the benefit of its people or the wider world. Of course the chances of this actually happening are slim, because actors with little regard for the basic needs of human beings are more often than not, for instance, poor stewards of the natural environment, and unlikely to justly securitize relevant ecosystems. Although I do not insist on a criterion specifying the justifiability of the securitizing actor, it is important to note that by conducting a just securitization, a morally dubious securitizing actor does not become a just entity.

My second abiding reason for not insisting on legitimate authority is that criterion 2, which specifies that referent objects have to be just and what this means, already does a large part of the job legitimate authority ensures in just war theories. Thus because just war theorists used to be exclusively concerned with the right to self-defence, it was important to specify that the entity to be defended by war was actually legitimate, or in other words, just. It is noteworthy in this context that scholars concerned with other-defence (i.e. humanitarian intervention) are relaxing or even jettisoning the requirement of legitimate authority, because in other-defence, ultimately more important that the legitimacy or justice of the defender is the justice of the referent object and just cause (Pattison, 2010; Fabre, 2012).

A third and pivotal reason for not including legitimate authority as a separate criterion for just securitization stems from an extrapolation of an observation made by Lene Hansen back in 2000, arguing that by prioritizing speech over the visual and the bodily, securitization theory is complicit in the production of silence. She put it as follows:

> It has to be acknowledged that if security is a speech act, then it is simultaneously deeply implicated in the production of silence: all speech involves an attempt to fix meaning, to define a particular situation and the subjects within it, and any successful speech act implies as a consequence the exclusion of other possible constructions of meaning. Silence is a powerful political strategy that internalises and individualises threats thereby making resistance and political mobilisation difficult. (Hansen, 2000: 306)

---

[30] Fabre (2012: 189), using an example by Nardin, argues as follows: "'a murderer is not forbidden to save a drowning child". What matters, rather is that he should be able to swim and rescue the child effectively – and then hand her to the appropriate parties.'

[31] It should be clear that a securitizing actor is unjust for the same reasons that render putative referent objects unjust (see Chapter 4, section 4.5 for social and political orders including states, and section 4.7 for individuals and small groups of individuals).

It seems to me that if JST were to insist on traditional legitimate authority, it too would be complicit in the production of silence or, perhaps better, it would be deaf and blind to the existence of securitizing actors other than legitimate states. Moreover, given that the Copenhagen School's original version of securitization theory was supposed to apply to more than simply states (cf. Chapter 2), a theory of just securitization needs to apply to these other actors.

With the reasons for the inclusion of non-state actors as securitizing actors now clear, we must recognize that by not requiring legitimate authority as traditionally understood (i.e. by focusing exclusively on (just) states as legitimate securitizing actors), JST is headed for trouble: anarchy. Thus, in the absence of such a criterion, what is to stop, for example, the formation of militia groups, within the borders of a just state, who take it upon themselves to address the threat posed by jihadi terrorism against the wider population? Of course, in many states this would be unlawful because only states hold, and are defined by, '*the monopoly of the legitimate use of physical force within a given territory*' (Weber, cited in Wolff, 2011: 960 emphasis in original). Morality, however, can be quite different from the law, and it would seem that without a criterion specifying legitimate authority, there is nothing stopping non-state actors acting in this way. Our moral intuition tells us, however, that this simply does not seem correct, because few would celebrate the breakdown of law and order. At the same time, however, we must recognize that renunciation of non-state securitizing actors simply on the grounds of them lacking traditional legitimate authority (e.g. by virtue of having been democratically elected) is not only insufficient, but also dangerous, because it might shut down legitimate resistance to oppression (cf. Finlay, 2015). Indeed, it is well-known that as a result of the global war on terror, many oppressive regimes label acts of resistance against them as terrorism (cf. Smilansky, 2004).

Just war theorists working on the ethics of non-state violence including terrorism have tried to address the problem of legitimate actorness by introducing the concept of *representative authority*; after all, the criterion of legitimate authority is concerned with who can speak for whom (e.g. Finlay, 2015: chapter 6). McPherson argues that: 'Nonstate terrorism's distinctive wrongness does not lie in the terrorism but rather in the resort to political violence without adequate licence from a people on whose behalf the violence is purportedly undertaken' (2007: 542). Representative authority matters for McPherson, Frowe explains, 'because peoples are entitled to self-determination' (2016: 196). This right is particularly acute in situations of threat and defence. As Jonathan Parry explains: 'Victims occupy a privileged position within the morality of defense – it is *their* interests at stake after all – and this gives them the *exclusive right* to decide whether and how those interests are defended' (Parry, 2017: 176; first emphasis in original, second emphasis added). Similarly, James Pattison, who utilizes just war theory to establish a duty for humanitarian intervention, holds that morally significant for legitimate authority is whether the intervenor 'represent[s] the opinions of those in the political community that is potentially subject to its humanitarian intervention' (2010: 140). His thinking stems in part from the morally relevant fact that the community on which intervention is imposed carries the burden of the intervention by being turned into a warzone (ibid.: 143). What Pattison calls the 'burdens argument' (ibid.: 143) is also the main driver in Chris Finlay's call for representative legitimacy. He argues: 'it ought to be up to those whose interests are most directly at stake to judge in each particular case when reasonable hope of avoiding full-scale war can be abandoned and when the enormous risks involved in recourse to Organized Offensive Violence ought to be taken' (Finlay, 2015: 182–183).

Representative legitimacy[32] is potentially important for JST. As discussed above (Chapter 2), referent objects are sometimes also the audiences of securitizing speech acts. And while the opinions of referent objects are routinely ignored in securitization (section 2.2.2), a theory of just securitization may very well require audience consent to securitization as one of its substantive principles. A securitization that has the backing of the referent object appears intuitively compelling, because it sets the ground rules for when other-securitization is permissible.

In spite of these benefits, there are seven reasons why I do not include such a principle as a necessary condition for just securitization. First, seeking the consent of a referent object wastes precious time, during which threats increase. Secondly, how exactly is consent[33] to be established? Specifically, who can legitimately speak for the referent object? What is to be done when consensus is achieved with a small majority? Furthermore, what if the referent is silenced by an oppressor? Thirdly, the referent object – including majorities[34] – can be wrong in rejecting securitization – and where global/

---

[32] Pattison refers to this as local external representativeness.

[33] Note here that consent – including by majority – is at one end of a possible spectrum. Some writers who recognize practical difficulties with consent and how to measure it stress merely consultation, some mix it up and stress that some form of consultation must take place while consent seems ideal. All this is very much reminiscent of the role of the audience in securitization, whereby Wæver and Co. do not stress acceptance (probably because consent it is hard to measure or attain), but merely that the threat has to be argued for, i.e. consultation must take place (Buzan et al., 1998: 25).

[34] See Parry, 2017: 180 for problems with majority consensus.

transnational threats are concerned – to everyone's peril.[35] Fourthly, it should be noted that Pattison and Finlay, who also face some of these problems, acknowledge that there are some cases when representative legitimacy is not required, for example, in cases where victims are unable to voice consent to liberation, for fear of reprisals (one may think of IS here) (Finlay, 2015: 185–189; see also Pattison, 2010: 141).[36] Fifthly, we must recognize that while ostensibly audience consent safeguards those subject to securitization, from not being subjected to securitization and the harms it brings; I think this principle does far more for the securitizing actor. Thus it works to absolve the securitizing actor from the accusation of paternalism.[37] Moreover, if the referent object consented to securitization, it is also the case that the referent object has little come-back when things go wrong. In other words, the burden of responsibility is shifted onto the referent object's shoulders.[38] Sixthly, representative legitimacy only works for human referent objects. It is not clear who can meaningfully represent ecosystems and non-human species (cf. Frowe, 2016: 198). Seventhly, and perhaps most importantly, whatever reasons putative non-pacifist referent objects may have for resisting securitization, all decisive reasons are already covered by the other substantive criteria of just initiation of securitization. That is to say, referents will object to securitization not because they have no say in it, but rather because there is no just cause, or because it lacks a reasonable chance of success,[39] or because it is disproportionate.[40] A further decisive reason why they might object informs McPherson's initial call for representative legitimacy.

---

[35] South Africa's President Mbeki's AIDS denial, that cost some 300,000 lives, comes to mind here.

[36] I also think that rights-based accounts of political violence are under much greater pressure to include representative legitimacy than my needs-based account, because such accounts are constrained by the victims' 'right to refuse assistance' (Finlay, 2015: 161) while they hold the 'exclusive right to decide whether and how these interests are defended' (Parry, 2017: 176).

[37] McMahan writes about a related benefit from consent for the intervenor when he argues: 'But if the intervention fails on balance to benefit those it was supposed to rescue, or proves to be unjustified for other reasons, its having been undertaken without the consent of the ostensible beneficiaries increases the culpability of the intervenor' (McMahan, 2010b: 54).

[38] We can find this in Balzacq (2015b, 109), who argues that the audience is normatively important because 'if things go wrong [we can hold] both the speaker and the audience … accountable for the effects'.

[39] Notice here that in Pattison's case, advocacy of representative legitimacy is driven not by moral reasons, but by the practical reason that consent increases the chances of an intervention succeeding.

[40] Altman and Wellman argue that 'the majority's judgement is not a criterion of permissible intervention; rather, it is evidence of whether a key criterion – the proportionality principle – is met' (2008: 245).

The deeply distinctive problem of nonstate terrorists now emerges. That they lack legitimate authority is only a rough indication of the problem. Political violence by nonstate actors is objectionable when they employ it on their own initiative, *so that their political goals*, their violent methods, and, ultimately, their claim to rightful use of force do not go through any process of relevant public review and endorsement. (2007: 542; emphasis added)

From this quote we can see that the primary reason why McPherson insists on representative legitimacy/consent is that he aims to ensure that political violence does not serve the political goals of the non-state group (securitizing actor) but the group on whose behalf violence is taken (or in the terminology used above he seeks to make sure that that securitization is referent object benefiting). In JST this is already covered by the criterion of right intention. In short, while representative authority seems intuitively compelling, it does not add anything not already covered by the suggested substantive criteria of JST (cf. McMahan, 2010b; Altman and Wellman, 2008).

My dismissal of a principle of legitimate authority as representative authority, however, leaves us with the problem of anarchy. Indeed, the problem is so severe that we may ask how then can the theory – and indeed the practice – of just securitization be feasible?

To answer this question we need to recognize that the problem of anarchy is perhaps most acute when non-state actors undermine state authority when they securitize. Thus, whilst the militia group securitizing jihadi terrorism inside a legitimate state is intuitively problematic, fewer people would lambast Sea Shepherd for lack of legitimate authority, when they try to securitize whales.[41] The key difference here, I think, is that Sea Shepherd's legitimate authority is no more or less than that of other actors, including states (with the exception of the UNEP perhaps), while jihadi terrorism as a threat to national security is legitimately addressed only by those same state actors. Yet this only holds so long as state actors provide security. Even Hobbes, for whom the primary duty of the state was the provision of security (Steinberger, 2002: 858; Sorrel, 2013), there exists a right to resist albeit with the proviso that at this point the social contract is annulled and the state has in effect ceased to exist (Steinberger, 2002). This is instructive for our purposes here, as it delineates *when* non-state actors within legitimate states can take it upon themselves to securitize issues ordinarily under the jurisdiction of the state. I hold that non-state actors are permitted to do this, and thus effectively *defy* the state, when

---

[41] They might object for other reasons. Notably, Greenpeace does not concur with Sea Shepherd's direct action tactics (cf. Chapter 2, section 2.2.3), as it is committed to non-violence.

states fail to do their duty to protect against an objective existential threat (cf. Fabre, 2012: 148). It should be noted that I do not wish to suggest that states have an obligation to securitize even objective existential threats, only that the threat has to be recognized and that a strategy to address it has to be in place (this may be deliberate non-politicization, cf. Chapter 5, section 5.4). This formulation has the additional advantage that it also allows non-state actors to securitize against those unjust regimes that pose objective existential threats to non-state groups within states (cf. Finlay, 2015: 19–76).

A case in point where a non-state actor justly reverted to self-securitization inside a state is that of the Tancítaro Public Security Force; this being the armed self-defence force in the Mexican avocado-producing town of Tancítero. This group formed because the Mexican government was unable, for financial reasons, to provide security for avocado farmers/producers, who were freely targeted by organized criminals extorting money, killing land-owners and kidnapping them for ransom (avocados are known as the green gold, because of the price they fetch in the international market, leaving farmers well-off) (Parish Flannery, 2017). It is noteworthy that in spite of the fact that some of the weaponry carried by this group is illegal in Mexico, the government tolerates this group.

To summarize, I have argued that inclusion of a criterion of legitimate authority is exclusionary, and as such not part of JST. I have also rejected the necessity of representative authority for just other-securitization. However, to protect against the breakdown of law and order as well as the over-proliferation of securitization, we must recognize that legitimate states are the primary agents of securitization in matters of national security because states have not only a primary duty to provide security, but – in virtue of the social contract – a primary right to do so. Should states fail to provide security, non-state actors may address such unaddressed objective existential threats. In other words, the right to securitization does not hang on legitimacy, but ultimately on whether there is an *unaddressed* objective existential threat.

5.5.2 *Last Resort*

The principle of last resort, whereby war is permissible only when all other options have been exhausted (i.e. literal strong last resort), is a staple element of most just war theories. Last resort seeks to 'ensure that war should not be fought unnecessarily' (McMahan and McKim, 1993: 523). Similar to legitimate authority, the principle of last resort has been subjected to a number of reformulations. Not, however, because of the changed nature of war, but rather because of the realization that 'literal strong last resort' is very hard, if not impossible, to satisfy as there are always other options that can be tried (see Walzer, 1992: xiv; Lazar, 2010; 2012: 29). This realization has led some just war theorists to argue: '[b]ecause actors could always attempt additional options or allow more time for existing efforts to achieve a just aim, a strict interpretation of this view [of last resort] would require pacifism' (Aloyo, 2015: 190–191). In order to deal with this problem, philosophers have suggested that last resort should be rethought as the last thing to be tried after other *plausible* and less harmful options have been tried at least once and failed to satisfy just cause (Frowe, 2011: 62). This certainly addresses the problem inherent to literal strong last resort, notably that last resort understood in this way seems attainable. Given this, last resort could thus usefully inform a theory of just securitization. Yet last resort is not part of JST; its absence clearly demands an explanation. In what follows, I aim to show that the reason is that JST is a theory about moral permissibility and that last resort is too stringent a criterion for this purpose because – when properly understood – its logic sits in the realm of moral obligation. To understand my reasoning it is important to realize that I understand last resort in line with its actual common-sense meaning of necessity, whereby necessity designates the thing/action *required* to achieve x. Or, in Lazar's words, necessity implies that 'there is *no other way* but the antecedent to avert the consequent' (2012: 14–15). I propose that we can be sure that no other option can deal with the problem (i.e. that last resort is satisfied) only once suitable alternatives have been tried and proved ineffective at satisfying just cause and securitization has emerged as the *only* and simultaneously last option yet to be tried. Once this point is reached, however, securitization is no longer merely morally permissible, but rather it is now *necessary* to securitize in order to achieve just cause.[42] In other words, last resort ought to be a substantive criterion of a theory of just securitization that focuses on obligation. Securitization, in turn, is permissible not when it is in the fact-relative sense necessary, but when all available evidence suggests securitization has comparatively better prospects of achieving the just cause than comparable alternatives (see section 5.4).[43] After all, judgements yielded by the 'evidence-relative perspective ... are much more in tune with our ordinary thinking about self-defence' (Lazar, 2012: 8) during which defenders simply do not have access to all the morally relevant facts about

---

[42] Provided all other criteria are met. Note also that the obligation to securitize rests on a range of other factors including the costs to the securitizing actors, the culpability of securitizing actors in threat creation, potentially requests by referent object audiences, etc. Last resort is merely the point in time.

[43] It goes without saying that all other criteria have to be satisfied too; this is simply about the point in time.

a situation, yet whereby we are still able to achieve views about permissibility. The fact that securitization is permissible before it is a last resort is satisfied is apposite in a further sense; after all, delaying securitization because of the harm it is likely to cause in order to satisfy last resort may well cause further harm in the process (Aloyo, 2015: 193).[44]

5.6 CONCLUSION

Just initiation or the just resort to securitization is a complex issue. This chapter has shown that in addition to just cause three further criteria should govern the decision to embark on securitization. In the order of the criteria listed, they refer to: 1) the requirement of sincerity of intention, specifying that the securitizing actor has to be sincere in her intention to safeguard the specified referent object of security; 2) macro-proportionality, which states that the expected good gained from securitization must be greater than the expected harm from securitization and which leaves room for the possibility that just cause is too trivial for securitization to be proportionate; 3) the requirement of the reasonable chance of success, which holds that securitization is not justified if, on all available evidence, it does not have a better chance of succeeding in achieving the just cause than other viable alternatives.

Not everyone will agree with each aspect of the criteria for the just initiation of securitization, including their exact wording, and on the necessity and level of certain thresholds (especially regards the scale of threat, the size of the referent object and the nature of the minimum floor for the satisfaction of basic human needs). Some people might object, for example, that the requirement for objective *existential* threats is too demanding, and that dangers and

---

[44] Much more can be said on the issue of necessity. While I believe that necessity should be understood in accordance with the commonsense meaning explained here, some very prominent just war scholars divert from this meaning of necessity. They take the necessity requirement for just wars to mean not *last* option (established ex post), but that 'the least harmful means of averting a threat' should be chosen (Frowe, 2016: 64). Lazar explains that this interpretation of necessity emerges when 'we consider what makes harm *unnecessary*' (2012: 15; emphasis in original). This interpretation of necessity is difficult to understand. 'To get an intuitive grasp on necessity and proportionality', Lazar (2017) offers the following helpful explanation: 'note that if someone threatens my life, then killing her would be proportionate; but if I could stop her by *knocking her out*, then killing her would be unnecessary, and so impermissible.' Beyond the difference between necessity and proportionality we can see from this why a war is impermissible when it does not satisfy necessity. Killing needs to be necessary to achieve just cause for it to be justifiable. In JST securitization and the harm it causes is not unnecessary when it is the best option for dealing with a threat (Cf. chapter 5, section 5.4).

vulnerabilities should not be excluded from a theory of just securitization. Others might think that representative authority ought to feature in a theory of just securitization, considering the role of the audience in securitization theory. Such disagreements will be part and parcel of the complex arguments proposed here, and the specifics are up to discussion inviting further research in this area.

6

Just Conduct in Securitization

6.1 INTRODUCTION

In line with just war theory, just securitization consists of two parts.[1] One is the just initiation of securitization, the other the just conduct during securitization. Whereas the former specifies the circumstances when exceptional measures may be used (i.e. when the move from politicization to securitization is permissible), the latter seeks to pose restrictions on the nature of the exceptional measures including on what executors of securitization including security professionals are permitted to do.

If not by that name, the 'justice during' securitization has been at the heart of heated debates in a number subjects for some time. These subjects include, besides critical security studies, also strategic studies, criminology, international law, constitutional legal studies, continental political theory, analytical political philosophy and (critical) terrorism studies. The last subject mentioned in this list provides the clue that such discussions have come to the forefront in the context of the (in)famous 'war on terror', a phrase no longer used even by its originator – the United States government. While the wars in Afghanistan and Iraq have all but come to a close as far as Western involvement is concerned,[2] a loose alliance of Western and other powers has been carrying out airstrikes against IS targets in Iraq and Syria, while drone warfare has become the Pentagon's strategy of choice (Malley and Finer, 2018). Domestically (in Europe and the United States) the securitization of terrorism too continues well beyond the use of this phrase. Today, the focus of domestic counter-terrorism is the threat posed by the return of foreign fighters from

---

[1] There is just termination as well, but as explained previously, just desecuritization cannot render an unjust securitization just, and vice versa.

[2] Please note, however, that in June 2017 the United States sent a 4,000 strong contingent to Afghanistan to help with the stalemate in the war there.

Syria and Iraq, as well as home-grown radicalization, with the terrorist attacks in inter alia Brussels, Paris, Florida, Nice, Berlin, Manchester, London and Barcelona carried out by often native/long-resident IS affiliates.

During the initial physical wars on terror, one major cause for concern triggering discussions about justice was the unlawful treatment of combatants by US soldiers – not only the gross extremes of torture at Abu Ghraib prison in Iraq, but also everyday human rights infringements at Guantanamo Bay and in other facilities. These remain very serious offences, which deserve thorough discussion, evaluation and punishment in accordance with international law. Ultimately, however, the treatment of combatants and non-combatants *in war* is more adequately addressed within the framework of the just war theory as opposed to one of just securitization. Indeed, in just war theory, *jus in bello* criteria already detail everything from how prisoners should be treated to the culpability of soldiers in unjust wars (see, for example, McMahan, 2009b; Orend, 2006; Bellamy, 2008) and some just war theorists deal explicitly with the problem of terrorism (Steinhoff, 2007a; Miller, 2009; Finlay, 2015).

A second major issue that has triggered the discussion of the just conduct during securitization is the balance between negative liberty (i.e. freedom from interference) and security. Thus in many countries – but especially in the United States and in the United Kingdom – the 'war on terrorism' has led to a curtailment of established and hitherto taken-for-granted civil liberties expressed in control orders, pre-charge detention, stop and search policies and – as we know from Edward Snowden – mass surveillance techniques. Many of the security measures used in the securitization of terrorism have been controversial. We can see this clearly not only from Snowden's revelations, but also from subsequent developments. Amnesty International's report on counter-terrorism in Europe (2017), for example, argues that 'sweeping new laws across the EU are driving Europe into a deep and dangerous state of permanent securitisation'.

Despite its name, domestically the 'war on terror' is not technically a war; instead it is better understood as a state-led securitization (see also Miller, 2009: 86, 118; Wilkinson, 2010: 135; Ford, 2013). As part of the securitization of the terrorist threat, governments of different states usually argue that if security is wanted, certain civil liberties must be sacrificed, or at least curtailed (see Waldron, 2010). In itself this is not what causes objections among the many people who have written on this subject; indeed most reasonable people would under certain circumstances and *in principle* be happy to give up some civil liberties (for example, not object – apart perhaps from the inconvenience – to having their bags, clothing and bodies searched before boarding a flight) in order to feel and *be* more secure from hijacking or bombs. What people object to in the war on terror and its aftermath is rather one of three things: 1) that the security measures used exceed the just cause and sometimes pursue an alternative agenda; 2) that the security measures are often more harmful than the threat itself; and 3) they take issue with how security practitioners behave in times of emergency, and for example, treat suspects, who might very well be innocent, inhumanely and often with total disregard for human rights.

These three observations are developed below into three criteria that determine just conduct during securitization. Because warfare is a more concrete thing than securitization, involving necessarily one type of action (killing) and a distinct group of people (combatants/soldiers), the match between the rules of *jus in bello* and just conduct during securitization is not entirely seamless and perhaps less organic than that between the rules of *jus ad bellum* and just initiation of securitization. Nevertheless the three criteria developed in this chapter broadly have precedence in the just war tradition, all criteria invoke *jus in bello* proportionality, while criterion 8 also invokes discrimination. Importantly, given that the number of combinations of securitizing actors, threats and security measures is potentially endless this chapter does not aim to provide a blueprint for what precisely can be done in each and every situation, instead it specifies what kind of considerations ought to inform the choice of security measures used, including what is impermissible behaviour for executors of securitization including – in state-led securitizations: security professionals.

Although I arrive at these criteria starting from the empirical context of the securitization of Islamic or jihadi fundamentalist terrorism, it goes without saying that the three criteria are not limited to this particular securitization and below. Where appropriate I also use other cases as illustrative examples. The securitization of terrorism presents merely a timely and familiar example that helps me and hopefully also the reader think through what might be required and why.

6.2 TARGETED SECURITY MEASURES

Regardless of the precise nature of security measures used in securitization, it is important to remember that JST holds that any such measures have a hope of being justified only when there is a just cause and when securitizing actors are informed by the same (cf. McMahan, 2005: 5). It follows that whatever is done to ensure the essential character of the just referent object, it is a just response only if it targets and does not exceed the threat, because the threat to it and nothing beyond the threat is what permits securitization in the first place. This requirement has precedence in the just war tradition as part of micro-proportionality which requires – among other things – 'that any offensive action should remain strictly *proportional* to the objective desired' (Moseley, 2008; my emphasis). The meaning of proportional here really refers to the use of appropriate force to the objective sought. Orend puts this well when he argues: 'Make sure, the [proportionality] rule commands, that the destruction needed to fulfil the goal is proportional to the good of achieving it. The crude version of this rule is: do not squash a squirrel with a tank, or swat a fly with a cannon. *Use force appropriate to the target*' (Orend, 2006: 119; emphasis in original). This interpretation of *in bello* proportionality goes back to the Geneva Conventions, which prohibit attack 'excessive in relation to the concrete and direct military advantage anticipated' (cited in McMahan, 2018b: Kindle 11513). Partially informed by this, I propose in this section the following principle for JST:[3]

Criterion 6: The security measures used must be appropriate and should aim to only address the objective existential threat that occasions securitization.

Security measures often exceed the threat securitization was supposed to target.[4] The most poignant empirical example of a securitization where the security measures taken exceeded the threat and became – to some – more threatening than the threat itself was/is the war on terrorism (or in other words, the securitization of jihadi terrorism) waged by the United States, the United Kingdom and their various willing allies. Many scholars have pointed out that even when factoring in the events of 9/11, terrorism killed fewer people per year in America than do road accidents, not to mention heart conditions. Two wars (Afghanistan and Iraq), complete with hundreds of thousands of civilian deaths, plus several wide-ranging changes to domestic law (e.g. the PATRIOT Act but also similar legislation in other countries), the use of torture, the prison at Guantanamo Bay, the practice of extraordinary rendition etc. simply greatly exceeded the threat posed by Al-Qaeda terrorism. Regime-

---

[3] My criterion here is also informed by the *in bello* principle of necessity. In the JWT this principle serves to delimit who or what count as legitimate targets for attack insofar as any military offensive must be necessary to generate a military advantage (Frowe, 2016: 110). As Janina Dill has shown, however, in international law among other things, 'necessity is a condition of proportionality' (Dill, 2015: 74). She argues: 'As far as war is concerned, proportionality implies an absolute obligation to minimise excepted collateral damage as much as possible. This minimisation effort in turn comprises the task of making sure that there would not have been an alternative military equivalent target with a more favourable proportionality calculus' (ibid.: 73–74).

[4] While there is some overlap here between this criterion and criterion 3 on right intention, wrong intention does not necessarily mean that the threat is exceeded; it could simply result in the threat not adequately targeted.

change, oil revenues or even unfinished family business (i.e. G. W. Bush finishing off what his father had left unfinished) have all been named as ulterior motives for the war in Iraq.

In the light of this, some academics have gone as far as to imply or suggest that there was no real threat, and they see the war on terror as a vehicle for – in the United Kingdom at least – creating a 'suspect Muslim community', whereby the target of many counter-terrorist measures was Muslim others (Pantakis and Pemberton, 2009; Croft, 2012). However, while the specific argument of a Muslim suspect community remains largely unfounded (Greer, 2010), it is also the case that there was a real threat emanating from Islamic fundamentalists intent not only on indiscriminately harming citizens of Western countries, and who executed their intentions in New York, Washington, London, Madrid and Bali, even if some of these were in direct response to the West's reactions to 9/11. Secondly it would be conspiratorial to believe that, for example, MI5 has not foiled a large amount of terrorist attacks in the years since the 7/7 bombings (cf. Manningham-Buller, 2007: 43–44). The same holds true of other branches of the secret services. Nevertheless, there can be little doubt that for many agencies within different national governments, the war on terror was a welcome 'discourse of danger' (Campbell, 1998) that provided security institutions with a raison d'être, governmental funding, and as Snowden has revealed, with a mandate to act zealously and practically monitor everyone they possibly could, including for purposes of industrial espionage.

Some scholars have argued that the security measures exceeded the threat for political reasons, because in the immediate aftermath of the 9/11 attacks, people wanted tangible action. Notably the PATRIOT Act passed through Congress and Senate with just one person objecting (Evangelista, 2008: 60); indeed at that time, inaction would have been deemed unpatriotic. After all, few events had captured the mind-set of ordinary Americans as much as the events of 9/11 (see Croft, 2006). Similar observations have been made of the United Kingdom. Andrew Neal, for example, has observed from his extensive studies of the UK parliament that: 'In counter-terrorism there is a long-held parliamentary convention of consensus' (2013: 127, see also De Londras, 2011: 87).

In addition, there are reasons to believe that psychological factors played a role in why the security measures employed exceeded the threat that occasioned it. How was it possible that a few men armed with box-cutters could kill several thousand innocent American civilians? And what could like-minded people achieve if only they had access to nuclear weapons? This, together with evidence that Al-Qaeda had a nuclear programme in place before 9/11 and even carried out explosive tests, as well as the fact that they had tried to buy stolen fissile material in the past and had tried to recruit nuclear weapons scientists (Bunn, 2010b; Bunn et al., 2005, 154) surely played a role in the excessive response to the terrorist threat. Be that as it may, none of these reasons justify the excessiveness of the security measures used, rendering the securitization of terrorism after 9/11 by the United States, the United Kingdom and others unjust for '*jus in*' securitization reasons.

Securitizations whereby the security measures used exceed the threat are not confined to agent-intended threats. Critically inclined scholars of environmental security, for example, worry that the climate security threat and projected figures of climate migrants (i.e. people displaced by climatic change) will be used to justify harsh immigration policies that serve economic, military or xenophobic interests (Hartmann, 2010). An empirical example of an excessive securitization of an agent-caused threat is provided by WHO's securitization of infectious disease, beginning in the mid-1990s and expanded in the early 2000s, which took the form of a global surveillance programme and exceeded the threat posed by viruses such as Severe Acute Respiratory Syndrome (SARS) and H5N1 (avian influenza), which together killed fewer than 285,000 people worldwide (Roos, 2012). Not only did WHO's securitization divert valuable resources from common and entirely preventable infectious diseases responsible for approximately 14.7 million death worldwide, but also there are good reasons to belief that securitization was driven by WHO's agenda to gain authoritative power in the area of infectious disease, which was the primary concern for Western countries, WHO's largest donors (Davies, 2008: 295–313). By contrast WHO, the UN's and relevant states' (i.e. those with outbreaks) security measures used in response to the Ebola crisis of 2014/15 did not exceed the threat, neither did they serve an ulterior motive. Here, the primary focus was on containing and obliterating the disease; security measures included curfews, lock-downs and travel restrictions. All of these were in place for a comparatively short time and served to bring the spread of the virus under control.

The discussion shows how scholars using JST can know whether or not security measures are appropriate and necessary. As a general rule, as far as agent-intended threats are concerned, securitizing actors need to tailor the exact nature of the response to the capabilities of an aggressor, which (when combined with intent) make the threat real, but which also designate the boundaries for the appropriateness of the response. For example, if the threat is from terrorism, the aim of securitization and all measures employed ought to be to deal with terrorists, not to use it as an opportunity to spy on the general population, erode civil liberties and to push through (often long-standing) foreign policy goals.[5]

Moving on to non-intended threats (i.e. agent-lacking threats and agent-caused threats), here in the absence of an aggressor complete with capabilities, we cannot say that the measures must be tailored to the capabilities of the aggressor. At best, we can say that the security measures need to be tailored to the source of the threat and that it should not pursue some ulterior agenda. This means that scholars examining such cases must be well-informed about the political situation, history and the context in which security measures are used. Important in particular is whether the threat identified as the just cause really is the subject of securitization, or whether it follows/pursues an ulterior agenda. It will therefore be important to establish what such ulterior agendas could be. In the WHO case discussed, for example, the author of the study, Sarah Davies, established who funds the WHO in the area of infectious disease, and the funders' objectives.

6.3 LEAST HARMFUL OPTION

Imagine a situation where we have two equally viable, targeted and effective (sets of) security measures, and that each one of these would solve the threat that occasions it without exceeding it, but that option B would cause, or risk, more overall harm[6] than option A. Which should be chosen, and why? In the following I will set out my reasons why option A must be chosen; overall, this section develops and defends the following corresponding criterion for just securitization.

Criterion 7: The security measures used must be judged effective in dealing with the threat. They should aim to cause, or risk, the least amount of overall harm possible; and do less harm to the referent object than would otherwise be caused if securitization was abandoned.

To make my case, consider the hypothetical securitization of climate change through two equally effective but not equally harmful options. As part of option A, climate change is securitized via a legally binding emissions reduction climate security regime. Importantly, as a case of securitization, this regime would be unlike any environmental regime currently in existence.

---

[5] Note here that securitization and riskification are sometimes hard to disentangle (cf. Chapter 3, section 3.7).

[6] By overall harm I mean harm to everyone, including – where appropriate – agents at the source of the threat, innocent third parties and referent objects (e.g. citizens of states).

It would be governed and enforced more rigorously than anything hitherto. It would make withdrawal illegal and enforce compliance thoroughly, for example, by applying economic sanctions against states and companies that do not comply with such a regime.[7] Should economic sanctions fail to have the desired effect – which is often the case – they would be followed by the loss of membership in world organizations including WTO and/or regional organizations such as the EU.

Under option B, securitization would consist of irreversible forms of environmental manipulation of a kind not done before, including ocean fertilization and enhanced weathering. Some of the suggested methods of geo-engineering (for an overview, see Royal Society, 2009), hold at least the potential to deal with the climate threat, and – should they work – they might even be sufficient with no further mitigation methods needed. The problem is however that it comes at a considerable risk. Not only is there no guarantee that it will actually work, but also so-called non-encapsulated methods (technological solutions where foreign materials are released into the oceans or the atmosphere) are virtually irreversible and, should they go wrong, could spell further disaster and bring about biosphere and human insecurity (ibid.). Environmental history is full of examples where technological fixes have led to unintended consequences. The green revolution, which saw a substantial increase in crop-yield in the developing world achieved by the use of pesticides and fertilizers, for example, led to increased levels of cancer and millions of pesticide-related deaths. Indeed, climate change itself is 'the unintended effect of the deployment of technologies once regarded as benign. Responding with further large-scale deployment of technologies may therefore simply exacerbate the problem' (Royal Society, 2009: 37). In short, for now and unless further conclusive research has been conducted, the potential harm of geo-engineering is too high, making A the preferred option.

Preference for the least harmful option is informed by JST's overall aim to curtail the amount of destruction and harm done by security politics. This requirement tracks the important intuitive moral principle, don't cause harm if you don't have too, which is also central to just war theories (Lazar, 2017). Such considerations usually are part of the micro-proportionality requirement, which specifies that 'the least harmful means available of achieving the good' must be chosen (Frowe, 2011: 107). In order to establish least harmful

---

7 As Robert Falkner writes about the Paris 2015 agreement: 'Even where parties are in breach of treaty provisions, they will not face punitive sanctions as they might in other international agreements such as those of the WTO' (2016: 1118).

means/options, users of JST must weigh up the expected harm different targeted[8] security measures are likely to cause those that have rendered themselves liable to being secured against and to innocent bystanders, and choose the option that causes the least overall morally weighted harm (where the harms to liable persons are significantly discounted compared to harm to non-liable persons).[9]

A potential problem emerges with this straightforward logic when strategy B, though anticipated to be more harmful than A, is at the same time expected to be vastly more effective. Thus what if – to stick with our example – only securitization as irreversible geo-engineering could deal with rising temperatures once and for all? Which option should be chosen, and why?[10] In such cases it seems intuitively right that it is permissible that the more effective yet – at least in the short term – more harmful option is selected. The reason for this is that the option that is initially more harmful might still be less harmful overall, provided it is able to deal with the source of the problem (climate change) for good, and as such prevent future harm.

It should be noted here that choosing the least harmful option also guards against the possibility of security measures doing more harm than not doing anything against the threat. That is, it guards against security measures doing more harm to the referent object than they seek to guard against. Once more, the many counter-terrorist measures employed in the war on terror are instructive. Thus a number of scholars have argued that legislation like the PATRIOT Act, which institutionalized the loss of some civil liberties, have led to a weakening of democracy, which is normally tantamount to individual rights and autonomy (Waldron, 2002). Similarly, Roger Scruton has argued that terrorism can on occasion threaten democracy by influencing domestic policies to such a degree that 'the people' are no longer fully in charge, leaving democracy compromised. Thus, terrorism can impinge on freedom of speech and also on the politics of religious exception. Scruton puts this as follows: 'Terrorism destroyed democracy when the Bolsheviks and the Nazis took over. As for the Islamists – well, they have already made free speech about religion all but impossible' (Scruton, 2007). Matthew Evangelista suggests that ill-treatment and wrongful incarceration of innocent terrorist suspects is likely to lead to resentment and a 'desire for vengeance' (Evangelista, 2008: 68). Neil Hicks reports that counter-terrorism has led to the global erosion of human

---

[8] In a sense of criterion 6.
[9] I am grateful to Jonathan Parry for this formulation.
[10] Note that in the Laws of Armed Conflict (LOAC), notably the Geneva Protocol of 1925, there are prohibitions against certain types of harmful weapons because they do not discriminate between combatants and non-combatants, that one can thus rule out from the start.

rights (Hicks, 2005: 209ff.). Mass-surveillance techniques and programmes on the scale revealed by Snowden have damaged diplomatic relations (here especially the revelation that the NSA tapped the phones of thirty-five world leaders); it has eroded trust in the democratic accountability of government and its institution, and it has put ordinary people at risk, as their data might end up in the hands of criminals and/or they could wrongly be framed as complicit in terrorist attacks. Moreover, as Luke Harding puts it: 'Paradoxically, in its quest to make Americans more secure, the NSA has made American communications less secure; it has undermined the safety of the entire internet' by inserting a 'back door' into the encryption software used to protect personal and corporate data such as health records and financial transactions (Harding, 2014: Kindle location 2393). Other such arguments abound.

The possibility that the security measures used can cause more harm to those they are supposed to protect (i.e. the referent object) than the very threat these measures seek to address, means that a corresponding criterion must not only specify that the security measures used must not only cause, or risk the least amount of overall harm possible, instead it must also specify that, security measures must do less harm to the referent object than there would be if securitization were abandoned.

6.4 JUST CONDUCT OF EXECUTORS OF SECURITIZATION

Many rules of the *jus in bello* are concerned with the rightful conduct of soldiers in war. Criteria for the just conduct of soldiers include, for example, the requirement of discrimination between combatants as legitimate and non-combatants as illegitimate targets, and the requirement of 'benevolent quarantine' whereby enemy soldiers may be captured, stripped of their weaponry, but not tortured (Orend, 2006: 110). Indeed, even the novel *jus ad vim* mostly simply concerns the conduct of soldiers in situations short-of-war (Ford, 2013; not so Brunstetter and Braun, 2013, 2011). When thinking about just securitization, we do not have the luxury of an easily identifiable group that *always* executes securitization, in part because securitization can – depending on threat-type – involve distinct executors of securitization. At best, we can say that state-led securitization is usually executed by some combination of the police, border guards, private security firms (often employed by states), the intelligence community and sometimes even the military but (depending on threat) may involve other actors such as healthcare professionals or the coast-guard. Moreover, in non-state securitizations there is not necessarily a discernible difference between the securitizing actor and the executor of securitization, but also there are no security professionals we can reliably pinpoint.

Despite this difficulty it should by now be obvious that if securitization has a hope of being justifiable then – even in times of emergency – executors of securitization including security professionals cannot simply conduct themselves as they please and free of constraint regarding the harm they are permitted to cause, including to those that have made themselves liable to being secured against.[11]

In line with this, my final criterion of just securitization must ensure that the conduct of executors of securitization is restricted by certain rules. Specifically I hold that when executors of securitization harm people they should be appropriately constraint by the rights of those people.

In liberal democracies, a prominent and effective way of restricting state power is the practice of human rights (Beitz, 2009). The inclusion of human rights in this context may seem counter-productive because – at least in part – securitization often necessitates the temporary suspension or infringement of individual rights. For example, the right to privacy is and can be infringed by surveillance in an effort to locate terrorists and criminals. And while the excessive use of this practice renders securitization unjust (cf. above), it does not make sense to prohibit infringements of the right to privacy. Indeed securitization could never be just if all possible human rights of all persons would have to be observed all of the time.However, the fact that it can – as part of a wider just securitization – be permissible to suspend some key relevant rights (notably, liberty, freedom of movement and privacy) does not mean that all human rights may be suspended wholesale. Arguing thus would permit excesses of violence, including indiscriminate and disproportionate killing, torture and police brutality undermining the intermediate need of physical security.[12] A concern with just conduct of executors of securitization including security professionals must serve to curtail the worst excesses of violence and the abuse of special powers in the name of security, pertaining in particular to 1) the proportionate use of lethal force and to 2) mistreatment of persons detained or

---

[11] This shows that micro-proportionality too must not only take account of proportionality$_w$ considerations (as it does when it seeks to constrain collateral damage) but also of proportionality$_n$ (McMahan, 2018b). Notably I will shortly argue that the use of lethal force in just securitization is proportionate only, and with one caveat, when there is an intended direct lethal threat.

[12] Note here again the mutually beneficial relationship between rights and needs, with rights 'vital means by which substantive human needs are better protected' (Doyal and Gough, 1991: 224).

handled/controlled[13] as part of securitization. I propose that the conduct of executors of securitization must as much as possible be informed by the adherence to a number of inalienable basic rights as stated in the United Nation's Universal Declaration of Human Rights, explicitly: the right to life, the right not to be tortured, and protection against arbitrary detention, exile and arrest. As we shall see, however, the right to life is not an absolute right; it can be overridden, depending on liability. The criterion this section will develop and defend reads as follows.

Criterion 8: Executors of securitization must respect a limited number of relevant human rights in the execution of securitization.

It is important to recognize that the use of lethal force can be morally permissible as part of securitization. Some threats (e.g. an aggressor developing chemical or nuclear weapons they intend to use) warrant a more harmful kind of response, notably a lethal one (e.g. a missile strike to take out this capability, including the aggressor[14]) than do, for example, a bunch of hackers who have broken into a government's computer system as part of a dare (some sort of 'hack-off') and succeeded in obtaining one or more national secret. A notable difference between these two examples is that the former is a direct lethal threat, while the latter is a non-lethal threat to the cyber-security of a political order/state. This difference matters. David Rodin has argued that in English law as well as under the European Convention on Human Rights, harm to property is excluded from rightful defence with lethal force (Rodin, 2002: 44). This means that within the jurisdiction of this law one cannot shoot a burglar, or a car thief.[15]

This logic is important because it suggests that 'the harms inflicted by attacks against persons and attacks against property are not just different in magnitude; they are different in *kind*. It is not simply that being killed is a worse injury than being robbed of everything that one owns; it is a different kind of injury, for one inflicts damage that may be reconstructed in full, whereas for the other, this possibility does not meaningfully exist' (Rodin, 2002: 45). In itself this does not change JST's logic of the just cause, whereby threats have to be real and existentially threatening to a just referent object. What it does do, however, is to help prescribe *when* executors of securitization

---

[13] By handled or controlled, I mean the security management of persons short of detention; a recent example is the handling by the Spanish police of the independence vote in Catalonia in the autumn of 2017.

[14] Note I hold that one missile strike does not amount to warfare, even though missile strikes are part of war.

[15] As Rodin points out, not all US states share this law.

are permitted to employ lethal force. Most obviously it allows us to say that when there is a direct lethal threat, securitization can involve lethal force.[16] To stick with our example of the hackers, their removal by means of lethal force on the part of the police or some special branch thereof, or even a military strike would be unjust, because they do not pose a direct threat to human life.

We know from previous chapters that security threats can be caused by agents intentionally as well as without intent. We also know that both agent-intended threats and agent-caused but unintended threats can be direct threats to human life. Does it matter for the justice of securitization, whether or not a direct threat is intended by the agent or not? Or in other words, are, for example, police permitted to use – as part of securitization – lethal force against carriers of a lethal infectious disease, for which no known cure exists? I propose that – with one notable exception – the answer to this question has to be no. In the same way as the just war theory discriminates between combatants and non-combatants, executors of securitization need to discriminate between aggressors and (to stick with the example) disease-carriers,[17] and identify, out of the two, only the former as legitimate targets for lethal force. Although – unlike non-combatants – carriers of infectious disease pose a direct lethal threat, they do not intend to do harm and as such they have not lost their right to life (the right not to be killed) (Rodin, 2002).

This said, there are, however, situations when carriers of a highly infectious and incurable disease forfeit the right not to be killed. This is the case when they do not accept that they – upon *knowing* that they are disease carriers – act in ways that threaten the life of other innocent people, for instance by breaking curfews or defying detention (cf. Wilkinson, 2007). The forfeiture of the right

---

[16] The tragic de Menezes case shows that it is possible that as part of securitization, innocent people may be killed; thus the securitization of terrorism in Britain involved a pre-emptive shoot-to-kill policy of suspected terrorists (O'Driscoll, 2008b: 154). In order to show that this does not automatically render securitization unjust, it is necessary to briefly consider the doctrine of double effect (DDE). An intrinsic part of *jus in bello*, DDE holds that the killing of non-combatants in war does not necessarily render the war unjust, provided that this was not intended but merely foreseeable (clearly, in the United Kingdom after 7/7 the killing of innocents might have been foreseen but never intended). In other words, it holds that there is a morally significant difference between intending and foreseeing to cause harm (Frowe, 2011: 140). This is particularly important for war fighting, because a war in which no non-combatants are killed is practically unachievable (ibid.: 141). However, given that this leaves DDE open to all kinds of abuses provided harm was not intended, Frowe (ibid.) explains that DDE comes with a proportionality requirement. Thus: 'the foreseen harm must be outweighed by the good that I intend to achieve'. In war, this might refer to a particular military campaign; for our purposes, it refers to security measures.

[17] Disease-carrier is an example. I mean all probable agents in agent-caused threats that pose direct threats to life.

not to be killed in such situations goes back to McMahan, who ties the liability to being killed through acting in particular ways to responsibility, which includes beyond the intention to do harm also reckless, negligent and risky behaviour (McMahan, 2009b: 159ff.; see also Frowe, 2014: 64–86 and 184; cf. Chapter 4, section 4.7).[18]

So far so good, but direct lethal threats are not the only threats that kill people. Recall that indirect lethal threats are, whilst not targeted at people, lethal to people because the resulting change in or the demise of the non-human entity or social and political order directly threated will still kill people (cf. Chapter 3, section 3.2.1). For example, substantial damage to an ecosystem can pose an indirect lethal threat to people. An indirect lethal threat can be the unintended consequence of an agent-intended threat. In a twist on our earlier 'hack-off' example used above, consider *Hacker*:

Hacker

Hackers break into a government's computer system with the intention to obtain one or more national secret in order to sell the same to a foreign and malign government that has the intention to use the information against the people within the state, for example, by carrying out targeted acts of sabotage on nuclear power plants, leading to these plants leaking nuclear fissile materials.

Hacker raises the question: can lethal force be used to deal with indirect lethal threateners? Or else, is it permissible to take out the hackers with a targeted missile strike that would kill them? Although the hackers themselves do not intend to kill people, I think – following Frowe (2014) – that the answer is quite possibly yes.[19] Frowe argues that provided a person is 'morally responsible for posing an unjust threat' (ibid.: 73) it is morally permissible to use lethal force against 'a person who contributes to the threat to Victim's life, but who is not going to kill Victim' (ibid.: 7). On Frowe's account 'a person is morally responsible for posing an unjust threat if she had reasonable opportunity to avoid posing the unjust threat and she intentionally failed to avail herself of that opportunity' (ibid.: 73). Frowe's detailed account serves to problematize the category of innocent bystanders and it ultimately allows her to argue that in war, all kinds of non-combatants that contribute to an unjust war may be liable to being killed. As such, her account looks at cases that are less straightforward

---

[18]   This list should also include mental illness that results in the loss of autonomy, as described in Chapter 3. Fabre (2012: 59) acknowledges this in her example of a psychotic gunman on a rampage losing the right not to be killed.

[19]   The example is for illustrative purposes only; I realize that one huge challenge for cyber-security and defence is that the origin of the threat is often unknown.

than the one discussed here. The most clear-cut case when one is morally responsible for posing an unjust threat is when 'one intentionally contributes to an endeavour that aims at inflicting harm' (ibid.: 11). Our hackers in *Hacker* clearly fall into that category, and as such have rendered themselves liable to defensive lethal force.

Indirect lethal threats can also emerge as the unintended consequence of agent-caused, but not intended threats. Consider, for example, *Water Pollution*:

Water Pollution

Residents of upstream riparian A unintentionally pollute and consequently destroy the ecosystem of the water to such an extent that it has lethal consequences for people residing in downstream riparians B, C and D; notably, when pollution has rendered their main diet fish toxic for human consumption. With little else to eat, people in B, C and D now face starvation.

In *Water Pollution*, the threat is caused by agents who do not realize that their actions are threatening to valuable ecosystems, let alone lethal to other people. Given that they are unaware that their actions are threatening, they could also not plausibly make use of any opportunity to avail the threat. To my mind at least this renders culprits morally irresponsible for posing the unjust threat.

Agent-caused threats can also be produced by harmful neglect. Consider *Climate Neglect*:

Climate Neglect

Executive of state A is fully aware of the causes and consequences of global climate change, but decides not to act accordingly, in an effort not to hamper A's short-term economic goals.

Including from the IPCC's many reports we know that failure to secure the climate can kill people (cf. Chapter 3, section 3.6). Indeed if we believe that the causal connections between extreme weather events, crop failures etc. are reliably attributable to rising temperatures, then this is already the case. This raises the question whether a lethal response is, in principle at least, permissible in cases where lethal threats emerge indirectly, after relevant agents fail to protect against the foreseeable events (e.g. safeguarding the climate). As in the *Water Pollution* case, actors do not intend to cause the threat to the stability of the global climate. One notable difference between the two cases is that in *Water Pollution* the threat is ignorantly caused, whereas in *Climate Neglect* the threat is culpably caused. In the latter case, the executive of state A knows that failure to act on climate change will lead to higher temperatures and more climate change. Does the difference between the two cases render those culpable of harmful neglect liable to lethal defensive force? As Frowe (2014) and McMahan (2005) argue, it seems intuitive that people can be liable to be killed if they negligently pose/contribute to threats. Given this, it also seems fairly intuitive that someone could be liable for failing to prevent a threat, at least if they do so culpably (i.e. in full knowledge of the threat, and they could prevent the threat at low costs to themselves). Given that lethal force is only permissible when it is necessary to achieve the goal of addressing the unjust threat, situations where the negligent are liable to being killed are, if at all, exceedingly rare. We can see why this is the case in *Climate Neglect*. In this case, killing those who neglect to act on climate change (i.e. the executive of state A) and thus threaten the lives of others – on its own – does simply not achieve that goal. Killing is only permissible if it serves some defensive purpose. Killing someone who negligently fails to prevent a threat can only be permissible if killing them is causally effective in preventing that threat. This condition seems unlikely to be met in *Climate Neglect*.

This concludes my analysis of liability and loss of the right to life. Moving on from lethal force, another key area for just conduct of executors of securitization concerns the treatment of individuals detained and/or handled as part of securitization. Skleparis (2016: 98) observes that during the migrant crisis in Greece, migrants were subjected to inhumane and degrading treatment at the hands of relevant security professionals (or as he, drawing on Bigo, calls them, '(in)security professionals'), including 'punches and kicks to the head and body'. The treatment of suspects and the disregard for human dignity has become an issue of concern also in the context of the war on terror. David Luban has pointed out that the often-mentioned trade-off between rights and security is really a fallacy. In his own words: 'As a respectable, middle-aged, native-born, white, tenured professor who leads a dull life, I know the odds are slender that I will ever need to invoke the right against self-incrimination or the right to a speedy, public trial, let alone the right not to be shipped off to the Jordanian police for interrogation' (Luban, 2005a: 243; see also Dworkin, 2003; Waldron, 2010). In other words, what is traded-off here is other people's rights (those who become involved with radical groups, or are simply and/or likely just suspected of it) for my security (the middle-class, Caucasian self who is very unlikely to be wrongfully suspected of any such involvement). Other people's rights concern us less than our own rights, in the same way as poverty in Africa affects many average Britons psychologically less than, for example, reports by the Trussell Trust that the number of UK families using food banks has seen a steep rise since the onset of the financial crisis and the government's subsequent drive for austerity. Luban suggests but ultimately does not pursue the idea that rights lost in the war on terror would be valued more if we imagined a situation whereby our children, as our nearest and dearest, would one day lose their rights after having flirted with radical groups. The underlying idea in Luban's hypothetical is of course that it would make us think of suspects, offenders and, for our purposes here, agents at the source of agent-caused threats (immigrants, disease carriers etc.) first and foremost as fellow human beings, which is not only what they are, but also how they ought to be treated.

JST agrees with this assessment. The theory does not sanction revenge or retaliation, which is to say: misgivings about the actions of suspects, offenders and other persons detained as part of securitization are not to be unduly punished by those in charge of detention. Securitization cannot be justified if the basic needs – including physical security – of suspects and offenders are excessively undermined. Indeed, these rules must apply prior to detention and in the controlling of people as part of securitization, for example to manage or disperse crowds.

As already stated, it should be clear that even lawful detention means that a suspect's human needs are compromised; after all, autonomy is curtailed, but it cannot mean that physical security too is taken away, as is most obviously the case when suspects are subjected to torture. JST is thus in full agreement with Article 10 of the International Covenant on Social and Political Rights, which specifies a right to humane treatment when deprived of liberty. In more detail, the Office of the High Commissioner for Human Rights General Comment no. 21 from 1992 specifies:

> Article 10, paragraph 1, of the International Covenant on Civil and Political Rights applies to any one deprived of liberty under the laws and authority of the State who is held in prisons, hospitals – particularly psychiatric hospitals – detention camps or correctional institutions or elsewhere. [It] imposes on States parties a positive obligation towards persons who are particularly vulnerable because of their status as persons deprived of liberty, and complements for them the ban on torture or other cruel, inhuman or degrading treatment or punishment contained in article 7 [i.e. no one shall be subjected to torture or to cruel, inhuman or degrading treatment or punishment. In particular, no one shall be subjected without his free consent to medical or scientific experimentation] of the Covenant. Thus, not only may persons deprived of their liberty not be subjected to treatment that is contrary to article 7, including medical or scientific experimentation, but neither may they be subjected to any hardship or constraint other than that resulting from the deprivation of liberty; respect for the dignity of such persons must be guaranteed under

the same conditions as for that of free persons. Persons deprived of their liberty enjoy all the rights set forth in the Covenant, subject to the restrictions that are unavoidable in a closed environment.

Lucia Zedner has helpfully suggested that this could be achieved by making sure that 'suspected terrorists be pursued within the ordinary criminal process (albeit accused of the most serious crimes) and considered as criminal defendants to whom the principles of criminal justice apply' (2009: 140). Specifically, this includes: '[t]he presumption of innocence and the privilege against self-incrimination, access to impartial legal advice and legal aid, rules of evidence, charge with a substantive offence, adequate time and facilities to prepare a defence, the right to confront witnesses, rules against hearsay evidence, and on the admissibility of evidence' (ibid.: 140; see also Ashworth and Zedner, 2014).

As part of securitization it is possible that individuals other than suspects and offenders are detained. Specifically in securitization of infectious disease, disease carriers might be detained and quarantined to stop the further spread of the disease. While this may be a proportionate and appropriate measure, it is important that humane treatment and dignity must also be awarded to those individuals. While it may not be possible to cure these people, the right to humane treatment means that they are cared for and not simply – once isolated – left to their own devices.

This completes the list of criteria determining just conduct during securitization. Two prominent issues remain outstanding in this context; the first concerns the question whether there are situations in which the criteria of the just conduct during securitization can be suspended without securitization becoming unjust. A second concerns the moral culpability of agents that are party to an unjust securitization. In the following I will address each issue in turn.

6.5 MORAL EXEMPTIONS TO JUST CONDUCT IN SECURITIZATION

A much-debated issue for just war scholars is the problem of dirty hands, which poses the question: 'Should political leaders violate the deepest constraints of morality in order to achieve great goods or avoid disasters for their communities?' (Coady, 2014). In the context of the war on terror, philosophers have discussed the problem of dirty hands under the thought experiment of the ticking time bomb, which has been described by Frowe (2011: 197) in the following terms:

Imagine that a terrorist has planted a bomb in a crowded shopping centre. You, the local Chief of Police, capture the terrorist, but they refuse to tell you where they have hidden the bomb. Only by torturing them can you get them to reveal the bomb's location. If you do not torture them for the information, the bomb will go off and hundreds, perhaps thousands, of people will be killed. Should you torture the terrorist?

Much simplified, philosophers' responses to this hypothetical thought experiment are split along the usual lines of deontology versus consequentialism (though, for an exception, see Bufacchi and Arrigo, 2007). Absolute deontologists hold that certain things are categorically morally wrong, including torture, killing people etc. They also point out that one will never have perfect information, that one simply can't be sure you have the right person, or that suspects will talk, and also that television programmes such as the American TV series '24', where the torture of 'baddies' is common fare, provide a distorted picture of reality (Luban and Engel, 2014). Consequentialists, specifically Utilitarians focus on the maximizing the overall good, and some (albeit few) have argued that the torturing of one guilty party can be morally justified if it helps to save many innocent people. Dershowitz (2002) infamously suggests the issuing of torture warrants regulating but also legitimizing torture.

Torture clearly breaks with criterion 8 of JST, which inter alia specifies the humane treatment of persons detained as part of securitization. The question is, whether there can be moral exceptions to this rule making torture morally permissible? Let us turn once again to the just war tradition for some guidance. In his uncompromising style Uwe Steinhoff is one of the few philosophers who advances a case for the moral permissibility of torture in some cases. He compellingly argues:

> What is so bad about torturing people, anyway? People also kill people. Soldiers kill people, policemen kill people, doctors kill people, executioners kill people and ordinary people kill people. Some of these killings are justified. So why shouldn't it be justified in some cases to torture people? After all, being killed seems to be worse than being tortured. Even most of the tortured people seem to see it this way; otherwise they would kill themselves in order to escape further torture … So if killing is sometimes justified, torture too must sometimes be justified. (Steinhoff, 2007b: 96)

He goes on to illustrate the moral permissibility of torture on the American film *Dirty Harry*, in which the lead character Harry (portrayed by Clint Eastwood) is able to ensure the survival of a kidnapped child only by torturing the kidnapper.[20] I agree with Steinhoff that few people – including

---

[20]   Harry shoots the kidnapper in the leg and later puts his foot onto the leg wound to inflict further pain.

myself – would object to Harry's actions, especially seeing that the victim is an innocent child, kept in a confined space where she slowly runs out of oxygen. It would appear then that Steinhoff is correct in claiming that torture is sometimes morally permissible. Steinhoff, however, also points out that bona fide ticking time bomb scenarios are rare, and he argues that Dershowitz-style institutionalization of torture is a mistake because it leads to the 'brutal-isation of the legal system' and thus ultimately to 'the brutalisation of its enforcer – which, in modern societies, is ultimately the state' (ibid.: 110).[21] In other words, while there are cases when torture is permissible, we ought to have laws and norms that treat torture as always criminal.

6.6 MORAL CULPABILITY AND INDIVIDUAL AGENTS IN UNJUST SECURITIZATION

So far I have argued that securitization can be unjust for reasons that pertain either to the initiation of securitization, or for reasons that relate to what is done during securitization, including the unjust conduct of executors of securitiza-tion. To say that something is 'unjust' is tantamount to saying that it is wrong, and from here it is only a small step to identifying the agents that are doing wrong. Clearly, in securitizations that are unjust because of the absence of a just cause, securitizing actors are, at a minimum, morally culpable. Former UK Prime Minister Tony Blair, for example, can be held morally responsible for overstating, indeed for deliberately exaggerating,[22] the risk allegedly posed by Iraq to international security in the run-up to the Iraq war (cf. Chilcot, 2016).

If securitization is unjust because of what executors of securitization (i.e. individuals who implement security measures, but are not responsible for the initiation of securitization) have done during securitization (for example, because they mistreated individuals detained under a state's terrorism laws) the executors of securitization are, at a minimum, morally culpable for their actions. None of this is particularly contentious. Indeed it is possible to go further and to argue that moral culpability is the basis of legal culpability. Some people believe that Tony Blair should have been indicted for his conduct in the run-up to the Iraq war; likewise some wish to see the prosecu-tion of G4S employees for the mistreatment of prisoners at Mangaung prison in South Africa in 2013, and will be satisfied with the guilty verdict returned in March 2014 for the three G4S employees Stuart Tribelnig, Terry Hughes

---

[21] Coady (2008: 299–300) appears to be more worried by unjust states claiming supreme emergency; indeed terrorism itself could be justified as such.

[22] www.theguardian.com/uk-news/2016/jul/06/iraq-inquiry-key-points-from-the-chilcot-report.

and Colin Kaler for the manslaughter of Jimmy Mubenga, who died in their custody at Heathrow Airport in 2010. In the context of war, prosecutions for grave misconduct are increasingly prominent; recent examples include the trial of Lynndie England, one of the US Army reserve soldiers responsible for torturing prisoners at Abu Ghraib prison, and the prosecution of a Royal Marine (later identified as Sgt Alexander Blackman) for the murder of an injured Taliban insurgent in Afghanistan in November 2013.[23]

The question I seek to answer in this section is this: what should we say about agents who take part in securitization that is unjustly initiated (for example, because it lacks a just cause), but who diligently follow the rules of conduct in carrying out their role? Have these individuals acted in a morally wrong way, so as to be culpable, or have they done nothing wrong and are morally innocent? Or is it the case that they have acted wrongly, but that their actions can and should be excused? Before I can begin with this analysis in earnest a disclaimer is in order; thus although this book is concerned with all possible securitizing actors, in securitizations outside of the context of the state or an equivalent hierarchical organization, this problem is likely to be less acute because there may be less of a distinction between securitizing actors and the actual executors of securitization. For this reason my analysis here is limited to state actors.

I want to begin to answer the above question by looking at the just war tradition for some guidance; because here the issue of the moral status of combatants in war is increasingly the subject of debate (see various in Rodin and Shue, 2008). I say increasingly because for many years, just war scholars simply accepted the 'independence thesis' made famous by but pre-dating Walzer's *Just and Unjust Wars*, which states 'the *ad bellum* status of the war in which a combatant fights does not affect his or her *jus in bello* rights and obligations (in other words, *jus in bello* is independent of *jus ad bellum*)' (Rodin, 2008a: 44). Revisionist just war theorists have questioned the logic of the independence thesis, which is also codified in the Laws of Armed Conflict (LOAC). In a nutshell, the issue is this: how can it be true that (i) a war is impermissible but (ii) killing in that war is permissible?[24] In addition to the issue of permissibility, revisionist just war scholars are interested in blameworthiness. Some argue that it cannot be right that soldiers fighting in a war that is unjust for *ad bellum* reasons are considered entirely blameless for their actions, proposing instead that such 'unjust warriors' are, at a minimum,

---

[23] Note that the conviction of murder in this case was quashed on appeal in 2017 and reduced to manslaughter.

[24] I am indebted to Jonathan Parry for this formulation as well as his help with key points in this chapter.

morally culpable for partaking in an unjust war (McMahan, 2008, 2009b; Orend, 2006: 109–110; Rodin, 2007a, 2008a). Defenders of the independence thesis hold against this that soldiers are often ignorant of world politics, stressing that soldiers are often very young and naïve when drafted, lacking the analytical skills necessary to decide whether a war is just or unjust. Or they accentuate that soldiers are often lied to by politicians on whose behalf they end up fighting the war. Others yet again stress the loyalty to institutions, the fact that soldiers follow orders and 'are just doing a job', and highlight the consequences of disobedience not only in terms of consequences for career development, but also personal shame (see, for example Ryan, 2008; Zupan, 2008).

Some, but not all, adherents of the dependence thesis in turn argue that just warriors should enjoy rights in warfare that exceed specifications of *jus in bello*. Others maintain that unjust warriors' *in bello* privileges should be restricted by lowering the bar of what it is permissible for them to do. This is known as the asymmetry thesis, which states 'that it is not the case that the same *jus in bello* rights and obligations are held by combatants on both sides of any conflict' (Rodin, 2008a: 44, fn. 1).

The most vocal proponent of both the dependence thesis and the asymmetry thesis is Jeff McMahan, who argues 'that it is morally wrong to fight a war that is unjust because it lacks a just cause' (McMahan, 2009b: 6). And consequently that by virtue of participating in unjust wars, unjust warriors have made themselves morally liable to military attack, while just warriors remain 'innocent', here in a sense of having done nothing to render them morally liable to being attacked (McMahan, 2008: 8). In other words, unjust warriors are legitimate targets for military attack by just warriors, while unjust warriors do not hold the privilege to attack just ones.

Let us now return to JST and contemplate what both the dependence thesis and the asymmetry thesis may mean in this context. From the point of view of the dependence thesis, all executors of securitization (for example, individual police officers, border and prison guards) are acting unjustly for partaking in securitizations that were unjustly initiated. The asymmetry thesis in turn prompts the question: do just and unjust executors of securitization (to be clear, in cases where the justice/injustice stems from violation of just initiation of securitization reasons) enjoy the same privileges and prohibitions? For obvious reasons, no one would wish to extend special privileges to unjust executors of securitization, but in my view, even extending such privileges to just executors (in Rodin's terminology, 'permissive asymmetry' (2007a: 599)) would simply render the criteria specifying just conduct in securitization insufficient. 'Restrictive asymmetry' (Rodin, 2007a: 600), in turn is easier;

after all, the logic of JST rests on the idea that unjust executors of securitization are morally prohibited from doing certain things just executors are permitted to do.

The most interesting puzzle these debates give way to is the question of whether executors of securitization are – from a moral point of view – prohibited from engaging in securitizations that are unjustly initiated (e.g. because they lack a just cause)? With this we have arrived back at the dependence thesis, which demands that we consider individual executors of securitization morally culpable for participation in unjust securitization. But does it really make sense to render individual unjust executors of securitization morally culpable? Should we not excuse – at least some – unjust individual executors of securitizations for partaking in unjust securitization on the grounds of ignorance, deception and loyalty to institutions, provided they actually have those excuses?

In order to answer these questions I suggest that we need to go further and contemplate what is at stake when we invoke the notion of 'moral culpability'. Judging by the debate between independence and dependence theorists, it seems to me that the main disagreement lies with whether or not just war theories concerned with morality *should* inform the laws of war. McMahan, for example, seeks to 'distinguish sharply and explicitly between the morality of war and the law of war' (McMahan, 2008: 35). By contrast, Shue wants the morality of war to be action-guiding: '[w]e do not need a "morality of war" if we can get a morally justified set of laws of war' (Shue, 2008, 89).

But what can we take from all this for JST? Throughout this book I have stated that JST is supposed to be action-guiding. Given that there are no 'laws of securitization' that a corresponding morality of securitization could aim to improve, we ought to perhaps think in terms of a normative theory of security that could become law. Importantly I do not wish to promote the latter as either possible or even desirable.[25] Instead, all I wish to claim here is that by adopting this way of thinking in developing a theory of just securitization, we are more likely to usefully limit our criteria to what would be acceptable to most reasonable people. This is important because as an action-guiding theory, principles of JST cannot be unreasonably demanding. For the case in hand this means that I hold, first, that individual unjust executors of securitization should be excused for their participation in unjust securitizations if there are good reasons to believe that they

[25] Waldron (1999) and Bellamy (2007), for example, argue that fundamental political problems (e.g. gun laws) should be subject to democratic decision-making, not the law.

were acting either in good faith that the securitization was just, or if they acted under duress. Second, at the same time, moral culpability must rest somewhere. I would suggest that instead of focusing on individual unjust executors of securitization, it might make more sense to focus on those in charge instead, individuals who might then be rendered accountable by corresponding laws.

It is obvious that much more could be said about the culpability of actors in securitization, but here is not the place to do so. Ultimately what one has to recognize is that all calls for rendering unjust soldiers morally culpable are informed by the desire to reduce the occurrence of unjust wars in the world. McMahan, for one, believes that 'if people generally believed that participation in an unjust or morally unjustified war is wrong – that could make a significant practical difference to the practice of war ... Many people, including active-duty soldiers, would be more reluctant to fight in wars they believed to be unjust' (2009b: 7). The same argument could be advanced with a view to securitization, and since it is the objective of JST to restrain both the incidence and destructiveness of securitization, this needs to be taken seriously.

In my view there are at least two moral and/or practical reasons to object to the idea that institution based executors of securitization should act on their own accord and conscientiously disobey orders.[26] The first is that it could significantly compromise the security of any given state and that of the people living within it. After all, policemen and women, border guards and so on refusing to act on orders may have wrongly interpreted securitization as unjust. Second, asking individual executors of securitization to take on this sort of role is very demanding, and risks leaving these individuals with a deep sense of personal insecurity, because if they decide incorrectly they are culpable.

---

[26] However, the German 'Soldatengesetz', which regulates the conduct of soldiers and punishes disobedience with up to three years in prison, also contains a paragraph specifying that soldiers are required to disobey orders, if following those orders would constitute a criminal offence. ('Ein Befehl darf nicht befolgt werden, wenn dadurch ein Straftat begangen würde. Befolgt der Untergebene den Befehl trotzdem, so trifft ihn eine Schuld nur, wenn er erkennt oder wenn es nach den ihm bekannten Umständen offensichtlich ist, dass dadruch eine Straftat begangen wird'. Gesetz über die Rechtsstellung der Soldaten § 11, www.gesetze-im-internet.de/sg/BJNR001140956.html. Moreover, since the 1998 Rome Statute of the International Criminal Court holds that following orders 'shall not relieve [a] person of criminal responsibility unless a) the person was under legal obligation to obey orders ... b) the person did not know the order was unlawful; and c) the order was not manifestly unlawful' (Gaeta, 1999: 173).

6.7 CONCLUSION

This chapter has discussed the complex issue of just conduct during securitization. We have seen that beyond establishing principles of just conduct guiding practitioners, many other pertinent moral issues arise, and indeed in this conclusion two final issues need further discussion. First is the question of whether or not all criteria of JST have to be met for securitization to be just. Second is the issue of whether securitization and a counter-securitization can be justified on both sides. I will commence with the first. Some scholars writing within the just war tradition have argued that adherence to all criteria of the just war is too stringent and that – in some cases – a war may be justified even without meeting all the criteria. This is the case with regards to some scholars who want to drop the requirement of the last resort (Aloyo, 2015), but more so with those scholars who have looked at humanitarian intervention from the point of view of the just war tradition. Pattison, for instance, rejects a categorical approach to humanitarian intervention whereby all possible criteria would have to be met for an intervention to be just in favour of a scalar approach (2010: 33, see also Tesón, 2005: 143–144). This concerns in particular the legitimacy of the intervener. Instead of requiring full legitimacy for the intervener, Pattison holds that it is sufficient if the intervener has an adequate degree of legitimacy for intervention to be morally acceptable (Pattison, 2010: 32). It is easy to see the rationale for this argument, thus it simultaneously facilitates humanitarian intervention (considered a good thing), and second it lightens the burden on the need to intervene for the fully legitimate states that there are. While a scalar approach to legitimate authority is not particularly relevant for JST as this theory does not require legitimate authority, it reveals something about the logic informing scalar approaches more generally. Thus a scalar approach – i.e. the idea that it might be sufficient if some but not all of the principles specifying just war are met – is driven by the objective to facilitate or ease (certain types of) war. As such, however, it is antithetical to the objective specified by many just war theorists and shared by JST, which is to constrain and limit the occurrence of war and securitization respectively. A scalar approach that would drop one of the criteria of JST as developed in this book would have the opposite effect, and is to be rejected.

Moving on to the second outstanding point, consider that Walzer once argued that: 'Someone must be responsible, for someone decided to break the peace of the society of states. No war, as medieval theologians explained, can be just on both sides' (Walzer, 1977: 59). This raises the question: can securitization and counter-securitization be just on both sides? When contemplating this issue for just securitization it should be clear that we are not concerned with two actors securitizing the same thing (i.e. the United Kingdom and the United States both securitizing Islamic terrorism), instead we are concerned with the issue of securitization and a second securitization that comes about as a result of the initial securitization (e.g. a response to it). In order to discuss this further, let us consider as an illustrative example the actions of Edward Snowden and his collaborators as an act of counter-securitization. As argued in Chapter 2, securitization by non-state actors refers to whatever most reasonable persons would agree constitutes exceptional action, and means mostly in terms of the amount of harm risked/caused or intended and/or the level of violence employed. While non-violent in character, there can be little doubt that Snowden's actions simultaneously risked, intended and caused a huge amount of harm to the governments of the United States and the United Kingdom. What is more, Snowden himself justified his action in terms of the language of existential threats. Specifically he argued: 'What they're doing [the NSA] poses "an existential threat to democracy"' (in Greenwald et al., 2013). At the same time, the action by the NSA and GCHQ which caused the whole affair in the first place was part of the securitization of terrorism; making Snowden's actions a useful example of counter – securitization, and allowing us to at least contemplate the question of the justness of securitization on both sides.

In accordance with JST, Snowden's actions are morally justifiable, if and only if, the securitization of terrorism (i.e. counter-terrorism) itself was not only unjustified, but constituted an objective existential threat to the object in need of protection, namely democracy, or more accurately to the people living within the respective democratic states. Since the states in question (the United Kingdom and the United States) satisfy basic human needs, they are – within the terms of the theory – morally justifiable referent objects. In my view it is an overstatement to say that democracy was at any point in time objectively existentially threatened by the surveillance techniques used by the NSA or GCHQ; what happened is better understood as a danger to values associated with liberal democracy in particular the right to privacy. This is not to suggest, however, that the United States and the United Kingdom's securitizations were justified. Not least in accordance with criterion 7, for example, we can say that the measures used during the securitization of terrorism (i.e. employment of extensive surveillance techniques) were disproportionally harmful, and should have been abandoned in favour of less harmful measures. Given that this case then does not allow a verdict regarding the question of whether securitization can be just on both sides, let us contemplate an alternative hypothetical scenario, one whereby democracy was objectively existentially threated by the surveillance techniques used. Yet in this case it is easily apparent that securitization was unjust at least on the state-actors side because it exceeded the threat (criterion 6) and it was unduly harmful (criterion 7).

From these examples, one may conclude that securitization and counter-securitization are unlikely to be justified on both sides, because – at least – one side is likely to have acted out of line with the principles of JST. Concluding thus, however, ignores that the situation is potentially radically altered when we are dealing with agent-caused but not intended threats.

I have argued in this book that we must differentiate between morally wicked (basically immoral) and moral people, whereby a person is morally wicked if they *intentionally* infringe other people's needs. I have also argued that morally wicked persons – provided they pose an existential threat to a just referent object – have made themselves targets to defensive emergency measures, whilst at the same time losing the moral right to counter these defensive measures with their own security measures. I have also said that objective existential threats to a just referent object can lack intent, and be agent-caused, and for example, pertain to large numbers of migrants overwhelming a state's welfare system. In other words, I have argued that securitization against agents at the sources of agent-caused but not intended threats can be justifiable.

An important difference between persons at the source of agent-caused threats and persons causing agent-intended threats is that the former are not morally wicked. Notably, migrants do not intend to do harm. As such, these persons have not lost their moral right to defend themselves against defensive measures (i.e. securitization), while they may also be defended by third parties.[27] This generates the possibility of a simultaneous just securitization by the threatened state against the migrants threatening a state, and a just counter-securitization on part of the migrants themselves, or indeed on behalf of the migrants by a third party. In short, the existence of intent-lacking threats means that securitization and counter-securitization can be justified on both sides.

---

[27] Fabre (2012: 61) advances a similar conclusion when she argues that in McMahan's hypothetical Ambulance case, whereby a speeding ambulance driver loses control over his vehicle and veers towards a pedestrian, both are permitted to defend themselves.

7

Just Termination of Securitization

Just war theories are increasingly accompanied by criteria determining how wars can be ended justly. For some scholars, the so-called just peace constitutes an 'ethical exit strategy' from just wars (Orend, 2006). For others, the just peace is unrelated to the justice of the preceding war; arguably, injustice in war makes the justice of peace all the more pressing (May, 2012). Whatever the reasons, just peace is fast becoming a staple of just war scholarship and just war theories are now considered incomplete without theories concerning the ending of war (cf. Evans, 2009).

I consider JST incomplete without also considering the just termination of securitization, or else just desecuritization.[1] My thinking is informed by two interrelated reasons. First, as I have argued throughout this book, securitization cannot be justified unless there is a just cause. Beyond delineating just securitization, this logic also means that the necessity of desecuritization is already a part of JST, because in the absence of a just cause, desecuritization is morally required. Second, just as distinct securitizations differ in terms of how justified they are, so do different desecuritizations. It would be naïve to assume that simply because desecuritization does not play out in the realm of the exception it is automatically morally unproblematic. In short, a comprehensive theory of the ethics of securitization must entail the ethics of the unmaking of securitization.

---

[1] Lene Hansen has argued that desecuritization is complementary (or, as she puts it 'the supplement') to securitization, in the sense that securitization is incomplete without desecuritization specifically because 'were there only securitisations [and not also desecuritization], there would be only hyper-politicisation and no "normal politics" for securitisation to separate itself from' (2012: 531). Put differently, we cannot understand what is distinct about securitization as a special form of politics without the normal politics captured in the idea of desecuritization.

This chapter begins by discussing the meaning of desecuritization in JST. I show that while in the Copenhagen School's writings desecuritization is understood alternatively as a process or an outcome, it is most accurate to conceive of desecuritization as a process, and the 'desecuritized state of affairs', in which formerly securitized issues are either politicized or depoliticized, as the outcome of that process. I go on to discuss the relationship between just securitization and just desecuritization; specifically I consider whether the latter depends on the former. From here I move on to the issue of who can desecuritize, and to the far trickier question of who has a duty to do this?

Having established this conceptual basis, the chapter then develops three principles guiding the ethics of desecuritization. The first principle is concerned with the last point in time when securitization must be unmade. In developing this criterion I consider the just war tradition's recent innovations of *jus terminatio* law, or else *jus ex bello*, which unlike *jus post bellum* raises the possibility that just termination of war is not simply the inversion of *jus ad bellum* criteria.

The second principle of just desecuritization I propose prescribes what precisely has to be 'unmade' as part of just desecuritization, how and to what extent. The third principle goes further. Recall from the introduction to this book that I hold that the overall aim of just desecuritization is to achieve a desecuritized state of affairs where actors objectively are and subjectively feel sufficiently secure to the extent that regress into a securitized state of affairs is unlikely. In line with this I argue that just desecuritization needs ideally to include a series of context specific restorative measures aimed at achieving security as a state of being.[2]

The chapter concludes by contemplating whether distinct types of desecuritizing actors and their blameworthiness in prior unjust securitization influences how much and what they have to contribute towards achieving security as a state of being in comparable situations.

---

[2] This is quite different from Wæver, who argues as follows: 'In the securitisation perspective, the dichotomy turns into a triad: Insecurity is the situation when there is a threat and no defence against it; security is a situation with a threat *and* a defence against it; but a-security (a situation that has been desecuritized or never securitised) is simply not phrased in these terms, it is not a question of *being secure* or not and there is not a perception of existential threats being present' (2003: 13 first emphasis in original, second added). Wæver, I think, is wrong here on the relationship between desecuritization and security, because here he does not observe the difference between security as a state of being which can be achieved in the absence of securitization and security as a social and political practice. I think in his aim to make clear that desecuritization is free from securitization, he also and perhaps inadvertently dispenses with security as a state of being (cf. Chapter 1, section 1.2).

7.2 WHAT IS THE MEANING OF DESECURITIZATION IN JUST SECURITIZATION THEORY?

In the securitization literature, desecuritization is generally understood as the reverse of securitization. Huysmans (1998) has referred to desecuritization as 'the unmaking of securitization'.[3] According to Wæver and the Copenhagen School, desecuritization leads to politicization, which is broadly defined as the state of affairs whereby 'an issue is part of public policy' (Wæver, 2003: 10). Described thus politicization refers to an *outcome*; whereas elsewhere in the Copenhagen School's framework desecuritization is the process of re-politicizing a formerly securitized issue. Drawing on prior single-authored work by Wæver they argue: 'desecuritization [is] the shifting of issues out of emergency mode and into the normal bargaining processes of the political sphere' (Buzan et al., 1998: 4).

If one accepts – as I have suggested elsewhere – that only official political authority is decisive of whether something is politicized, it is possible to argue that desecuritization may *lead* to either the situation where the former security issue is depoliticized or to the situation where it continues to be part of official politics (Floyd, 2010; Cui and Li, 2011). Depending on a range of issues, either outcome may be deemed morally right or wrong, good or bad, or else just or unjust. With reference to the environmental sector of security I have suggested in previous work that environmental problems require political solutions and that therefore 'in almost all cases, desecuritisation as politicisation is morally right, whereas a desecuritisation as depoliticisation is morally wrong' (Floyd, 2010: 186).[4]

Yet the environmental sector is a special case and problems with this logic become apparent as soon as we consider other sectors of security and other securitizing actors than states. In the first instance, in the absence of formal political authority it might be hard to say when something is not politicized, because everything that is not securitized can be said to be politicized. Second, even if we circumvent this problem and say, as I did in my work on environmental security, that once desecuritized a former security issue is politicized if it remains on the political agenda of former securitizing actors or an equivalent

---

[3]   It is generally accepted that desecuritization occurs – in time – after securitization has occurred. For a dissenting view, however, see Bourbeau and Vuori (2015) who conceptualize desecuritization moves as strategies of pre-empting securitization. Whilst there can be little doubt that strategies of pre-empting securitization exist and are worthy of investigation, I would advise against calling them de-securitization, after all, one cannot defuse a bomb without the fuse having been lit, the timer having been set, etc.

[4]   I am guilty here of the same crime as the Copenhagen School, insofar as I do not distinguish between outcome and process, to be clear, I mean outcomes in this instance.

agent (e.g. new leadership of an existing political group); whether or not this is preferable in any given situation is ultimately issue-dependent and quite possibly beyond the grasp of further theorization. In the societal sector, for instance, indefinite awareness of difference between ethnic groups formerly engaged in conflict (overt or otherwise) might be counterproductive and could lead to renewed tensions between parties. In the context of theorizing the role of forgiveness and reconciliation for a just peace, Andrew Rigby highlights this danger when he writes: 'Whatever new memories and interpretations of the past are created in the process of forgiveness, they are formed on the basis of the old. Under certain circumstances these deeper memories can resurface, resurrecting the old resentment, bitterness and the desire to avenge the past crimes and injustices suffered at the hands of the historical enemy' (2005: 188). In short, in security sectors other than the environmental sector, unceasing political attention to the former security issue may not be beneficial to keeping the peace.

Finally, when desecuritization is defined exclusively in terms of its outcome, we cannot say anything meaningful about its ending. Seventy-plus years after the end of WWII in Europe, for instance, are we still living with desecuritization right now, or have we moved on? Given that desecuritization can lead to the situation where the former security issue is either politicized or depoliticized, at best we can know with certainty that desecuritization is not simply over when an issue has become depoliticized. Fortunately, however, any attempt to evaluate the morality of desecuritization in terms of outcomes risks misunderstanding the meaning of desecuritization. Thus desecuritization is not an outcome or a state of affairs, but rather it is a sum of actions,[5] which is to say a *process* (i.e. the unmaking of security policy and action) that has a *desecuritized state of affairs* as its outcome. In the latter, an existing security issue can be either politicized or depoliticized, and quite naturally, for different issues, one or the other may be better. As Figure 7.1 shows by means of either renewed securitization or politicization, a return to securitization is possible from both.

Thinking about desecuritization as a sum of actions also allows us to specify an end-point of desecuritization, as it is complete when security language and measures have been abandoned and – where appropriate – when restorative measures are complete. Using this definition, and instead of focusing on the outcome of desecuritization only, we can say with certainty, for example, that desecuritization after WWII in Europe is long over and a desecuritized state of affairs has long been the norm. To summarize, understood as a sum of actions,

---

[5]   I am grateful to Jonathan Floyd for helping me to see this clearly.

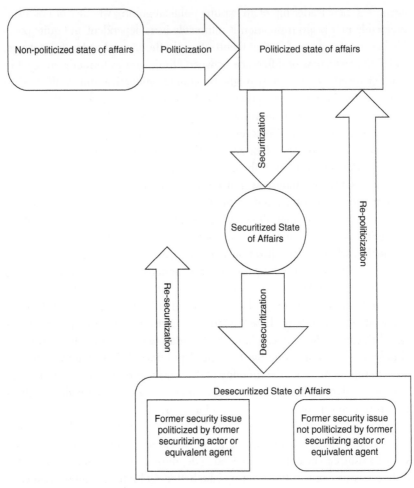

FIGURE 7.1 Progression and Difference Between Processes and Outcomes in Relation to Politicization, Securitization and Desecuritization[6]

desecuritization becomes a short-term event that can be identified, studied and morally evaluated.[7]

[6] Arrows depict processes and textboxes outcomes.

[7] Although just peace scholars write about just peace and thus seemingly an outcome (May, 2012: 10–14 in particular argues that peace is the object, hence the outcome of war), criteria specifying *jus post bellum* really concern the justice of the peace settlement (see specifically Hayden, 2005: 169, and Orend, 2006: 180, indeed the latter's idea of ethical exit strategy, is indicative of outcome, not process). This is to say, the concern is with just process (peace

7.3 DOES JUST DESECURITIZATION NEED TO FOLLOW FROM JUST SECURITIZATION?

If desecuritization is the unmaking of securitization, one issue that is relevant in my aim to prescribe criteria for just desecuritization is whether the nature of the prior securitization influences the nature of desecuritization. Or put differently, can just desecuritization follow from an unjust securitization? In the just war tradition the analogous question of whether a just peace can follow from an unjust war is contested. As mentioned already by Orend, a just peace is an 'ethical exit strategy' for contesters of just wars only (2002: 56). Following Orend, it could thus be argued that just desecuritization can only follow from just securitization. With reference to the Iraq war, however, Walzer has argued that a better (i.e. more just) political order can emerge even from an unjust war (Walzer, 2004). A political order following a war may be better on balance – insofar as it meets the rights and needs of people – than the order it replaced, even though such an order remains illegitimate. Orend is correct that a post-war peace is legitimate only when the new rulers came to govern as a result of a just war (see Simmons, 1999),[8] yet this does not mean that it is also more just.[9] In fact the opposite can be true and a new order following unjust securitization can be more just.

In addition, Bellamy gives us another reason why the justice of desecuritization should be judged separately from that of the justice of securitization. Hence he has pointed out that *not* separating 'just war' and 'just peace' produces 'counter-intuitive outcomes'. In the case of the Iraq war, for example, 'it would mean that for those who opposed the invasion of Iraq, the only just course of action would be immediate withdrawal of allied forces' (Bellamy, 2008: 622). When, in Walzer's terminology a 'just occupation', featuring rebuilding, investment and the training of police seems the better and more just alternative. This is not to suggest

---

settlement) as opposed to just outcome (peace). Nevertheless the expectation is, of course that just procedure will produce a just outcome. That is: a just peace settlement will produce a just and thus lasting peace (see Fabre, 2018: Kindle location 13774, for some poignant observations on different types of peace following from war).

[8] Following A. John Simmons, 'to show that an act or arrangement is justified (optimal or permissible) is to show that it is best or good enough on balance' (1999: 741, fn.5), while legitimacy is about lawful authority to rule. In Simmons' words: 'showing a state to be legitimate involves showing that it actually has … certain kinds of morally unobjectionable relations with those it controls; justifying the state only involves showing, against the anarchist, that it is possible for a state to have such relations and that having states at all is advantageous' (ibid.: 744, fn.15).

[9] May (2012: 15) goes further. He argues that 'even in an unjust war, the party who is aggrieved may still have done things during the war that it now has a duty to repair.'

that a just peace can retrospectively justify an unjust war, but only that actors who have done wrong in the past can make amends and do the right thing subsequently. For this same practical reason, I suggest that we should consider the justice of desecuritization separately from the justice of securitization. As we shall see, however, the justice or injustice of the preceding securitization is important when considering the nature of restorative measures in just desecuritization.

My argument thus far also raises the question of whether an unjust desecuritization renders an otherwise just securitization unjust? This is important, because in line with this, it could be objected that my account of just securitization is incomplete, and that a commitment to just desecuritization should form an additional criterion determining just securitization.[10] In answering this question it needs to be remembered, however, that the outcome of securitization is not a desecuritized state of affairs. Instead securitization is a process with a distinct outcome, namely a securitized state of affairs; and we cannot judge the justice of one process (securitization) in terms of either a) the justice of another process (desecuritization), or b) the justice of the outcome of that other process (i.e. a desecuritized state of affairs). In other words, securitization and desecuritization are intimately related, but ultimately separate processes with distinct outcomes. And the justice of either should be evaluated separately from the other.

7.4 WHO CAN DESECURITIZE?

For the purposes of JST desecuritization is best understood as a process, that is to say as the sum of actions that undo securitization, and not, for example, as an outcome (i.e. a state of affairs), or even – as some claim – the aim of 'security policy' (de Wilde, 2008: 597; cf. introduction to this volume). Indeed if the latter was true, fewer people would object to securitization on normative grounds. The meaning different scholars ascribe to desecuritization is important not only because we need to know what we are actually talking about when we are conducting research in this area, but also because it determines *who* the agents of desecuritization are or can be. Many elaborations on desecuritization have in common that they are informed by normative ideals.[11] The reasons for this can be traced back to the Copenhagen School. Although members of that school consider desecuritization a political choice made by actors, they also seek to inform securitizing actors of their own view that *ceteris paribus* desecuritization is a better solution to a security problem

---

[10]   I am grateful to Adam Quinn for bringing this to my attention.
[11]   Including elaborations on who can desecuritize, see for example, Aradau (2004).

than securitization (Wæver, 1999: 337; cf. Chapter 1, section 1.41). One reason why scholars endorse desecuritization is that it enables them to take responsibility for the securitizations they may have unleashed as part of their own text; often responsibility is 'based on experiences' with (de)securitization (Floyd, 2010: 27; see also Hansen, 2012: 534). Notably in Wæver's case, the relevant (research) experience here is détente, which he defines as 'negotiated desecuritisation; negotiated limitation of the use of the security speech act' (1997: 227). Importantly however, in détente and similar desecuritizations, which Hansen describes as 'change through stabilisation' (2012: 539), we must recognize that the actual desecuritizing actors are not scholars, but policymakers who are responsible for securitization.

In parallel to the idea that not only states but also non-state actors (including scholars) can mount securitizing moves and even successful securitizations, some securitization scholars have argued that desecuritization is not the prerogative of securitizing actors, but desecuritization as resistance is an option open to a wide range of actors. Juha Vuori, for example, has argued that desecuritization can be thought of as resistance which is to say, 'as a counter-strategy or-move to securitization' (2011a: 191). An 'act of desecuritization' as resistance, for him, sees the relevant actors proclaim that 'we no longer accept (X is an existential threat to Y)' (Vuori, 2011a: 191). To illustrate his point he provides the example of protesters in the floundering GDR, who through the slogan 'we are the people' no longer accepted that the West posed an existential threat to the people of East Germany, which in turn led the ruling SED party to accept defeat (ibid.: 207, fn.16). Nevertheless, Vuori also conceives of desecuritization as an 'active performative ... as terminating the institutional fact of a securitized issue' (ibid.: 191). And he stresses that although desecuritization moves can be articulated by anyone, 'the success of desecuritization may depend on actors with sufficient formal or other sociopolitical capital to perform or promote desecuritization' (Vuori, 2011b: 119). All this suggests that desecuritization is subject to similar power dynamics as is securitization. Accordingly, anyone can utter a 'desecuritizing move' – and say resist any given securitization – but only some actors will have sufficient sociopolitical capital to, as Vuori puts it: terminate 'institutional facts' (2011a: 191). In short, the ability to desecuritize, to undo step-by-step security language and security measures, remains the prerogative of sufficiently powerful actors. Following Vuori, we might say that scholars – at most – can perform desecuritizing moves (really desecuritizing requests, cf. Floyd, 2017), not desecuritization.

The actors that are most easily able to terminate securitization are the very same actors who have put security language and action in place i.e.

securitizing actors. However, desecuritization can also be instigated by for example consecutive administrations or governments, thus by the same type of actor, but ultimately different individuals. Indeed quite often incoming governments will deliberately undo whatever their predecessors did in order to leave their own political mark on the times. Depending on the level of institutionalization of securitization, however, even these actors will find desecuritization sometimes hard to achieve. For example, throughout his time in office, President Obama was unsuccessful in his efforts to shut down Guantanamo Bay prison camp. The closure of this facility is effectively blocked by Congress, which has passed legislation barring trial of inmates in federal prisons. Extradition of prisoners to third countries or release of those inmates who do not constitute a risk to their relevant home countries remains impossible because of the high risk that they will be tortured there. In short, unless Congress changes legislation, no one knows what to do with the inmates, and for the time being, the camp remains open (The Guardian, 2013). Although presumably rarer, we can also not rule that securitization can be unmade by third parties, for example, when independent mediators are invited to settle conflict.

7.5 WHO IS REQUIRED TO DESECURITIZE?

Above, I have argued that while desecuritizing requests are performable by everyone (provided that they have functional vocal cords, the ability to write and that they are not otherwise silenced (Hansen, 2000)); desecuritization is limited to those actors that can undo the institutional facts of securitization. I have also said desecuritization can be carried out not only by securitizing actors (of the securitization now to be undone), but also by the same type of actor yet different individuals (e.g. a rebel movement's new leadership or a state's new administration/government) and even by third parties. Yet on what grounds, if any, are putative desecuritizing actors that played no part in securitization required to desecuritize? Indeed, beyond the simple observation that they are the only actors that could meaningfully do this, for what reason are any of the possible desecuritizing actors required to desecuritize? In what follows I will try and offer an answer by drawing heavily on David Miller's concept of remedial responsibility and his connection theory (see Miller, 2007: 81–109). To do this it is first of all important to be clear about all possible desecuritizing actors and their role in the securitization now in need of undoing. At least five distinct combinations are possible:[12]

---

[12]   D and E could be further subdivided into whether or not the preceding securitization was just.

A. desecuritizing actor is the same as the securitizing actor of the preceding unjust securitization;
B. desecuritizing actor is the same as the securitizing actor of the preceding just securitization;
C. desecuritizing actor is the same the securitizing actor of the preceding unjust securitization, but the securitization is/was excusable;
D. desecuritizing actor is other than the securitizing actor, but the same type of actor within a given order as was the securitizing actor (for example, a new government or administration);
E. desecuritizing actor is a third party.

I shall proceed by arguing that in cases A, B and C, desecuritizing actors are outcome-responsible, which is to say responsible for their own actions and decisions, and within it, that both A and B are morally responsible, which is to say blame- or praiseworthy for their actions. I shall argue that all three are required to desecuritize as a matter of remedial responsibility. Following Miller, I argue that remedial responsibility can also be placed at the feet of actors not outcome responsibility, provided these actors have benefited from the securitization or have a unique capacity to undo it. In short, I show that D too is required to desecuritize as a matter of remedial responsibility. I shall argue that E is not required to desecuritize, but nevertheless permitted to do so.

It is not particularly contentious to argue that actors are outcome-responsible. In Miller's terms, outcome responsibility refers to 'whether a particular agent can be credited or debited with a particular outcome' (2007: 87). Moral responsibility is technically a form of outcome responsibility, but not everyone who is outcome responsible (i.e. causally responsible for an event) is also morally responsible and consequently blame- or praiseworthy. Notably, C is outcome-responsible for securitization, but because here actions were excusable,[13] not morally responsible. A and also B are both outcome- and morally responsible for securitization.

In addition to outcome responsibility, whereby agents are responsible for the consequences of their action (notably, we can establish outcome responsibly by asking who is responsible for bringing about a given state of affairs), a second type of responsibility exists. Miller explains: 'With remedial responsibility we begin with a state of affairs in need of remedy ... and we then ask whether there is anyone *whose responsibility* it is to put that state of affairs right'

---

[13] I have alluded to the possibility of securitizing actors being excused for acting wrongly on more than one occasion throughout this book, for example, when securitizing actors had the right intention but falsely believed the referent was just.

(Miller, 2007: 98; my emphasis). Miller goes on to show that remedial responsibly rests with those that are morally responsible, as this does not only 'create a mechanism for getting P out of that condition' but also it puts right 'the moral imbalance between [the morally responsible actor] and P' (ibid.: 100). For Miller, remedial responsibility also rests with those that are outcome- but not morally responsible because we should 'expect, in general, to bear the costs' for our actions (ibid.: 101). In other words, we can now see that A, B and C are obliged to desecuritize as a matter of remedial responsibility, whereby remedial responsibility is grounded in an actor's causal role in bringing about a state of affairs.

So far, we have established that desecuritizing actors that were also the architects of securitization they are now charged with undoing have not only the means to do so but they are required to do so as a matter of remedial responsibility. But what of those cases where the only plausible desecuritizing actor is *other* than the securitizing actor of the preceding securitization? For example, when the original securitizing actor is no longer around? Miller holds that remedial responsibility can apply in cases where there is a palatable injustice but no agent who is either morally or outcome-responsible to put the injustice right. Remedial clearly comes from the word remedy, thus in Miller's words: 'remedial responsibility potentially applies whenever we encounter a situation in need of remedy' (2007: 98). He argues that '[V] should be considered remedially responsible for P's condition when he is linked to P in one or more [way]' (ibid.: 99). The way in which this linkage exists is the essence of Miller's connection theory. In the context of D I shall argue that his ideas of connection by benefit and/or by unique capacity[14] are what matters (see ibid.: 102–104). I shall further argue that in the context of E, responsibility does not apply.

Miller's idea of 'benefit' in the context of remedial responsibly captures the idea that even if one actor [V] has 'played no causal role in the process that led to P's deprivation [s/he is nonetheless responsible if s/he has] benefited from that process – for instance, resources that would otherwise have gone to P have been allotted to [V]' (ibid.: 102). It is easy to see why D may have been a morally innocent (in the relevant sense) beneficiary of

---

[14] To be clear, Miller identifies with community a third connection, whereby actors are said to be remedially responsible because they are attached to P through community ties (family, nationhood and so on). I have excluded this here because I think in the examples for D below, community is subsumed by capacity. Especially if we think of 'the capacity to act' in terms of Pierre Bourdieu's 'social capital' rests on the standing of an actor in a community and his/her ability to culturally relate.

securitization. For example, in cases where D is a new government or administration, they may have been elected – in part – because the initial securitization (be it just or unjust) was, or became, deeply unpopular with the electorate.

Another reason why D may be considered remedially responsible is in cases where D might have the *unique capacity* to desecuritize. Clearly the next best (other than outcome-responsible) actors able to undo institutional facts of securitization are the official actors who have replaced the securitizing actor.

Turning now to E, the question is on what grounds are actors that are neither the securitizing actor, nor actors that have benefited from securitization in any way, remedially responsible for unmaking securitization? Miller argues that such actors are remedially responsible if they are most 'capable of supplying the remedy' (Miller, 2007: 103). However, I think that at this point the notion of remedial responsibility, at least when it comes to desecuritization, breaks down. To my mind, Miller's idea to stretch the notion of responsibility this far must be considered in the context of his wider theory of global justice. It appears that it is easier to motivate third parties to act on grave issues of global injustice if we can declare them *responsible* to act on it, as opposed to simply identifying a need and asking them to respond to that need.[15] When it comes to desecuritization capacity alone does simply not make for responsibility, indeed requiring this would have bizarre and counterproductive implications whereby powerful states would be required to meddle in the internal affairs of weaker states, when such interference can – rightly or wrongly – be perceived as a source of insecurity and thus give cause (justly or otherwise) for securitization. I therefore think that it is not only impossible but also unwise to *require* E to act on desecuritization. Importantly, however, this does not preclude third parties from doing the right thing (i.e. when the need arises, desecuritize in a just way), after all – except for cases where securitization is morally required – desecuritization is always morally permissible.

In summary, actors are required to desecuritize when they are remedially responsible. Remedial responsibility results from outcome or moral responsibility for securitization. Beyond that, actors who have benefitted from securitization and/or who have unique capacity to desecuritize are remedially responsible and on that basis obliged to desecuritize.

---

[15] In my opinion a comparable logic can also explain the rise of human rights over human needs. Thus unlike rights, needs do not imply duties, obliging anyone to act (see Floyd, 2011b).

7.6 TIMING

Let us now move onto the substantive criteria of just desecuritization, the first of which concerns the final point in time when securitization must be unmade. The principle I defend and develop in this section is as follows:

Criterion 9:[16] Desecuritization of just securitization must occur when the initial and related new objective existential threats have been neutralized, whereas desecuritization of unjust securitization must occur immediately.

It is a curious fact that most scholars interested in *jus post bellum* do not spend much time discussing when wars should be terminated, but instead write purely about the rights and obligations of victors and sometimes the vanquished (May, 2012) in peace settlements. David Rodin speculates that this oversight is a function of the fact that just war theory is concerned with necessity in so far as we either fight to victory or succumb in defeat (Rodin, 2008b: 54). Contra this, Rodin (2008b) but also Moellendorf (2008), argue that considerations of *jus post bellum* must include (indeed be preceded) by considerations of *jus terminatio* (or else *jus ex bello* for Moellendorf, 2008, 2015) and consider not merely how wars should end, but *when* wars should be terminated. Much simplified these writers quibble with the idea that *terminatio* law 'is simply the symmetrical inverse of the initiation of war and therefore that we can be governed by precisely the same *ad bellum* conditions that governs war's initiation' (Rodin, 2008b: 55 emphasis in original). Instead they propose 'that moral judgements regarding the ... termination of war must be sensitive to the ever-changing landscape of war' (Moellendorf, 2008: 130). In line with this, scholars theorizing *jus terminatio* advocate the continuous application of the principles of the just war throughout the war effort (Fabre, 2015; McMahan, 2015). Doing this reveals the possibility that even just wars may have to be terminated before just cause is satisfied, for instance when the chances of success become diminished because a new military invention strengthens the opposing side so much that the war cannot succeed (Fabre, 2015: 634). I do not find this particularly contentious, after all here the just continuation of war is obviously judged against the same criteria that were used to determine the initial justice of the war. It seems logical that wars that were justified to begin with may no longer be justified once the war is in progress, and clearly the same holds true for securitization.[17]

---

[16] Although just desecuritization can occur irrespective of the justifiability of the preceding securitization, and my three criteria for just desecuritization could have been labelled 1–3, I have decided to use numbers 9–11 for them in this book. I made this choice to avoid confusion when different criteria are discussed in different chapters of the book.

[17] Moellendorf (2018) summarizes his argument for the independence of *jus ex bello* from *jus ad bellum* in the following terms: '1. Whether resorting to war is justified depends on conditions

In my view far more challenging is that continuous application of the criteria of the just war also allows for the possibility that a war that was initially judged unjust because it lacked a just cause can gain a just cause in the process of war.[18] Moellendorf and Rodin both propose that there are circumstances when a war that was initially considered unjust for *ad bellum* reasons would be unjust to terminate because so doing would be more harmful. Moellendorf gives the following example: 'If grave humanitarian danger provides just cause for intervention, then surely it justifies continuing a war, even if the war originally did not satisfy the principle of just cause. In general the strongest case for such an argument would be a new and highly plausible prediction of genocide' (2008: 128). Similarly Rodin argues that as 'war aims evolve … opportunities [are created] to expand the moral permission to continue fighting, sometimes far beyond what could have be countenanced by application of *ad bellum* principles at the conflict's start' (Rodin, 2008b: 56 emphasis in original).

While I agree that prematurely terminating a war that was initiated for unjust reasons may run the risk of greater overall harm than continuing with it would, I also think that this way of thinking is potentially dangerous because it could undermine the entire purpose of the JWT, which is to prevent unjust wars in the first place. Thus, if practitioners realize that it can become permissible to continue initially unjust wars because of the changing nature of any given war over time, then what incentive is there to adhere to the rules of the JWT is the first place?[19] Moellendorf holds against this that 'professional soldiers are not eager to pursue protracted wars, based on changed mandates, especially when such wars are costly to the lives of their troops and the reputation of their armies' (2015: 660). Securitization, however, is different to war. Security professionals generally do well out of securitization and many

---

each individually necessary and jointly sufficient. 2. Each of the aforementioned conditions also applies to the justification of continuing a war. 3. After war begins, either the states of affairs relevant to the satisfaction of one or the aforementioned conditions, or reasonable beliefs about the states of affairs, may change, such that the truth value of one or more of the individually necessary and jointly sufficient conditions changes. 4. Therefore, the morality of continuing a war is distinct from the morality of resorting to war' (Location 13306 of 16735).

[18] It should be noted here that securitization's justness can also change over time because criteria other than those comprising just cause are suddenly met. To my mind, however, only the possibility of gaining a just cause in securitization previously lacking a just cause is challenging for the continuation of securitization. This is because of the priority status of just cause, whereby the other principles cannot be satisfied unless just cause is met (McMahan, 2005). Consequently we may say that a securitization that was unjust because at its outset it lacked, for example, a reasonable chance of success but as securitization progresses it defied that initial judgement was simply judged wrongly at its outset (see also Moellendorf, 2018: 13316 of 16735).

[19] Note that neither writer holds that a new just cause would make initial resort to war justified.

would welcome a changed mandate, after all a new threat justifies budgets and ensures their own continuous existence.

I also think that the *jus terminatio* runs the risks of ignoring the fact that a new just reason could largely be the product of an unjust securitization. For example, it is possible that an initial securitization of jihadi terrorism that lacked a just reason (i.e. absence of objective existential threat) by a state actor (that is itself a just referent object because it satisfied a moral minimum of basic human needs) leads to radicalization among Muslims and hence the rise of jihadi terrorism and therewith an actual just reason (see Fabre, 2015: 643 for a similar example). This example – let's call it *Jihadi Terror* – alludes to the possibility that unjust securitization could be used and abused to eventually generate a just reason and hence permit securitization, or at least securitization that we consider ethically problematic because of its emergence but nevertheless morally preferable to desecuritization (Rodin, 2015). It seems to me further that the possibility that just reason could be the product[20] of unjust securitization is the very reason why the continuation of securitization is not straightforward, but needs unpicking. Consider thus that in cases where the new just reason emerges irrespective of unjust securitization, the continuation of securitization seems justified. Consider, for example, *Migration Economy Collapse*:

Migration Economy Collapse

State A (which is itself a just referent object) unjustly securitizes migration, even though numbers are low and well below existential threat level, but while doing this is suddenly and independently faced with unprecedented and existentially threatening numbers of migrants from state B, all due to the sudden collapse of B's economy and resultant civil war.

Here, the continuation of securitization is justified precisely because the initial securitization had no role in producing a threat, while continuing with securitization now simply serves to protect a threatened good. In short, here the continuation of securitization is equal to a new securitization. I also think that in cases where securitizing actors falsely believed that they had a just cause and acted on the basis of right intention, securitization even of self-made

---

[20] It should be noted here that while unjust securitizing actors can produce just causes, produc-tion of security threats, especially for agent-intended threats is not entirely self-made. For example, in my view there can be little doubt that NATO's eastwards expansionism since the end of the Cold War has largely produced the current situation of insecurity with Russia (Mearsheimer, 2014). However, without Putin being the way he is (i.e. set on expansionism, 'stuck in the past', determined to rule) coupled with Russia's poor economic situation, NATO's actions alone are perhaps unlikely to have created that situation. In short, the security threat from Russia is not entirely a product of NATO's actions.

just reasons is justified, because here the actors' initial unjust securitization was excusable (cf. Chapter 5, section 5.2).[21] The pressing question is thus this: ought a securitization whose just reason is effectively *produced* by an initial unjust securitization that lacked both a just reason and right intention to continue? To help us answer this question, consider *Migration Panic*:

Migration Panic

Driven purely by political gain, the executive of just state A securitizes migration from adjacent state B, from which numbers are low and well below existential threat level. In doing this, however, they unintentionally create a panic among the population of traditional emigrant (to A) states C and D. The extent of the panic is such that it leaves populations in these states so worried that they too will become the target of such securitization by A that they begin to emigrate in such large numbers to A, that immigration from C and D constitutes an objective existential threat to A.

It seems to me that the main reason why *Migration Panic* is different to *Migration Economy Collapse* is that here the securitizing actor is morally *responsible* for creating the just reason for securitization. And if they are morally responsible, do they not simply deserve to be threatened? Ultimately I think that this issue requires a lengthier treatment than I am able to offer here,[22] for the time being I would like to suggest – albeit tentatively – that the just cause trumps, in a sense that whether or not just cause is a product of prior unjust securitization does not negatively impact on the permissibility of continuing with (now just) securitization. This is so for two reasons. First, there are limitations on the kinds of harms that are justifiable in the correction of a wrong. With reference to *Jihadi Terror*, for example, we can say that unjust securitization of terrorism does not render jihadi terrorism a necessary or proportionate response, ergo (now) just securitization of jihadi terrorism on behalf of a just referent object can continue.[23] The scenario described in *Migration Panic*, however, is different, because here we are not dealing with threats intended to harm state A, but rather migration as agent-caused threat. It seems to me, however, and this is my second point in support of continuation of securitization, that crucial here is that the people likely to be harmed by the threat are not only the state-level actors responsible for the initial unjust

---

[21] Again, provided the referent object is just.

[22] Crucial in this are considerations whether the past is relevant to our present evaluations (see for example, McMahan, 2015).

[23] It might be helpful to think of the initial securitization of terrorism in the example of *Jihadi Terror* as unjustified at time T_1, but as justified at T_2 (cf. Fabre, 2015), given that securitization was unjustified at T_1, however, securitizing actors remain blameworthy.

securitization, but the people living in state A, and these people are not deserving of the harm they are likely to encounter because they are innocent bystanders. It is also possible that the security threat might have been produced by a previous government, and not the people that govern now. In summary, we can say that it does not follow from the fact that an agent is culpable for the existence of a threat that an agent is wrong to use force against an unjustified threat.

With these considerations in mind we can now say that the final point in time when just securitization *must* be terminated is when the initial or a *related* new objective existential threat to a just referent object has been neutralized. It also follows that unjust securitization is to be terminated immediately in cases lacking a just reason and/or just referent object of security. Whereas, for example, in cases where securitization is unjust because of the nature of the security measures employed, the latter must at once be transformed, or else securitization must be abandoned and desecuritization must commence.

Although specifying last point in time is important for just termination of securitization, it must be remembered that desecuritization *can* occur prior to the neutralization of the objective existential threat *without* the resulting desecuritization being unjust. This is because under JST, not even the existence of objective existential threats *requires* recourse to securitization; it merely permits it.[24] If securitizing actors find a way to address any given objective existential threat without continuing with securitization then that desecuritization might still be just. Colin McInnes and Simon Rushton, for example, argue that the UN is gradually desecuritizing HIV/AIDS because 'securitization is not the only way of getting attention [the realization is rather that] "developmentization" may work too' (2013: 130).

It is important to remind ourselves that objective existential threats are threats to the essential character of actors, orders and other entities regardless of whether they are being responded to accordingly (including whether they are intersubjectively recognized as such). In order to get an analytical grip on different threats, in Chapter 3 I have distinguished between agent-intended, agent-lacking and agent-caused (but not intended) threats. In the context of just and unjust desecuritization we have to think about the point when threats residing in these three analytical categories have been neutralized, and also about how we can know that this is so. Things are easiest perhaps for agent-

---

[24]   There will be cases when securitization is morally obliged, however, because the criterion of last resort is demanding (cf. Chapter 5, section 5.5.2), more often than not – among permissible securitizations – securitization will simply be that (i.e. permissible), but not required.

intended threats. Thus such threats are no longer real when a (former) 'aggressor' no longer intends to do harm. To observe the change in intentions it will be necessary to examine whether an aggressor's language has changed and, because language alone is not conclusive of intent and can be changed for the purposes of deception, we need to examine also if his or her behaviour has changed. A good example is that of the Revolutionary Armed Forces in Colombia (FARC), which during the lengthy peace process with the Colombian government not only abandoned threatening language, but also gradually changed their behaviour. Notably, just before signing the peace deal in 2016, FARC signed a ceasefire and officially changed from being a terrorist organization to a political movement. FARC has also abandoned its long-standing 'revolutionary tax' imposed on local businesses in FARC-controlled areas and used to sustain the group (Weston Pippen, 2016). Moreover as part of the peace agreement FARC is also abandoning its jungle camps and is disarming (Vyos and Forero, 2016).

Agent-intended threats are also no longer real when an aggressor no longer has the capabilities to follow through with a threat. It was argued in Chapter 3 that one of the biggest assets of Al-Qaeda and IS is the ability of such organizations to recruit manpower. When terrorist organizations fail to attract people to their cause, they simply won't have enough or any henchmen to carry out suicide bombings, in which case they would no longer constitute existential threats to states or even people within states.

As far as I can see, agent-lacking objective existential threats occur mostly in the environmental sector of security and refer to natural disasters including floods, earthquakes and tsunamis. There are potentially two points in time when such threats can be said to be no longer threatening: A) immediately after their occurrence, or B) when a minimum floor of human needs satisfaction among those affected by the natural disaster is achieved. Given that the aftermath of natural disasters often kills and/or adversely affects more people (for example, through the prevalence of disease and lawlessness)[25] than the initial disaster, neutralization must be defined in accordance with option B.

In the event of agent-caused threats, some cases will be straightforward and in order to establish whether a threat has been neutralized, scholars and practitioners will simply need to collect evidence that the threatening beha-viour, which was unintentionally, but not necessarily ignorantly and as such innocently caused, has been terminated. For example, assuming, and purely

---

[25] For example, since the devastating 2010 earthquake in Haiti, which left several tens of thousands of people dead and many more homeless, a cholera epidemic ensued. As of May 2013 there were 657,117 cases and 8,096 deaths (CDC, 2013).

for the sake of argument, that irregular migrants constitute a real threat to the EU but that this threat was in part caused by Germany's open-door policy (see Chapter 3, section 3.6.1), threat neutralization would amount to a statistically significant reduction in the number of irregular migrants heading for the EU, perhaps because of a reversal of Germany's open-door policy. But far from all agent-caused threats are straightforward, and for many there will be no comparable points at which such threats can be said to have been neutralized. Indeed neutralization is likely to be a gradual process. A securitization of climate change via a hypothetical exceptional climate regime of the kind discussed in Chapter 6 section 6.3, for example, should not be disbanded at the first sign of success, but should continue until behaviours have changed and signatory states have developed less carbon-intense and more sustainable lifestyles.[26]

7.7 ACTION

I have said so far that desecuritization is to be understood as the unmaking of securitization. To understand what this means, however, we need to remind ourselves that in this book, securitization was defined as a combination of security language and most importantly security action, specifically security measures. If this is so then desecuritization must consist of both the reverse of security language and security measures. In this section I propose the following principles for just desecuritization:

Criterion 10: Desecuritization should ideally be publically declared, and corresponding security language and security measures should be terminated with immediate effect.

Security language, as all specific political terms, can be reversed by simply dropping the use of the terminology in question. This happens quite often in political life. I have mentioned earlier, for example, that the US government has now dropped the term 'war on terror', while for example, former UK PM David Cameron's use of the term 'big society', which was supposed to designate community and voluntary projects over state funding in austere times (for example, to keep public libraries open and running), disappeared without a trace just a few years after its invention. Where just desecuritization is concerned, however, I propose that rather than simply dropping securitizing language, desecuritization would be cemented if it begins with a public announcement. The requirement of public proclamation of peace can be found in the *jus post bellum* (Hayden, 2005:

---

[26] Note I am not suggesting that climate change requires securitization, only that once a just securitization of climate change is initiated that it makes little sense to abandon it too hastily.

169; Orend, 2007: 580). While I have found the reasons for this requirement are often not made explicit,[27] we can extrapolate (from research conducted by mainstream constructivists) that public proclamation of peace is closely bound up with the idea of generating a lasting peace. Constructivist researchers have found evidence that a hypocritical[28] public commitment to certain internationally accepted standards of behaviour (norms) can be turned to a force for good in world politics, that is to say, into real commitment to the cause. This may happen in the following way:

> If – and only if – a public sphere exists which can make compelling demands upon states to redeem their rhetoric, normatively orientated critics can work to force great powers to live up to their strategically chosen rhetoric. Holding the powerful to their public commitments opens up possibilities for the weak to exercise power over the strong by shaming them with their own words. (Lynch, 2008: 175; see also Schimmelfennig, 2005: 157)

In other words, the idea is that in democracies at least, the general public can hold desecuritizing actors to their commitment to desecuritization even if the desecuritizing actor is insincere. It is for example not inconceivable that a government's secret security services continues to access ordinary, innocent individuals' phones, emails and Facebook accounts as a matter of habit and technological capability, even after the security threat that gave rise to these measures has been neutralized.

While few securitization scholars would object to the desirability of holding desecuritizing actors accountable, many would question the possibility of a desecuritizing speech act (Hansen, 2012: 530). Some scholars (e.g. Behnke, 2006: 65) would hold against this that desecuritization by public announcement is logically impossible as declaring something no longer a threat 'would be invoking the language and logic of security' (Hansen, 2012: 530). Arguably, however, this objection bites only for those variants of securitization theory that believe in the securitizing force of language; it has no bearing on my framework of securitization where security speech by securitizing actors amounts to no more than a warning and/or a promise, but never to successful securitization (see Chapter 2, section 2.2.2; Floyd, 2010: 53–54).

Indeed beyond the unmaking of security language, much more important – given my definition of securitization – is the termination of security measures. A precedent for this suggestion can again be found in the *jus post bellum*. Rigby (2005: 181) argues, for example, that just peace involves 'disarming, demobilisation and re-integration of combatants'. Orend (2006: 181)

---

[27] Orend suggests that: 'People who have suffered through a war do indeed deserve to know what the substance of the settlement is' (2006: 179).

[28] Lynch defines hypocritical as an: 'intentionally deceptive moral stance' (2008: 170).

recommends 'demilitarization and disarmament'. In line with this, I hold that just desecuritization requires the immediate, and ideally complete termination of all measures taken in response to a threat, which – it is vital to remember – actors are permitted to take only in the presence of a just cause. This point is important, because as Andrew Neal has convincingly shown, when the first emergency, that legitimized security measures, fades, desecuritization is not guaranteed, but rather 'emergencies become normalized' and are legislated for (Neal, 2012a: 260).

Yet how feasible is it to require the unmaking of security measures, and thus to insist, for instance, on the removal of military/policing hardware, the tearing down of fences/walls and or the reversal of laws? Historic examples show that if desecuritization is wanted, all of these can be achieved. For example, after the end of the Cold War, NATO and Russia signed the Partnership for Peace deal in 1994, which included cooperation in military matters, a general thawing of hostilities, and also the removal of military hardware from key strategic positions.[29] Similarly the allied victors of the Second World War (France, the United States, the United Kingdom and Russia) who divided defeated Germany into four parts, have now largely withdrawn from the country and whatever of their military capability remains there today, is there in a capacity as friend and ally. Sticking with Germany, after the fall of communism, the Berlin Wall was literally torn down, showing that if the political will is there, even physical barriers can be removed.

The reversal of law supporting securitization is properly the hardest to achieve, because although a specific threat might have been neutralized, a type of threat can continue to exist, rendering specific legislation necessary in perpetuity. For example, while the spectre of Islamic fundamentalist terrorism might eventually disappear from Western Europe, the possibility of terrorism motivated by different reasons is always there; this much was shown by the case of Anders Behring Breivik in Norway or by the National Socialist Underground terror group in Germany. Arguably thus the kinds of terrorism legislation that have been passed in many different states since 9/11 are a necessity, and many practices such as the limitation of liquids on board aeroplanes are here to stay. This said, it is also the case that in Britain at least most new police powers awarded under the Terrorism Act and thus written into law are temporary measures that – as part of desecuritization – could simply not be renewed. Historical evidence supports that laws can be unmade; homosexuality, for example,

---

[29] Since Russia's military intervention in Ukraine, NATO has suspended all cooperation with Russia, and the issue has become re-securitized (Sperling and Webber, 2017).

was once widely punishable with imprisonment but is now decriminalized in a majority of countries.

7.8 LONG-TERM AIM

A security threat is desecuritized when corresponding security language and security measures have been terminated in the way described above. A desecuritized state of affairs is, however, likely to be short-lived unless diverse actors and groups *are* and *feel* sufficiently secure, which is to say, secure to the extent that they have no cause to deteriorate into securitization. Concretely this means that desecuritization itself needs to be conducted in such a way that it does not give rise to old or new grievances. Grievances could (wrongly or rightly) be interpreted as objective existential threats, and as such be the (just) reason for either the renewed securitization of the same issue, including by different actors, or for securitization that comes as a response to unjust desecuritization (I call this reactionary securitization). In this section I want to advance the idea that the chances of achieving sufficient security as a state of being are maximized when the process of just desecuritization includes context specific restorative measures. By restorative measures I principally mean measures that aim to *restore* relationships that were adversely affected by securitization, including between former foes,[30] but also between securitizing actors and innocent bystanders. The thought that restorative measures reduce the likelihood of renewed and/or reactionary securitization is influenced by the *jus post bellum* which specifies the need for rehabilitation, forgiveness and reconciliation (cf. Rigby, 2005; Hayden, 2005; Orend, 2006) if a lasting peace is wanted.[31] The criterion I wish to advance and defend in this subsection is as follows:

Criterion 11: In order to avoid renewed and/or reactionary securitization, desecuritizing actors should undertake context-specific restorative measures.

Importantly, I hold that the need for restorative measures is relevant not only for the termination of unjust securitization, but also for the termination of just securitization because not all adversely affected groups will recognize just securitization as just, plus just securitization harms people, including innocent bystanders, too.

---

[30] Lu (2018) speaks of alienation in the context of *post bellum* justice.
[31] Assume here that only a just peace would last.

In the following I want to sketch out some considerations concerning possible restorative measures across the three threat categories: agent-intended, agent-caused and agent-lacking threats; a full treatment of the issue is, however, beyond the scope of this chapter.

As far as desecuritization of formerly securitized agent-intended objective existential threats is concerned, it is important to remember that – where the desecuritizing actor is the same as the securitizing actor – we are dealing with two groups of people that were until very recently engaged in (sometimes overt violent) conflict. Both sides are likely to have sustained casualties and/or have been subjected to harm, and some members of either group are likely to want revenge, not peace. In short, the likelihood of renewed securitization is high. This raises the question, how can the probability that parties will seek revenge be reduced, thus reducing the possibility of renewed securitization? Peace research and conflict resolution studies suggest that the chances of renewed conflict are minimized by reintegrating formerly conflicting parties into society. The buzzword used by many scholars, as well as by the Organization for Security and Co-operation in Europe (OSCE), who are very active in this area, is reconciliation. In the OSCE publication *Security Community*, Middle East scholar Daniel Serwer highlights the importance of reconciliation.

> [A]t the societal level lack of reconciliation has consequences. It is a formula for more violence. If we remain trapped in it, we end up in a cycle of violence. Victims, feeling loss and the desire for revenge, end up committing aggression against those they believe to be perpetrators, who eventually react with violence. (Serwer, 2013: 26)

Reconciliation takes many forms. The OSCE's reconciliation work in Srebrenica, Bosnia and Herzegovina, for example, focuses on strengthening 'the country's "civic architecture", working in the courtroom, the classroom and the committee room.' For instance, in the classroom category, 'almost thirty history textbooks have been revised to remove instances of hate speech and an exclusive ethnic narrative, and almost 100 history teachers have been trained' (Burton, 2013: 30).

When contemplating restorative measures, including those that are part of reconciliation, it is important to uphold the distinction between desecuritization as a process and its outcome: the desecuritized state of affairs. Accordingly I do not want to go as far as to suggest that a culture of forgiveness should be established, as this would be tantamount to the issue being politicized once desecuritization is complete. To recap, after desecuritization and in the desecuritized state of affairs an issue may be politicized or depoliticized, whichever is better in terms of achieving security, as a state of affairs is issue-dependent and outside of theorization. Restorative measures should thus not blur the line between process and outcome of desecuritization; instead they are considered short-term measures that aim to reduce the chances of renewed and reactionary securitization.

What precisely reconciliation involves is context-dependent, yet as one observer puts it, reconciliation can only be assisted, not imposed (Burton, 2013: 31). Among possible reconciliation measures are truth commissions that seek to establish the 'aggressor's' wrongdoing, giving space to agents at the source of an unjust threat to repent and to apologize. Peace research has shown that official apologies to those harmed also help (Andrieu, 2009). The peace process in Colombia serves once again as a good example, with the FARC commanders expected to admit to 'their role in atrocities and face punishment, which could include restrictions on their movements, reparations to victims' families and supplying those families with details about what happened to loved ones' (Vyos and Forero, 2016).

It is however not only 'aggressors' that have to make up for unjust deeds. In cases where securitization was unjust, truth commissions could act as fora for unjust securitizing actors to issue official apologies, while they could also serve to establish the wrongdoing of executors of securitization. A further restorative measure could be punitive measures in the form of the public prosecution of unjust executors of securitization; and potentially even prosecution of police chiefs etc. who followed the rules of just conduct in securitization, but who acted in securitization that was unjustly initiated (cf. Chapter 6, section 6.6).

Reactionary securitization is different to renewed securitization insofar as it comes in response to unfair terms and conditions of desecuritization. The chances of this occurring are increased if innocent bystanders harmed by securitization are not adequately recognized. Besides public apologies, compensation payments are a useful measure to reduce the chances of reactionary securitization. Indeed this measure already exists. Notably, the family of Jean Charles de Menezes was paid an undisclosed sum by the London Metropolitan Police in compensation (The Guardian, 2009). Likewise Bisher al-Rawi, Jamil el Banna, Richard Belmar, Omar Deghayes, Binyam Mohamed and Martin Mubanga, all of whom were allegedly tortured by British forces and wrongfully incarcerated at Guantanamo Bay prison camp, were paid undisclosed sums in compensation by the UK government (BBC

News, 2010).[32] Notably, my argument here is not that these individuals will mount reactionary securitization to unjust desecuritization, but rather that their treatment – including as part of desecuritization – can feed nascent or existing grievances inspiring groups to launch reactionary securitization, for example, by joining the cause of a terrorist movement.

Moving on to agent-caused but unintended threats, I suggest we start by asking which relationships here need restoring that have been adversely affected by securitization? At least three possibilities exist. First – using the example of the securitization of migration – the relationship between the subject of securitization (e.g. migrants) and the referent object (e.g. a nation-state and the people within it). In this scenario it matters whether or not securitization was just or unjust. Thus while unjust securitization would require disclosure why it was considered necessary, and public apologies by or on behalf of the securitizing actor, apologies are not considered necessary for just securitization because no wrong was committed. However, here in order to prevent renewed securitization of the same issue by other groups (for example, right-wing groups as opposed to states), desecuritization should aim towards reconciliation of subject and object of securitization. One possible step here is, I think, Claudia Aradau's (2004) suggestion of 'dis-identification' of migrants as primarily that and to consciously view, and in public dialogue represent them as workers, carers, mothers etc. instead. This would also help to avoid potential reactionary securitization. Note that I have said that reactionary securitization ought to be understood as a backlash against unjust desecuritization. Desecuritization is unjust when an issue is not fully desecuritized in a sense of criterion 10. We can thus see that reactionary securitization is also a form of counter-securitization. Returning to the example, it seems to me that unless the securitization of migration is done justly, which includes *fully*, migrants and those who seek to protect them will continue to feel threatened in society and may find it necessary to secure themselves.

Second is the relationship between those who have caused the threat by harmful neglect and the referent object of securitization. Here perhaps the most vital part of restorative measures is public apologies for causing the threat and also perhaps an independent investigation on how the threat was caused. The aim of this would be to ensure that such mistakes are not repeated, thus reducing the chances of a need for renewed securitization.

---

[32]   FIO requests by the author concerning the sums of money in both cases where turned down by the Met and No 10 Downing Street. In the latter case it was made explicit that the pay-out was not tantamount to an admission of guilt on the part of the government. Notably, such pay-outs must be understood in terms of remedial responsibility by ties of community, not by moral or outcome responsibility (see Miller, 2007: 104).

Finally and third is the relationship – where applicable – between the securitizing actor and innocent bystanders harmed by securitization. Such harm may be sustained also in just securitization. Imagine for example that at the global level climate change was securitized in the way suggested in Chapter 6 (section 6.3) and an exceptional carbon emissions reduction regime was negotiated and subsequently enforced by a new dedicated compliance body with fall-back to the UN Security Council in case of non-compliance. In order to comply with such a regime, states would enforce harsh new emergency legislation, which might prohibit certain types of carbon-intensive industry altogether adversely affecting hundreds, perhaps thousands of people whose livelihoods are tied up with that industry. Ultimately the state in question would expect that these people will find work in new green collar jobs and invest heavily into retraining. Regardless of the justice of securitization in this specific case, my point is that in addition to ensuring, as part of desecuritization, the state would have to compensate people for the loss of their livelihood. This example is by no means outlandish; already the drive for allegedly 'green' shale gas, and potential conflicts with landowners, is an issue in both the United States and the United Kingdom. And it is only a matter of time before owners will be removed from their property to facilitate drilling and (presumably) be compensated for the loss of land.[33]

Restorative measures in desecuritization of agent-lacking threats take a different form. They are – at least in part – often quite literally about restoration in a sense of re-building. I have argued above that the threat from natural disasters continues after the event and that it can be said to have been neutralized only when a minimum floor of human needs satisfaction is met. The aim of restorative measures here must then be to reduce the chances of renewed disaster, and as such the need for renewed securitization in the future. Besides rebuilding, one such measure would be educating people about natural disasters (why did it happen and what precautions should vulnerable people take in the event of it happening again). In the aftermath of the 2004 tsunami in Indonesia, for example, there has been a focus on concerted education on tsunami risk management and understanding early

---

[33] Fracking is already a hugely controversial issue in Europe. While banned in Germany and France, it constitutes an important part of energy security in the UK. Resistance among residents is high and compensation plays a big part in meeting residents' resistance. Writing in *The Independent* in January 2014, Nigel Morris observes that: 'At the moment communities are offered £100,000 for each well at which exploratory drilling takes places, plus 1 per cent of the eventual profits from that well. Under this formula, communities could receive between £5m and £10m over a 25-year period.'

warning system for locals (GIZ, 2013). Another measure would be facilitating the relocation of people away from disaster areas.

To summarize, I have argued in this section that just desecuritization needs to include a number of positive, constructive steps beyond simply undoing securitization. Such positive steps are context-specific, but – for agent-intended and agent-caused threats – they primarily need to aim at restoring relations that are either broken or that have been adversely affected by securitization. Two such relationships matter in particular. The first is that between the agent at the source of the threat and the securitizing actor/referent object of securitization, the second is between innocent bystanders harmed by securitization and the securitizing actor or the referent object.

7.9 CONCLUSION

This chapter was about just termination of securitization, or in other words, just desecuritization. I have argued that unlike securitization, desecuritization is morally obligatory because securitization is time limited by the just reason. However not every actor is in the position to – in Vouri's terms – undo the institutional facts of securitization. I have suggested that we can differentiate between the following types of desecuritizing actor:

A. desecuritizing actor is the same as the securitizing actor of the preceding unjust securitization;
B. desecuritizing actor is the same as the securitizing actor of the preceding just securitization;
C. desecuritizing actor is the same the securitizing actor of the preceding unjust securitization, but securitization is/was excusable;
D. desecuritizing actor is other than the securitizing actor, but the same type of actor within a given order as was the securitizing actor (for example, a new government or administration).

I have argued that all four of these are – albeit for different reasons – remedially responsible for undoing securitization, and as such have a duty to desecuritize. While I have explained in this chapter when and how desecuritization should ideally proceed, one question that remains is this: in comparable situations, do all types of desecuritizing actor have to do the same amount towards putting in place restorative measures? To be clear, I assume that in any given desecuritization of a single-actor securitization[34] it is unlikely that more

---

[34] By single-actor I mean a state, or a non-state movement as opposed to a collective of states (i.e. the EU or NATO).

than one type of desecuritizing actor is present, because D emerges only when A, B or C is no longer present, while only one of A, B, or C is present in any given desecuritization. This means that I am not looking to ascertain who needs to do more in one and the same desecuritization, instead I am interested in the question whether desecuritizing actors that have done no wrong, or comparatively less wrong, regarding a preceding securitization have – in comparable situations – to do less towards justly undoing securitization than those morally responsible for a preceding unjust securitization?[35]

On the face of it, it seems plausible to argue that those desecuritizing actors that are morally responsible for an unjust securitization (i.e. A) should do more than either C or D.[36] Although it is not a perfect comparison, a possible ranking can be deduced from the burgeoning literature on climate ethics, where many people argue for the polluter pays principle,[37] which holds that those who have caused the problem of climate change should foot the bill. There are limitations that compromise the utility of this principle, notably the fact that most of the carbon was emitted before anyone knew carbon emissions could alter the climate. This is but one of the reasons why some scholars have suggested polluters are not morally culpable, advocating instead that the beneficiary should pay (see Neumayer, cited in Caney, 2010b). While – for the purposes of just desecuritization – this has no effect on A, who we know to be morally culpable, this logic is relevant for D, in so far as it suggests that desecuritizing actors that benefited from a preceding securitization (i.e. D) – specifically perhaps in cases were securitization was unjust – ought to do more than those desecuritizing actors who can be excused for unjust securitization (C), provided perhaps that their actions are fully and not only minimally excusable.[38] Consequently the following sliding scale, from highest to lowest (in terms of the amount of restorative measures they'd have to put in place) emerges: A, D and C.[39] I am not clear where B would fit into this scale, but this

---

[35] I assume, for the purposes of argument that all actors have the same ability to undo securitization.

[36] I bracket B here, because seeing that here securitization was just, desecuritization is likely to require less in the way of restorative measures.

[37] I would like to thank Jonathan Herington for this suggestion.

[38] In this book I have only touched on the topic of when securitizing actors may be excused for unjust securitization; needless to say, much more can and needs to be said on when this is the case, including on whether securitizing actors can be fully or partially excused for unjust securitization.

[39] This scale is potentially relevant for desecuritization by collectives (see Sperling and Webber, 2017 for a theory of collective securitization). I have argued elsewhere that within collectives (i.e. the EU or NATO), individual actors (i.e. individual member states) culpable of threat-creation to collectives ought to pay more towards the financial costs of collective securitization (cf. Floyd, 2019a) than actors who did not create the threat later securitized by the collective.

might not matter, because although what I have suggested is intuitively compelling, I am not sure this argument stands to reason, and with some trepidation I suggest that – in comparable situations – the amount all types desecuritizing actors have to do towards restoring relations is the same for all possible types of actor.[40] To understand my logic it is important to remember that the purpose of just desecuritization in general and restorative measures in particular is to avoid renewed or reactionary securitization. In other words, just desecuritizing actors are obliged to do *whatever it takes* to maximize the chances of achieving security as a state of being. For D this might mean that they – comparatively speaking – have to do a lot or not much at all, but it cannot give way to the principle that they – *ceteris paribus* – automatically have to do less than C or A in a comparable situation, especially not if the preceding securitization was unjust. In other words the blameworthiness of desecuritizing actors for securitization does not necessarily translate into a need to do more when it comes to restorative measures than those applicable to desecuritizing actors not involved in a preceding securitization.

This said, there are pragmatic limits to what D can meaningfully do; for example, in what sense D can apologize for another actor's actions. Those wronged or harmed by securitization would – quite rightly – be entitled to apologies from A and C. We can also expect that those desecuritizing actors blameworthy for preceding unjust securitization ought to bear more costly (to themselves) restorative measures, as is the case, for example, when relevant actors face prosecution. To summarize, my point is that while in principle the amount of restorative measures may not differ for different types of desecuritizing actors, the nature of these actions is likely to be influenced by the role of desecuritizing actors in the preceding securitization (i.e. whether they were responsible for securitization and also whether they were guilty of unjust securitization).

Following this logic of a differential burden depending on culpability it makes sense to argue, for example, that individual actors within collectives that were the primary architects of an unjust securitization ought to share a greater burden of undoing securitization than those that are – at least – partially excused for unjust securitization. While this may be so, this straightforward logic is complicated by a number of variables including, for example, whether unjust securitizing actors were fully or partially excused, capacity of different desecuritizing actors, and much besides. Miller goes as far as to suggest that: 'It is not plausible to say, in general that outcome responsibility trumps benefit or vice versa' (2007: 106).

[40]   Miller comes to a similar judgement, see (2007: 105, 109).

Conclusion

Whatever their disciplinary home, most scholars studying security give their view on the rightness or wrongness of a decision to address an issue in security mode and on the security measures used to address a threat. Similarly many practitioners of security – especially in light of the controversial securitization of terrorism – are increasingly under pressure to consider the same thing. Nevertheless, ethical concerns and security as its own area of enquiry and theorizing is only just beginning to garner attention, and thus far no systematic normative theory of security (i.e. one that enables scholars to morally evaluate past and present securitizations, while simultaneously aiding security practitioners to decide when and how to securitize) exists. It was the aim of this book to fill this gap in the literature. Taking its lead from the long-established just war tradition, this book has suggested that ethical thinking on security should take the form of a theory of just securitization made up of sets of principles designating just initiation of securitization, just conduct during securitization and just termination of securitization (just desecuritization). Securitization is understood in this book as a special form of politics, one whereby issues gain top priority and are addressed using exceptional measures. Theorizing the morality of security by developing principles of just securitization has the advantage that it covers the whole spectrum of possible security policies across all security sectors, involving all conceivable referent objects, threats and providers of security. Importantly, unlike many other interventions by scholars concerned with security and ethics, emphasis on securitization has the advantage that it does not focus on security as a valuable state of being or a good, instead it conceives of security as a political/social practice that has no intrinsic value, but that can be justified provided that a number of conditions are met (including, that it is done for the right reason and that it is informed by the right intention).

This book set forth a version of just securitization theory I have referred to throughout by the capitalized Just Securitization Theory. JST has a number of distinctive features, but most importantly it focuses on objective existential threats as just reasons for securitization, it makes the satisfaction of basic human needs the benchmark for the justifiability of potential referent objects, and it is concerned with the moral permissibility of securitization only. Unlike other variants of the concept of securitization, in JST successful securitization depends on the implementation of security speech into action. As such, JST maintains a functional distinction between scholars and practitioners of security; in other words, while scholars can comment on the morality of any given securitization (including: they can request securitization), the decision to securitize is that of securitizing actors, who preside over the means to enact exceptional measures.

This book was informed by three research questions:

1) When, if ever, may an issue be securitized?
2) If an issue is securitized, how should the securitization be conducted?
3) If an issue is securitized, how and when must the securitization be reversed?

Assisted by a large and varied number of illustrative, sometimes (semi-) hypothetical, examples I have sought to answer these questions in this book.

In the process I have set forth eight principles determining just securitization. These principles are supposed to hold regardless of the origin of the threat, the nature of the referent object (i.e. the entity threatened and to be made safe by securitization) and the provider of security. In more detail I have argued that securitization is morally permissible only in the presence of a just cause which in turn is made up of an objective existential threat to a just referent object of security. Referent objects are just provided they satisfy basic human needs, specifically autonomy and physical health. I further insisted on a sincerity of intention condition, whereby the right intention for securitization is the just cause. Just initiation of securitization was complemented by a criterion specifying macro-proportionality, which held that the expected good gained from securitization must be judged greater than expected harm from securitization. I further specified that just securitization needs to take account of the probable consequences of treating an issue in security mode. Specifically, securitization has to have a reasonable (i.e. greater than that of non-securitization alternatives) chance of succeeding in achieving the just cause.

The second of the two research questions was discussed as part of the development of the principles designating just conduct during securitization. I argued that the security measures used must be appropriate for dealing with the threat in question, and not serve some ulterior motive. A second criterion was concerned with reducing harm as much as possible; I argued that while the nature of the security measures differs according to the source of the threat, as well as the nature of the referent object, securitizing actors must consider the harm caused by the measures, and aim to choose the least overall harmful option available. In addition, I argued that securitization is unjust if the measures used are more harmful to the referent object than the threat they seek to solve. A third and final criterion specified just conduct of executors of securitization, including security professionals. I argued that although securitization necessarily involves the infringement of some human rights, executors of securitization should when they – as part of securitization – harm people be appropriately constraint those people's rights to life, freedom from torture and arbitrary detention.

Like recent versions of the just war theory, JST goes beyond theorizing simply the moral permissibility of securitization. Instead, it also considers the issue of just termination of securitization. In JST, desecuritization is conceptualized as a process (not an outcome) that occurs (in time) *after* securitization. This has meant that unlike securitization, which in JST remains a political choice decided by securitizing actors, not scholars, desecuritization is obligatory for actors who are remedially responsible for unmaking the preceding securitization, either on the basis of outcome responsibility or by connection. Although securitization and desecuritization are then interrelated processes, in JST the justice of one is judged independently of the justice of the other. In other words, an unjust desecuritization does not render a just securitization unjust and vice versa.

JST specifies three principles of just desecuritization, concerning 1) the timing when desecuritization must ensue (notably, I have argued that a securitization can remain just only for as long as there is a just cause); 2) the dismantling of the security measures taken, as well as the reversal of security language; and 3) a series of restorative measures aimed at reducing the possibility of renewed and/or reactionary securitization.

In addition to providing criteria determining the justice of securitization and desecuritization, the wider research argument also revealed a number of difficult issues such as that of the moral culpability of executors of securitization who have followed the rules of just securitization, but who have acted in securitizations that were unjustly initiated (Chapter 6, section 6.6). Or the question of whether just desecuritizing actors who played no part in securitization have fewer restorative responsibilities than desecuritizing actors culpable of unjust preceding securitization (Chapter 7, section 7.9), or the issue of whether securitization and a relevant counter-securitization can be just at the same time (Chapter 6, section 6.7). I have in this book advanced answers to these and other difficult questions, but I recognize that more can and needs to be said on all of them, as well as on all of the substantive principles advanced.

Beyond contributing to security studies, this book also contributes to the just war tradition. This is especially the case because some just war theorists are increasingly interested in wars that do not involve kinetic force, and as such, phenomena that may be called securitization. By thinking about what the just war tradition's criteria mean for securitization, JST speaks to just war theorists interested in these softer versions of war.

I have mentioned on more than one occasion on the preceding pages that the argument is conceived as very much a first word on just securitization. I hope that other scholars will devise theories of just securitization of their own volition. This is important because I believe that research on the principles of just securitization has more than just the potential to impact positively on the scholarly study of security and/or on the decisions and actions of practitioners. Beyond that it could – provided the idea of just securitization becomes widely known, which, in turn, is likely to happen only if just securitization becomes a research area in its own right – equip the public with tools to question the ethics of the decision to securitize including the security measures used and thus hold security practitioners accountable. In other words, the long-desired (in some parts of critical security studies) goal of emancipation can quite conceivably be achieved through just securitization.

The room for competing theories of just securitization is vast. One reason for this is that my interpretation of securitization is only one among many possible interpretations of the concept. For example, a theory of just securitization that theorizes securitization as an intersubjective process and focuses on audience acceptance of the speech act as pivotal would look quite different to the principles proposed as part of JST. Among other things, such a theory of just securitization would have to focus on ethical language, that is, on what kind of things securitizing actors are allowed to utter when it comes to securitizing speech acts, while they would also have to focus on what kind of audiences make ideal ethical adjudicators of the speech act and other new issues besides.

Another reason for the open-endedness of just securitization research is that JST focuses only on the circumstances when securitization is morally permissible, when it is equally valid and important to ask: when, if ever, is securitization morally required? A theory of just securitization that prioritizes the obligation to securitize is bound to be quite different from JST. Unlike JST, its objective would not be to reduce the number of securitizations in the world, but to use the mobilization power inherent to securitization to achieve security as a state of being. With this in mind, potential advocates of such a theory might utilize a scalar as opposed to a categorical approach to principles of just securitization (e.g. one where not all principles advanced as part of such a theory have to be met all of the time), largely to facilitate the ease with which securitization can take place. Theories of just securitization that focus on moral obligation could differ widely from one another depending on whether their proponents broadly concurred with cosmopolitan/global or communitarian/statist ethics.

Moreover, theories of just securitization could also derive their inspiration from virtue ethics, and, for example, devise principles that determine what makes for a virtuous securitizing actor. Theories of just securitization could supposedly also take a permissive view of the justice of securitization and seek to develop principles that specify the circumstances when securitization is forbidden.

In future, just securitization research also needs to engage with the issue of what can reasonably be expected of security practitioners when it comes to the issue of ethics and security.[1]

These concluding remarks show that there is huge potential for research in the area of just securitization. In fact the diversity and thus potential for just securitization research is such that it could become a meta-theoretical framework organizing thinking on ethics and security in general, in the same way as thinking about the morality of war is systematized by the just war tradition. Whatever happens in terms of just securitization research from here on in, this book has shown not only that questions concerning the morality of security ought to be taken seriously by anyone interested in the study and/or practice of security but also that clear and systematic answers are possible.

---

[1] This issue was considered outside the remit of this book; in part because a comprehensive answer is likely to involve the consultation of security practitioners in the way the practice turn literature suggests.

References

Alkire, S. (2002) *Valuing Freedoms: Sen's Capability Approach and Poverty Reduction*. Oxford: Oxford University Press.

Aloyo, E. (2015) 'Just War Theory and the Last of the "Last Resort"', *Ethics and International Affairs*, 29(2), 187–201.

Altman, A. and Wellman, C. H. (2008) 'From Humanitarian Intervention to Assassination: Human Rights and Political Violence', *Ethics*, 118 (2), 228–257.

Amnesty International (2017) 'Europe: Dangerously Disproportionate: The Ever-Expanding National Security State in Europe', www.amnesty.org/en/docu ments/euro1/5342/2017/en/.

Amoore, L. and de Goede, M. (eds.) (2008) *Risk and the War on Terror*. London: Routledge.

Andrieu, K. (2009) '"Sorry for the Genocide": How Public Apologies Can Help Promote National Reconciliation', *Millennium – Journal of International Studies*, 38(1), 3–23.

Anscombe, E. (1957) *Intention*. Oxford: Basil Blackwell.

Aradau, C. (2004) 'Security and the Democratic Scene: Desecuritization and Emancipation', *Journal of International Relations and Development*, 7, 388–413.

Aradau, C and Van Munster, R. (2007) 'Governing Terrorism Through Risk: Taking Precautions, (un)Knowing the Future', *European Journal of International Relations*, 13(1), 89–115.

Aradau, C. Huysmans, J. Neal, A. and Voelkner, N. (2014) *Critical Security Methods: New Frameworks For Analysis*. Abingdon: Routledge.

Arizona Border Recon (2018) 'Rules of Engagement', accessed 19 June 2018, www.ariz onaborderrecon.org/wp-content/uploads/2016/01/AZBR-POLICY- ROE-RE V12022015.pdf.

Ashby Wilson, R (ed.) (2005) *Human Rights in the War on Terror*. Cambridge: Cambridge University Press.

Ashworth, Andrew and Zedner, Lucia (2014) *Preventative Justice*. Oxford: Oxford University Press.

Aus DFAT (Department of Foreign Affairs and Trade) (2013) 'Kiribati country brief', accessed 14 August 2013, www.dfat.gov.au/geo/kiribati/kiribati_brief.html.

Austin, J. L. (1965) *How to do Things with Eords* (ed. J.O. Urmson). New York: Oxford University Press.

Baker, Deane-Peter (2007) 'Defending the Common Life: National – Defence After Rodin'. In David Rodin (ed.) *War, Torture and Terrorism*. Oxford: Blackwell Publishing, 19–34.

Ball, J. (2016) 'Types of Volcanic Eruptions', http://geology.com/volcanoes/types-of-vo lcanic-eruptions/.

Balzacq, Thierry (2005) 'The Three Faces of Securitization: Political Agency, Audience and Context', *European Journal of International Relations*, 11(2), 171–201.

(2010) 'Constructivism and Securitization Studies'. In Myriam Dunn Cavelty and Victor Mauer (eds) *The Routledge Handbook of Security Studies*. Abingdon: Routledge, 56–72.

(2011a) 'Enquiries into Methods: A New Framework for Securitization Analysis'. In Thierry Balzacq (ed.) *Securitization Theory: How Security Problems Emerge and Dissolve*. Abingdon: Routledge, 31–54.

(2011b) 'A Theory of Securitization: Origins, Core Assumptions, and Variants'. In Thierry Balzacq (ed.) *Securitization Theory: How Security Problems Emerge and Dissolve*. Abingdon: Routledge, 1–30.

(ed.) (2011c) *Securitization Theory: How Security Problems Emerge and Dissolve*. London: Routledge.

(ed.) (2015a) *Contesting Security: Strategies and Logics*, Abingdon: Routledge.

(2015b) 'The "Essence" of Securitization: Theory, Ideal Type, and a Sociological Science of Security', *International Relations*, 29(1), 103–113.

Léonard, Sarah, and Ruzicka, Jan (2016) '"Securitization" Revisited: Theory and Cases', *International Relations*, 30(4), 494–531.

Barnett, Jon (2001) *The Meaning of Environmental Security: Ecological Politics and Policy in the New Security Era*. London: Zed Books.

BBC (2014) 'Ethics Guide: What is Just War?', www.bbc.co.uk/ethics/war/just/what.shtml.

BBC News (2010) 'Government to compensate ex-Guantanamo Bay detainees', www.bbc.co.uk/news/uk-11762636.

Beck, Ulrich (1992) *Risk Society: Towards a New Modernity* (Vol. 17). London: Sage.

Beeby, Alan and Brennan, Anne-Marie (2008) *First Ecology: Ecological Principles and Environmental Issues*. Oxford: Oxford University Press.

Behnke, Andreas (1999) '"Postmodernizing" Security', paper presented at ECPR Joint Session of Workshops, Mannheim, 26–31 March.

(2006) 'No Way Out: Desecuritization, Emancipation and the Eternal Return of the Political', *Journal of International Relations and Development*, 9(1), 62–69.

Beitz, C. R. (2009) *The Idea of Human Rights*. Oxford: Oxford University Press.

Bellaby, Ross (2012) 'What's the Harm? The Ethics of Intelligence Collection', *Intelligence and National Security*, 27(1), 93–117.

Bellamy, Alex J. (2006) *Just Wars: From Cicero to Iraq*. Cambridge: Polity Press.

(2008) 'The Responsibilities of Victory: *Jus Post Bellum* and the Just War', *Review of International Studies*, 34, 601–625.

and McDonald, Matt (2004) 'Securing International Society: Towards an English School Discourse of Security', *Australian Journal of Political Science*, 39(2), 307–330.

Bellamy, Richard (2007) *Political Constitutionalism: A Republican Defence of the Constitutionality of Democracy*. Cambridge: Cambridge University Press.

Berenskoetter, F. (2007) 'Friends, There Are No Friends? An Intimate Reframing of the International', *Millennium*, 35(3), 647–676.

Bigo, Didier (2002) 'Security and Immigration: Toward a Critique of the Governmentality of Unease', *Alternatives*, 27(1 supp.), 63–92.

(2008) 'International Political Sociology'. In Paul Williams (ed.) *Security Studies an Introduction*. Abingdon: Routledge, chapter 9.

Bin Laden, Osama (2006a) 'Declaration of War against the Americans Occuping the Land of the Two Holy Places'. In David C. Rapoport (ed.) *Terrorism: Critical Concepts in Political Science*. Abingdon: Routledge, 271–294.

(2006b) 'Jihad against Jews and Crusaders'. In David C. Rapoport (ed.) *Terrorism: Critical Concepts in Political Science*. Abingdon: Routledge, 295–297.

Blackburn, Simon (2005) *Oxford: Dictionary of Philosophy* 2nd edn. Oxford: Oxford University Press.

Bohman, James and Rehg, William, 'Jürgen Habermas'. In Edward N. Zalta (ed.), *The Stanford Encyclopedia of Philosophy* (Winter 2011 edn), http://plato.stanford.edu/archives/win2011/entries/habermas/.

Booth, Ken (1991) 'Security and Emancipation', *Review of International Studies*, 17(4), 313–326.

(2001) 'Ten flaws of Just War'. In Ken Booth (ed.) *The Kosovo Tragedy: The Human Rights Dimensions*. London: Frank Cass Publishers, 314–324.

(2005) 'Emancipation'. In Ken Booth (ed.) *Critical Security Studies and World Politics*. Boulder CO: Lynne Rienner, 181–187.

(2007) *Theory of World Security*. Cambridge: Cambridge University Press.

(2012) 'Challenging the Ideas that Made Us: An Interview with Ken Booth'. In Shannon Brincat, Laura Lima and João Nunes (eds), *Critical Theory in International Relations and Security Studies: Interviews and Reflections*. Abingdon: Routledge.

and Wheeler, N. J. (2008) *The Security Dilemma: Fear, Cooperation and Trust in World Politics*. Basingstoke: Palgrave.

and Wheeler, N. J. (2013) 'Uncertainty'. In Paul Williams (ed.) *Security Studies: An Introduction*. Abingdon: Routledge, 137–154.

Bourbeau, Philippe (2011) *The Securitization of Migration*. Abingdon: Routledge.

and Vuori, J. A. (2015) 'Security, Resilience and Desecuritization: Multidirectional Moves and Dynamics', *Critical Studies on Security*, 3(3), 253–268.

Brandt, Richard (2003) 'Towards a Credible Form of Utilitarianism'. In Stephen Darwell (ed.) *Consequentialism*. Oxford: Blackwell Publishing.

Brandt Ford, S. (2013) 'Jus ad vim and the just use of lethal force-short-of-war'. In Fritz Allhoff, Nicholas G. Evans and Adam Henschke (eds) *Routledge Handbook of Ethics and War*. Abinghdon: Routledge, 63–75.

Brock, Gillian (2009) *Global Justice: A Cosmopolitan Account*. Oxford: Oxford University Press.

Browning, Christopher S. and McDonald, Matt (2013) 'The Future of Critical Security Studies: Ethics and the Politics of Security', *European Journal of International Relations*, 19(2), 235–255.

Brunstetter, Daniel and Braun, Megan (2011). 'The Implications of Drones on the Just War Tradition', *Ethics & International Affairs*, 25(3), 337–358.

(2013) 'From jus ad bellum to jus ad vim: Recalibrating Our Understanding of the Moral Use of Force', *Ethics & International Affairs*, 27(1), 87–106.

Buchanan, Allen (2007) 'Justifying Preventive War'. In Henry Shue and David Rodin (eds) *Preemption: Military Action and Moral Justification*. Oxford: Oxford University Press, 126–142.

Bufacchi, Vittorio and Arrigo, Jean Maria (2007) 'Torture, Terrorism and the State: A refutation of the Ticking-Time Bomb Argument', *Journal of Applied Philosophy*, 3, 23.

Bull, Hedley (2002) *The Anarchical Society: A Study of Order in World Politics*, 3rd edn. Basingstoke: Palgrave Macmillan.

Bunn, Matthew (2010a) 'Nuclear terrorism: A strategy for prevention'. In Michael E. Brown, Owen R. Coté Jr, Sean M. Lynn-Jones and Steven Miller (eds) *Going Nuclear: Nuclear Proliferation and International Security in the 21st Century*. Cambridge, MA: MIT Press, 329–367.

(2010b) 'Nuclear Smuggling: The Expert View', *The Guardian*, 7 November 2010.

and Wier A. (2005) 'The Seven Myths of Nuclear Terrorism', *Current History*, 104 (681), 153–161.

Bunzel, Cole (2015) *From Paper State to Caliphate: The Ideology of the Islamic State*. The Brookings Project on U.S. Relations with the Islamic World Analysis Paper No. 19, March 2015.

Burgess, J. Peter (ed.) (2010) *The Routledge Handbook of New Security Studies*. Abingdon: Routledge.

Burke, Anthony (2013) 'Security Cosmopolitanism', *Critical Studies on Security*, 1(1), 13–28.

Lee-Koo, Katharina and Matt McDonald (2014) *Ethics and Global Security: A Cosmopolitan Approach* (Routledge Critical Security Studies). Abingdon: Routledge.

Burton, Fletcher M. (2013) 'Bosnia and Herzegovina: Breaking the Vicious Cycle', *Security Community: The OSCE Magazine*, 2 June, 28–31.

Buzan, Barry(1996) 'The Timeless Wisdom of Realism?' In Steve Smith, Ken Booth and Marysia Zalewski (eds) *International Theory: Positivism & Beyond*. Cambridge: Cambridge University Press, 47–65 .

(2010) 'The English School and International Security'. In Myriam Dunn Cavelty and Victor Mauer (eds) *The Routledge Handbook of Security Studies*. Abingdon: Routledge, 34–44.

(2015) 'The English School: A Neglected Approach to International Security Studies'. *Security Dialogue*, 46(2), 126–143.

and Lene Hansen (2009) *The Evolution of International Security Studies*. Cambridge: Cambridge University Press.

Campbell, David (1998) *Writing Security: United States Foreign Policy and the Politics of Identity*, revd edn. Minneapolis, MN: University of Minnesota Press.

Caney, Simon (2005a) *Justice beyond Borders*. Oxford: Oxford University Press.

(2005b) 'Cosmopolitan Justice, Responsibility and Global Climate Change', *Leiden Journal of International Law*, 18, 747–775.

(2006) 'Environmental Degradation, Reparations, and the Moral Significance of History', *Journal of Social Science*, 37(3), 464–482.

(2010a) 'Climate Change and the Duties of the Advantaged', *Critical Review of International Social and Political Philosophy*, 13(1), 203–228.

(2010b) 'Climate Change, Human Rights, and Moral Thresholds'. In S. M. Gardiner, S. Caney, D. Jamieson and H. Shue (2010) *Climate Ethics: Essential Readings*. Oxford: Oxford University Press, 163–177.

Carmola, Kateri (2005) 'The Concept of Proportionality: Old Questions and New Ambiguities'. In Mark Evans (ed.) *Just War Theory: A Reappraisal*. Edinburgh: Edinburgh University Press, 93–113.

CDC – Centres for Disease Control and Prevention (2013) 'Cholera in Haiti', http://wwwnc.cdc.gov/travel/notices/watch/haiti-cholera.

Chandler, David and Hynek, Nik (eds) (2011) *Critical Perspectives on Human Security: Rethinking Emancipation and Power in International Relations*, Prio Series. Abingdon: Routledge.

Chapman, P. (2012) 'Entire nation of Kiribati to be relocated over rising sea level threat', *Daily Telegraph*, 7 March 2012, www.telegraph.co.uk/news/worldnews/a ustraliaandthepacific/kiribati/9127576/Entire-nation-of-Kiribati-to-be-relocated-o ver-rising-sea-level-threat.htm.

Chilcot, J. (2016) 'The Report of the Iraq Inquiry Executive Summary, House of Commons', www.iraqinquiry.org.uk/media/247921/the-report-of-the-iraq-inquir y_executive-summary.pdf.

Ciută, Felix (2009) 'Security and the Problem of Context: A Hermeneutical Critique of Securitization Theory', *Review of International Studies*, 35, 301–326.

Clifford, George. M. (2017) 'Just Counterterrorism', *Critical Studies on Terrorism*, 10(1), 67–92.

Coady, C. A. J (2008) *Morality and Political Violence*. Cambridge: Cambridge University Press.

(2014) 'The Problem of Dirty Hands', *The Stanford Encyclopedia of Philosophy* (Spring 2014 edition), https://plato.stanford.edu/archives/spr2014/entri es/dirty-hands/.

Cochran, Molly (2008) 'The Ethics of the English School'. In Christian Reus-Smit and Duncan Snidal (eds.) *The Oxford Handbook of International Relations*. Oxford: Oxford University Press, 286–297.

Collier, Paul (2013) *Exodus: How Migration Is Changing Our World*. Oxford: Oxford University Press.

Collins, Alan (2005) 'Securitization, Frankenstein's Monster and Malaysian Education', *The Pacific Review*, 18(4), 567–588.

(ed.) (2007, 2012 and 2016) *Contemporary Security Studies*. Oxford: Oxford University Press.

Cooper, Neil and Mandy Turner (2013) 'The Iron Fist of Liberal Intervention Inside The Velvet Glove of Kantian Idealism: A Response to Burke', *Critical Studies on Security*, 1(1), 35–41.

Corry, Olaf (2012) 'Securitisation and "Riskification": Second-order Security and the Politics of Climate Change', *Millennium: Journal of International Studies*, 40(2), 235–258.

Côté, Adam (2016) 'Agents without Agency: Assessing the Role of the Audience in Securitization Theory'. *Security Dialogue*, 47(6), 541–558.

Crawford, Neta C. (2007) 'The False Promise of Preventative War: The "New Security Consensus" and a More Insecure World'. In Henry Shue and David Rodin (eds) *Preemption: Military Action and Moral Justification*. Oxford: Oxford University Press, 89–125.

Croft, Stuart (2006) *Culture, Crisis and America's War on Terror*. Cambridge: Cambridge University Press.

(2012) *Securitizing Islam*. Cambridge: Cambridge University Press.

and Terriff, T. (eds) (2000) *Critical Reflections on Security and Change*. London: Frank Cass Publishers.

Cui, Shunji and Li, Jia (2011) '(De)securitizing Frontier Security in China: Beyond the Positive and Negative Debate', *Cooperation and Conflict*, 46: 144–165.

Daily Telegraph (2009) 'Chris Packham: "Giant pandas should be allowed to die out"', 22 September 2009, www.telegraph.co.uk/earth/wildlife/6216775/Chris-Packham-Giant-pandas- should-be-allowed-to-die-out.htmlDalby, Simon (2009) *Security and Environmental Change*. Cambridge: Polity.

Daniels, N. (2013) 'Reflective Equilibrium', *The Stanford Encyclopedia of Philosophy* (Winter 2013 Edition), http://plato.stanford.edu/archives/win2013/entries/reflective-equilibrium/.

Davies, S. (2008) 'Securitizing Infectious Disease', *International Affairs*, 84(2), 295–313.

Dean, H. (2010) *Understanding Human Need*. Bristol: The Policy Press.

De Londras, Fiona (2011) *Detention in the 'War on Terror': Can Human Rights Fight Back?* Cambridge: Cambridge University Press.

Den Boer, M. and Kolthoff, E. (2010) (eds), *Ethics and Security*. The Hague: Eleven International Publishing.

Dershowitz, A. (2002) *Why Terrorism Works*. New Haven CT: Yale University Press.

Detraz, Nicole (2012) *International Security and Gender*. Abingdon: Routledge.

Deudney, Daniel (1990) 'The Case Against Linking Environmental Degradation and National Security', *Millennium*, 19(3), 461–476.

De Wilde, Jaap (2008) 'Environmental Security Deconstructed'. In H. G. Brauch, J. Grin, C. Mesjasz, P. Dunay, N. Chadha Behera, B. Chourou, U. Oswald Spring, P. H. Liotta and P. Kameri-Mbote (eds) *Globalisation and Environmental Challenges: Reconceptualising Security in the 21st Century*. Berlin: Springer-Verlag, 595–602.

(2012) 'Review of *Security and the Environment: Securitization Theory and US Environmental Security Policy*, London: Cambridge University Press 2010', *Perspectives on Politics*, 10(1), 213–214.

Dexter, Helen (2016) 'War, Ethics and the Individual'. In Jonna Nyman and Anthony Burke (eds) *Ethical Security Studies*. Abingdon: Routledge, 174–188.

Dill, Janina (2015) *Legitimate Targets?: Social Construction, International Law and US Bombing*. Cambridge: Cambridge University Press.

   (2016) 'Forcible Alternatives to War: Legitimate Violence in 21st Century International Relations'. In Jens David Ohlin (ed.) *Theoretical Boundaries of Armed Conflict and Human Rights*. Cambridge: Cambridge University Press, 289–316.

Dingott Alkopher, Tal and Blanc, Emmanuelle (2017) 'Schengen Area Shaken: The Impact of Immigration-Related Threat Perceptions on the European Security Community', *Journal of International Relations and Development*, 20(3), 511–542.

Donnelly, Jack (2008) 'The Ethics of Realism'. In C. Reus-Smit and D. Snidal (eds) *The Oxford Handbook of International Relations*. Oxford: Oxford University Press, 150–162.

Donovan, G. H., Butry, D. T., Michael, Y. L., Prestemon, J. P., Liebhold, A. M., Gatziolis, D., and Mao, M. Y. (2013) 'The Relationship Between Trees and Human Health: Evidence from the Spread of the Emerald Ash Borer', *American Journal of Preventive Medicine*, 44(2), 139–145.

Dopagne, J. (2011) 'The European Air Traffic Management Response to Volcanic Ash Crises: Towards Institutionalised Aviation Crisis Management', *Journal of Business Continuity & Emergency Planning*, 5(2), 103–117.

Doyal, Len and Ian Gough (1991) *A Theory of Human Needs*. Basingstoke: Macmillan.

Doyal, Lesley with Len Doyal (2013) *Living with HIV and Dying with Aids*. Farnham: Ashgate.

Duffield, M. (2012) Challenging Environments: Danger, Resilience and the Aid Industry, *Security Dialogue*, 43(5), 475–492.

Duffield, M. and N. Waddell (2006) 'Securing Humans in a Dangerous World', *International Politics*, 43(1), 1–23.

Duffy, R. (2015) 'Responsibility to Protect? Ecocide, Interventionism and Saving Biodiversity.' Paper presented at the PSA.

Dunne, Tim and Wheeler, Nick J. (2004) '"We the Peoples": Contending Discourses of Security in Human Rights Theory and Practice', *International Relations*, 18(1), 9–23.

Dunn Cavelty, Myriam and Victor Mauer (2010) *The Routledge Handbook of Security Studies*. London: Routledge.

Dworkin, R. (2003) 'Terror and the Attack on Civil Liberties', *New York Review of Books*, 50(17).

Dyzenhaus, D. (2010) 'The "organic law" of Ex Parte Milligan'. In Austin Sarat (ed.) *Sovereignty, Emergency, Legality*. Cambridge: Cambridge University Press, 16–56.

Eckersley, R. (2007) 'Ecological Intervention: Prospects and limits', *Ethics and International Affairs*, 21(3), 292–316.

Elbe, S. (2006) 'Should HIV/AIDS be Securitized? The Ethical Dilemmas of Linking HIV/AIDS and Security', *International Studies Quarterly*, 50(1), 119–144.

   (2010) *Security and Global Health*. Cambridge: Polity Press.

Ericson, R. (2007) *Crime in an Insecure World*. Cambridge: Polity Press.

Erskine, T. (2003) 'Introduction: Making Sense of Responsibility in International Relations: Key Questions and Concepts'. In Toni Erskine (ed.) *Can Institutions have Responsibilities? Collective Moral Agency and International Relations*. Basingstoke: Palgrave, 1–18.

European Commission (2013) Press Release on Statement by the European Commission on the Capital Controls imposed by the Republic of Cyprus, Brussels, 28 March.

Evangelista, M. (2008) *Law, Ethics, and the War on Terror*. Cambridge: Polity Press.

Evans, M. (2005) 'Moral Theory and the Idea of a Just War'. In Evans, M. (ed.) *Just War Theory: A Reappraisal*. Edinburgh: Edinburgh University Press, 1–24.

  (2009) 'Moral Responsibilities and the Conflicting Demands of Jus Post Bellum', *Ethics & International Affairs*, 23(2), 147–164.

Fabre C. (2012) *Cosmopolitan War*. Oxford: Oxford University Press.

  (2015) 'War Exit', *Ethics*, April, 631–652.

  (2018) 'War's Aftermath and the Ethics of War'. In Seth Lazar and Helen Frowe (eds), *The Oxford Handbook of the Ethics of War*. Oxford: Oxford University Press, ch. 26.

Falk, R. (2005) 'Legality and Legitimacy: The Quest for Principled Flexibility and Restraint', *Review of International Studies*, 31, 33–50.

Falkner, R. (2016) 'The Paris Agreement and the New Logic of International Climate Politics', *International Affairs*, 92(5), 1107–1125.

Farwell, James P. (2014) 'The Media Strategy of ISIS', *Survival*, 56(6), 49–55.

Feldman, L. C. (2010) 'The Banality of Emergency: On the Time and Space of "Political Necessity"'. In Austin Sarat (ed.) *Sovereignty, Emergency, Legality*. Cambridge: Cambridge University Press, 136–164.

Fierke, K. M. (2007) *Critical Approaches to International Security*. Cambridge: Polity Press.

Finlay, C. (2015) *Terrorism and the Right to Resist: A Theory of Just Revolutionary War*. Cambridge: Cambridge University Press.

Floyd, Jonathan (2017b) 'Rawls' Methodological Blueprint', *European Journal of Political Theory* 16(3), 367–381.

  (2016) 'Analytics and Continentals: Divided by Nature but United by Praxis?', *European Journal of Political Theory*, 15(2), 155–171.

  (2017b) *Is Political Philosophy Impossible? Thoughts and Behaviour in Normative Political Theory*. Cambridge: Cambridge University Press.

Floyd, Rita (2007a) 'Towards a Consequentialist Evaluation of Security: Bringing Together the Copenhagen School and the Welsh School of Security Studies', *Review of International Studies*, 33(2), 327–350.

  (2007b) 'Human Security and the Copenhagen School's Securitization Approach: Conceptualising Human Security as a Securitising Move', *Human Security Journal*, 5, 38–49.

  (2010) *Security and the Environment: Securitisation Theory and US Environmental Security Policy*. Cambridge: Cambridge University Press.

  (2011a) 'Can Securitization Theory Be Used in Normative Analysis? Towards a Just Securitization Theory', *Security Dialogue*, 42(4–5), 427–439.

  (2011b) 'Why We Need Needs-Based Justifications of Human Rights', *Journal of International Political Theory*, 7(1), 103–115.

  (2013a) 'Analyst, Theory and Security: A New Framework for Understanding Environmental Security Studies'. In R. Floyd and Richard A. Matthew (eds) *Environmental Security: Approaches and Issues*. Abingdon: Routledge, 21–36.

(2013b) 'Whither Environmental Security Studies: An Afterword'. In R. Floyd and Richard A. Matthew (eds) *Environmental Security: Approaches and Issues*. Abingdon: Routledge, 279–288.

(2015) 'The Question of Value Added: A Reply to Burke', *Critical Studies on Security*, 3(2), 162–166.

(2017b) 'Parallels with the Hate Speech Debate: The Pros and Cons of Criminalising Harmful Securitising Requests', *Review of International Studies*, doi:10.1017/S0260210517000328.

(2019a) 'Collective Securitization in the EU: Normative Dimensions', *West European Politics*, First view at https://doi.org/10.1080/01402382.2018.1510200.

(2019b) 'States, Last Resort and the Obligation to Securitize', *Polity*, forthcoming.

(2019c) 'Securitizing the Environment'. In Matthew, R., Murphy, C., Nizkorodov, E., Goodrich, K., Hooper, A., Maharramli, B., Purcell, M. & Wagle, P. (ed.) *Routledge Handbook of Environmental Security*. Abingdon, New York: Routledge (in press).

and S. Croft (2011) 'European Non-traditional Security theory: From Theory to Practice', *Geopolitics, History, and International Relations*, 3(2), 152–179.

Ford, S. B. (2013) 'Just Use of Lethal Force-Short-of-War'. *Routledge Handbook of Ethics and War: Just War Theory in the 21st Century*. Abingdon: Routledge, 63–75.

Fotion, N. (2000) *John Searle*. Teddington: Acumen Publishing.

Frederiksen, H. D. (2004) 'Water: Israeli strategy, implications for peace and the viability of Palestine' Macro Center Working Papers Paper 9, http://docs.rwu.ed u/cmpd_working_papers/9.

Fredman, S. (2007) 'The Positive Right to Security'. In Benjamin J. Goold and Liora Lazarus (eds) *Security and Human Rights*. Oxford: Hart Publishing, 307–324.

Freedom House (2018) Kiribati country entry, https://freedomhouse.org/report/free dom-world/2018/kiribati.

Frowe, Helen (2011) *The Ethics of War and Peace*. Abingdon: Routledge.

(2014) *Defensive Killing*. OUP: Oxford.

(2016a) 'On the Redundancy of Jus ad Vim: A Response to Daniel Brunstetter and Megan Braun', *Ethics & International Affairs*, 30(01), 117–129.

(2016b) *The Ethics of War and Peace*, 2nd edn. Abingdon: Routledge.

Gaeta, P. (1999) The Defence of Superior Orders: The Statute of International Criminal Court Versus Customary International Law, *European Journal of International Law*, 10(1), 172–191.

Gasper, D. (1996) 'Needs and Basic Needs – a Clarification of Foundational Concepts for Development Ethics and Policy'. ISS Working Paper 210, The Hague.

(2007) 'Conceptualising Human Needs and Wellbeing'. In Ian Gough, J. Allister McGregor and Laura Camfield (eds) *Wellbeing in Developing Countries: From Theory to Research*. Cambridge: Cambridge University Press, 47–70.

Gearty, C. (2013) *Liberty & Security*. Cambridge: Polity Press.

GIZ (Deutsche Gesellschaft für internationale Zusammenarbeit) (2013) 'Project for Training, Education and Consulting for Tsunami Early Warning System (PROTECTS) – Capacity Development in Local Communities', www.giz.de/e n/worldwide/16692.html.

Gosepath, S. (2011) 'Equality', *The Stanford Encyclopedia of Philosophy* (Spring 2011), http://plato.stanford.edu/archives/spr2011/entries/equality/.

Gough, Ian (1994) 'Economic Institutions and the Satisfaction of Human Needs', *Journal of Economic Issues*, 28(1), 25–66.

(2000) *Global Capital, Human Needs and Social Policies*. Basingstoke: Palgrave.

(2013) 'Lists and Thresholds: Comparing the Doyal-Gough Theory of Human Need with Nussbaum's Capabilities Approach'. In Comim, Flavio and Nussbaum, Martha C., (eds) *Capabilities, Gender, Equality: Towards Fundamental Entitlements*. Cambridge: Cambridge University Press.

(2017) *Heat, Greed and Human Need: Climate Change, Capitalism and Sustainable Wellbeing*. Cheltenham: Edward Elgar Publishing.

Allister McGregor, J. and Laura Camfield (2007) 'Theorising Wellbeing in International Development'. In Ian Gough, J. Allister McGregor and Laura Camfield (eds) *Wellbeing in Developing Countries: From Theory to Research*. Cambridge: Cambridge University Press, 3–43.

Greenwald, G., MacAskill, E. and Laura Poitras (2013) 'Q&A with NSA Whistleblower Edward Snowden: "I do not expect to see home again"' *The Guardian*, www.theg uardian.com/world/2013/jun/09/edward-snowden-nsa-whistleblower-surveillance.

Greer, S. (2010) 'Anti-terrorist Laws and the United Kingdom's "Suspect Muslim Community"', *British Journal of Criminology*, 50, 1171–1190.

Griffin, James (2009) *On Human Rights*, Oxford: Oxford University Press.

Guardian, The (2009) 'Police pay compensation to De Menezes family', 23 November, www.theguardian.com/uk/2009/nov/23/de-menezes- family-compensation-stockwell.

(2013) 'US House defence bill blocks Obama's plan to close Guantánamo Bay prison', 14 June, www.theguardian.com/world/2013/jun/14/house-defense-bill-oba ma-guantanamo.

Gudmundsson, M. T., Thordarson, T., Höskuldsson, Á., et al. (2012) Ash Generation and distribution from The April–May 2010 Eruption of Eyjafjallajökull, Iceland, *Scientific Reports*, 2.

Guzzini, S. (2011). Securitization as a Causal Mechanism. *Security Dialogue*, 42(4–5), 329–341.

Hague, W. (2013) 'Data Snooping: Law Abiding Citizens Have "Nothing to Fear", says Hague – video', 9 June, The Guardian, www.theguardian.com/uk/video/2013/jun/ 09/data-snooping-law-abiding- citizens-nothing-fear-hague-video.

Hansen, Lene (2000) 'The Little Mermaid's Silent Dilemma and the Absence of Gender in the Copenhagen School', *Millennium*, 29(2), 285–306.

(2006) *Security as Practice: Discourse Analysis and the Bosnian War*. Abingdon: Routledge.

(2012), 'Reconstructing Desecuritisation: The Normative-Political in the Copenhagen School and Directions for How to Apply It', *Review of International Studies*, 7(4), 525–546.

Harding, L. (2014) *The Snowden Files: The Inside Story of the World's Most Wanted Man*. London: Guardian Faber Publishing, Kindle edition.

Hartmann, B. (2010) 'Rethinking Climate Refugees and Climate Conflict: Rhetoric, Reality and the Politics of Policy Discourse', *Journal of International Development*, 22, 233–246.

Hayden, P. (2005) 'Security beyond the State: Cosmopolitanism, Peace, and the Role of Just War Theory'. In M. Evans (ed.) *Just War Theory: A Reappraisal*. Edinburgh: Edinburgh University Press, 157–176.

Hayward, C. (2013) 'Situating and Abandoning Geoengineering: A Typology of Five Responses to Climate Change', *Political Science & Politics*, 46(01), 23–27.

Herington, Jonathan (2012) 'The Concept of Security'. In Micheal Selgelid and Christian Enemark (eds) *Ethical and Security Aspects of Infectious Disease Control: Interdisciplinary Perspectives*. Abingdon: Ashgate Publishing, 7–25.

(2013) 'The Concept of Security: Uncertainty, Evidence and Value', PhD diss., Australian National University.

(2015) 'Liberty, Fear and the State: Philosophical Perspectives on Security'. In P. Bourbeau (ed.) *Security: Dialogue across disciplines*. Cambridge: Cambridge University Press.

Hicks, N. (2005) 'The Impact of Counter Terror on the Promotion and Protection of Human Rights: A Global Perspective'. In Richard Ashby Wilson (ed.) *Human Rights in the 'War on Terror'*. Cambridge: Cambridge University Press, 209–224.

Holsti, K. J. (2004) *Taming the Sovereigns*. Cambridge: Cambridge University Press.

Honig, B. (2009) *Emergency Politics: Paradox, Law, Democracy*. Princeton, NJ: Princeton University Press.

Hoogensen Gjørv, G. (2012) 'Security by Any Other Name: Negative Security, Positive Security, and a Multi-Actor Approach', *Review of International Studies*, 38(4).

and Svein Vigeland Rottem (2004) 'Gender Identity and the Subject of Security', *Security Dialogue*, 35(2), 155–171.

Hurka, T. (2005) 'Proportionality in the Morality of War', *Philosophy & Public Affairs*, 33(1), 34–66.

Hussain, D. (2009) 'Fencing off Bangladesh', The Guardian, 5 September, www.the guardian.com/commentisfree/2009/sep/05/bangladesh-india-border-fence.

Huysmans, Jeff (1998) 'Desecuritization and the Aesthetics of Horror in Political Realism', *Millennium: Journal of International Studies*, 27(3), 569–589.

(2000) 'The European Union and the Securitization of Migration', *Journal of Common Market Studies*, 38(5), 751–777.

(2002) 'Defining Social Constructivism in Security Studies. The Normative Dilemma of Writing Security'. *Alternatives* 27 supplement, 41–62.

(2006) *The Politics of Insecurity: Fear, Migration and Asylum in the EU*, Abingdon: Routledge.

(2011) 'What's in an Act? On Security Speech Acts and Little Security Nothings', *Security Dialogue*, 42(4–5), 371–383.

(2014) *Security Unbound: Enacting Democratic Limits*, Abingdon: Routledge.

Hynek, Nik, and Chandler, David (2011) 'Introduction: Emancipation and Power in Human Security'. In David Chandler and Nik Hynek (eds.) *Critical Perspectives on Human Security: Rethinking Emancipation and Power in International Relations*, Prio Series. Abingdon: Routledge, 1–10.

(2013). 'No Emancipatory Alternative, No Critical Security Studies', *Critical Studies on Security*, 1(1), 46–63.

Ignatieff, M. (2004) *The Lesser Evil: Political Ethics in the age of Terror*. Toronto: Penguin Books.

Jackson, N. J. (2006) 'International Organizations, Security Dichotomies and the Trafficking of Persons and Narcotics in Post-Soviet Central Asia: A Critique of the Securitization Framework'. *Security Dialogue*, 37(3), 299–317.

Jackson, R. (2000) *The Global Covenant: Human Conduct in a World of States*. Oxford: Oxford University Press.

Jamieson, Dale (1993) 'Method and Moral Theory'. In Peter Singer (ed.) *A Companion to Ethics*. Oxford: Blackwell Publishing, 476–487.

Jarvis, L. and Legrand, T. (2016) '"I am somewhat puzzled." Questions, Audiences and Securitization in the Proscription of Terrorist Organisations', *Security Dialogue*, 48(2), 149–167.

Jepson, P. and Ladle, R. (2010) *Conservation*. Oxford: Oneworld.

Jervis, R. (1976) *Perception and Misperception in International Politics*. Princeton, NJ: Princeton University Press.

Justus, F.K., (2015) 'Coupled Effects on Kenyan Horticulture Following the 2008/2009 Post-election Violence and the 2010 Volcanic Eruption of Eyjafjallajökull'. *Natural Hazards*, 76(2), 1205–1218.

Karyotis, G., and Skleparis, D. (2013) 'Qui Bono? The Winners and Losers of Securitising Migration', *Griffith Law Review*, 22(3), 683–706.

Kennedy, D. (2012) 'Lawfare and Warfare'. In James Crawford and Martti Koskenniemi (eds) *The Cambridge Companion to International Law*. Cambridge: Cambridge University Press, 158–183.

Kerr, R. A. (2010) 'Iceland's Volcano Proving Tough to Predict', www.sciencemag.org/ news/2010/04/icelands-volcano-proving-tough-predict.

Kessler, O. (2010) 'Risk'. In J. Peter Burgess (ed.) *The Routledge Handbook of the New Security Studies*. London: Routledge.

Kiribati Government (2012) 'Kiribati Development Plan', www.ausaid.gov.au/coun tries/pacific/kiribati/Documents/kiribati–development–plan–2012–2015.pdf.

Kurki, M. (2008) *Causation in International Relations*. Cambridge: Cambridge University Press.

Lazar, Nomi C. (2013/2009) *States of Emergency in Liberal Democracies*. Cambridge: Cambridge University Press.

Lazar, Seth (2010) 'The Responsibility Dilemma for Killing in War', *Philosophy & Public Affairs*, 38, 180–213.

(2012) 'Necessity in Self-Defense and War', *Philosophy & Public Affairs*, 40(1), 3–44.

(2017) 'War', *The Stanford Encyclopedia of Philosophy*, https://plato.stanford.edu/ar chives/spr2017/entries/war/.

Lazarus, L. (2007) 'Mapping the Right to Security'. In Benjamin J. Goold and Liora Lazarus (eds) *Security and Human Rights*. Oxford: Hart Publishing, 325–346.

Leander, A. (2010) 'The Privatization of International Security'. In Myriam Dunn Cavelty and Victor Mauer (eds) *The Routledge Handbook of Security Studies*. Abingdon: Routledge, 200–210.

Léonard, S., and Kaunert, C. (2011) 'Reconceptualizing the Audience in Securitization Theory'. In T. Balzaq (ed.) *Securitization Theory: How Security Problems Emerge and Dissolve*, 57–76.

Lichtenberg, J. (2008) 'How to Judge Soldiers Whose Cause is Unjust'. In David Rodin and Henry Shue (eds) *Just and Unjust Warriors: The Moral and Legal Status of Soldiers*. Oxford: Oxford University Press, 112–130.

Lipschutz, R. (1995) *On Security*, New York: Columbia University Press.

Living Rainforest, This (2013) 'Anti-cancer: Rosy Periwinkle', www.livingrainforest.org/ about-rainforests/anti-cancer-rosy-periwinkle/.

Loader, I. and Walker, N. (2007) *Civilizing Security*, Cambridge University Press.

Lu, C. (2018) 'Reconciliation and Reparations'. In Seth Lazar and Helen Frowe (eds) *The Oxford Handbook of the Ethics of War*. Oxford: Oxford University Press, ch. 28.

Luban, D. (2005a) 'Eight Fallacies About Liberty and Security'. In Richard Ashby Wilson (ed.) *Human Rights in the 'War on Terror'*. Cambridge: Cambridge University Press, 242–257.

(2005b) 'Liberalism, Torture, and the Ticking Time Bomb', *Virginia Law Review*, 91, 1425.

(2007) 'Preventative War and Human Rights'. In Henry Shue and David Rodin (eds) *Preemption: Military Action and Moral Justification*, Oxford: Oxford University Press, 171–201.

and Engel, M. J. (2014) 'Intersections of Torture and Power: An Interview with David Luban', *Georgetown Journal of International Affairs*, 15(2), 110–116.

Lynch, M. (2008) 'Lie to Me: Sanctions on Iraq, Moral Argument and the International Politics of Hypocrisy'. In R. M. Price (ed.) *Moral Limit and Possibility in World Politics*. Cambridge: Cambridge University Press, 165–196.

MacFarlane, S. N. and Foong Kong, Y. (2006) *Human Security and the UN: A Critical History*. Bloomington, IN: Indiana University Press.

Mærli, M. B. (2011) 'The Threat of Nuclear Terrorism'. In Olav Njølstad (ed.) *Nuclear Proliferation and International Order: Challenges to the Non-Proliferation Treaty*. Abingdon: Routledge, 107–126.

Mahr, K. (2018) 'How Cape Town Was Saved from Running Out of Water', The Guardian, 4 May 2018.

Malley, R. and Finer J. (2018) 'The Long Shadow of 9/11: How Counterterrorism Warps U.S. Foreign Policy', *Foreign Affairs*, July/August, 58–69.

Manningham-Buller, E. (2007) 'Partnership and Continuous Improvement in Countering Twenty-First Century Terrorism', *Policing*, 1(1), 43–45.

Mautner, Thomas (2000) *The Penguin Dictionary of Philosophy*, London: Penguin Books.

May, L. (2012) After War Ends: A Philosophical Perspective, Cambridge: Cambridge University Press.

Mayer, Stephan F. Cynthia McPherson Frantz, Emma Bruehlman-Senecal and Kyffin Dolliver (2009) 'Why Is Nature Beneficial?: The Role of Connectedness to Nature', *Environment and Behavior*, 41(5), 607–643.

McCarthy, J. J. (ed.) (2001) *Climate Change 2001: Impacts, Adaptation, and Vulnerability: Contribution of Working Group II to the Third Assessment Report of the Intergovernmental Panel on Climate Change*. Cambridge: Cambridge University Press.

McDonald, B. (2010) 'Global Health and Human Security: Addressing Impacts from Globalization and Environmental Change', in R. A. Matthew, J. Barnett, B. McDonald and K. L. O'Brien (eds) *Global Environmental Change and Human Security*. Cambridge, MA: MIT Press, 64–67.

McDonald, Matt (2008) 'Securitization and the Construction of Security'. *European Journal of International Relations*, 14(4), 563–587.

(2012) *Security, the Environment and Emancipation: Contestation over Environmental Change*. Abingdon: Routledge.

McInnes, Colin and Rushton, Simon (2013) 'HIV/AIDS and Securitization Theory', *European Journal of International Relations*, 19(1), 115–138.

McLeod, O. (2008) 'Desert', *The Stanford Encyclopedia of Philosophy*, http://plato.sta nford.edu/archives/win2008/entries/desert/.

McMahan, Jeff (2005) 'Just Cause for War', *Ethics and International Affairs*, 19(3), 1–21.

  (2008) 'The Morality of War and the Law of War'. In David Rodin and Henry Shue (eds) *Just and Unjust Warriors: The Moral and Legal Status of Soldiers*. Oxford: Oxford University Press, 19–43.

  (2009a) 'Intention, Permissibility, Terrorism, and War', *Philosophical Perspectives, Ethics*, 23, 345–372.

  (2009b) *Killing in War*. Oxford: Oxford University Press.

  (2009–10) 'Proportionality in Self-Defense and War' Note to Stanford Political Theory Workshop, unpublished.

  (2010a) 'The Just Distribution of Harm Between Combatants and Noncombatants', *Philosophy & Public Affairs*, 38(4), 342–379.

  (2010b) 'Humanitarian Intervention, Consent, and Proportionality'. In N. Ann Davis, Richard Keshen and Jeff McMahan (eds) *Ethics and Humanity: Themes from the Philosophy of Jonathan Glover*. Oxford: Oxford University Press, 45–73.

  (2012) 'Rethinking the "Just War" Part 1 and 2.' *The New York Times*.

  (2014) 'Liability, Proportionality, and the Number of Aggressors, Penultimate draft, August 2014, unpublished manuscript.

  (2015) '*Proportionality and Time*' Ethics, April, 696–719.

  (2018a) Foreword. In Larry May (eds) *The Cambridge Handbook of the Just War*, Cambridge: Cambridge University Press, ix-xiii.

  (2018b) 'Proportionality and Necessity in *Jus in Bello*'. In Seth Lazar and Helen Frowe (eds) *The Oxford Handbook of the Ethics of War*. Oxford: Oxford University Press, ch. 21.

  and McKim, Robert (1993) 'The Just War and the Gulf War', *Canadian Journal of Philosophy*, 23(4), 501–541.

McPherson, L. K. (2007) 'Is Terrorism Distinctively Wrong?', *Ethics*, 117(3), 524–546.

McSweeney, B. (1999) *Security, Identity and Interests: A Sociology of International Relations*. Cambridge: Cambridge University Press.

Mearsheimer, J. J., 2014. Why the Ukraine Crisis Is the West's Fault. *Foreign Affairs*, 93 (5), 77–89.

Mely Caballero, A., Emmers, R. and Amitav Acharya (eds) (2006) *Non-Traditional Security in Asia: Dilemmas in Securitization*. Abingdon: Ashgate Publishing.

Mertens, T. and Goodwin, M. (2007) 'Democracy and Torture: When the People Decide'. In J. Hocking and C. Lewis (eds) *Counter-Terrorism and the Post-democratic State*, Cheltenham: Edward Elgar, 28–47.

Middleton, N. (2008) *Global Casino* (4th edn). London: Hodder Education.

Mill, J.S. (1985) *On Liberty*, London: Penguin Classics.

Millennium Ecosystem Assessment (MEA) (2003) *Ecosystems and Human Well-being: A Framework for Assessment*. Washington, DC: Island Press.

Miller, David (2007) *National Responsibility and Global Justice*. Oxford: Oxford University Press.

(2008) 'Global Justice and Climate Change: How should responsibilities be distributed?' Tanner Lectures on Human Values, delivered at Tsinghua University, Beijing, 24–25 March.

(2016) *Strangers in Our Midst*. Cambridge, MA: Harvard University Press.

Miller, S. (2009) *Terrorism and Counter-Terrorism*. Oxford: Blackwell Publishing.

Moaz, Z. (2009) 'Threat Perception and Threat Manipulation: The Uses and Misuses of Threats in Israel's National Security, 1949–2008'. In Oren Barak and Gabriel Sheffer (eds) *Existential Threats and Civil-Security Relations*. Lanham, Lexington Books, 179–217.

Moellendorf, D. (2008) 'Jus ex Bello', *Journal of Political Philosophy*, 16(2), 123–136.

(2015) 'Two Doctrines of Jus ex Bello', *Ethics*, 125, 53–673.

(2018) 'Ending Wars'. In Seth Lazar and Helen Frowe (eds) *The Oxford Handbook of the Ethics of War*. Oxford: Oxford University Press, ch. 25.

Morris, N. (2014) 'People living in fracking areas set to get more compensation', The Independent, 8 January, www.independent.co.uk/news/uk/politics/people-living-in-fracking-areas-set- to-get-more-compensation-9047653.html.

Moseley, (2008) 'Just War Theory', *Internet Encyclopedia of Philosophy*, www.iep.utm.edu/justwar/.

Mueller, J. E. (2006) *Overblown: How Politicians and the Terrorism Industry Inflate National Security Threats, and Why We Believe Them* (New York: Simon and Schuster).

Mulgan, T. (2001) *The Demands of Consequentialism*. Oxford: Clarendon Press.

Muslim Issue Worldwide, The (2013) 'Woolwich terrorist: transcript of the complete rant', http://themuslimissue.wordpress.com/2013/05/23/uk-muslim-murderer-in-woolwich-the-complete-rant/

Nagel, T. (1986) *The View from Nowhere*, Oxford: Oxford University Press.

(1997) *The Last Word*. Oxford: Oxford University Press.

Nasr, J. (2015) Germany needs migrants as workforce dwindles, but must pay for them' Reuters News https://www.reuters.com/article/us-europe-migrants-germany-economy-idUSKBN0TT24Z20151210?feedType=RSS&feedName=worldNews

Neal, Andrew (2010) *Exceptionalism and the Politics of Counter-terrorism*. Abingdon: Routledge.

(2012a) 'Normalization and Legislative Exceptionalism: Counterterrorist Lawmaking and the Changing Times of Security Emergencies', *International Political Sociology*, 6, 260–276.

(2012b) 'Terrorism, Lawmaking and Democratic Politics: Legislators as Security Actors', *Terrorism and Political Violence*, 24(3).

(2013) 'Legislative Practices'. In Mark B. Salter and Can E. Mutlu (eds) *Research Methods in Critical Security Studies*. Abingdon: Routledge, 125–128.

Neocleous, M. (2008) *Critique of Security*. Edinburgh: Edinburgh University Press.

and Rigakos, G. S. (eds) (2011) *Anti-Security*. Ottawa: Red Quill Books.

Newman, E. (2014) 'Human Security at 20: Reconciling Critical Aspirations with Political Realities', unpublished paper presented at 'The Laws of security: Reconceptualising Security at the Intersections of Law, Criminology & International Relations' 12 and 13 June, Law School, University of Leeds.

New Zealand Herald (2010) 'Hard line Warrior in war to save the Whale', www.nzherald.co.nz/nz/news/article.cfm?c_id=1&objectid=10619393.

North, Richard (2016) 'Principles as Guides: The Action-Guiding Role of Justice in Politics', *The Journal of Politics*, 79(1), 75–88.

Norton-Taylor, R. (2015) 'Up to 30,000 Foreign Fighters Have Gone to Syria and Iraq since 2011– report', *The Guardian*, 17 November.

Nunes, J. (2016) 'Security, emancipation and the ethics of vulnerability'. In Jonna Nyman and Anthony Burke (eds) *Ethical Security Studies: A New Research Agenda*. Abingdon: Routledge, 89–101.

Nussbaum, M. (2011) *Creating Capabilities*. Cambridge, MA: Harvard University Press.

Nyman, J. (2016a) 'Pragmatism, Practice and the Value of Security'. In Jonna Nyman and Anthony Burke (eds) *Ethical Security Studies: A New Research Agenda*. Abingdon: Routledge, 131–144.

(2016b) 'What is the Value of Security? Contextualising the Negative/Positive Debate', *Review of International Studies*, 42(5), 821–839.

and Anthony Burke (eds) (2016) *Ethical Security Studies: A New Research Agenda*, Abingdon: Routledge.

Oberman, K. (2015) 'The Myth of the Option War: Why States Are Required to Wage the Wars They Are Permitted to Wage', *Philosophy & Public Affairs*, 43(4), 255–286.

O'Brien, K., St Clair, A. L. and Kristoffersen, B. (2010) 'Towards a New Climate Science'. In Karen O'Brien, Asuncion Lera St Clair and Berit Kristofferson (eds) *Climate Change, Ethics and Human security*. Cambridge: Cambridge University Press, 215–227.

O'Donovan, O. (2003) *The Just War Revisited*. Cambridge: Cambridge University Press.

O'Driscoll, Cian (2008a) *Renegotiation of the Just War Tradition and the Right to War in the Twenty-First Century*. Basingstoke: Palgrave Macmillan.

(2008b) 'Fear and Trust: The Shooting of Jean Charles de Menezes and the War on Terror', *Millennium*, 36(2), 339–360.

and Lang, A. F. J. (2013) *The Just War Tradition and the Practice of Political Authority*. In O'Driscoll, C., Lang, A. F. J. and Williams, J. (eds) *Just War: Authority, Tradition, and Practice*. Washington, DC: Georgetown University Press, 1–16.

OECD (2015) Indicators of Immigrant Integration, www.oecd.org/els/mig/Indicators-of-Immigrant-Integration-2015.pdf.

Office of the High Commissioner for Human Rights (1992) General Comment No. 21: Replaces general comment 9 concerning humane treatment of persons deprived of liberty (Art. 10), http://www.unhchr.ch/tbs/doc.nsf/(Symbol)/3327552b9511fb98c12563ed004cbe59?O pendocument.

Office of the President of the Republic of Kiribati (2011) 'Kiribati Climate Change', www.climate.gov.ki/changing-climate/.

Olesker, R. (2018) 'The Securitisation Dilemma: Legitimacy in Securitisation Studies', *Critical Studies on Security*, 1–18.

Oppenheimer, C. (2003) 'Climatic, Environmental and Human Consequences of the Largest Known Historic Eruption: Tambora Volcano (Indonesia) 1815', *Progress in Physical Geography*, 27(2), 230–259.

(2016) 'The Year Without Summer', *In Our Time*, Radio 4, 21 August.

Orend, Brian (2002) 'Justice after War', *Ethics and International Affairs*, 16(1), 43–56.

(2006) *The Morality of War*. Peterborough, ON: Broadview Press.

(2007) 'Jus post bellum: The Perspective of a Just-War Theorist', *Leiden Journal of International Law*, 20, 571–591.

Owens, P. (2010) 'The Ethics of War: Critical Alternatives'. In Duncan Bell (ed.) *Ethics and World Politics*. Oxford: Oxford University Press, 309–323.

(2012) 'Human Security and the Rise of the Social', *Review of International Studies*, 38(3), 547–567.

Pala, C. (2014) 'Kiribati President Purchases "Worthless" Resettlement Land as Precaution Against Rising Sea', Inter Press Service News Agency, www.ips news.net/2014/06/kiribati-president-purchases- worthless-resettlement-land-as-pre caution-against-rising-sea/.

Pantazis, C. and Pemberton, S. (2009) 'Reconfiguring Security and Liberty: Political Discourses and Public Opinion in the New Century', *British Journal of Criminology*, 52, 651–667.

Parfit, Derek (1984) *Reasons and Persons*, Oxford: Oxford University Press.

(2011) *On What Matters*, Vol. 1. Oxford: Oxford University Press.

Paris, R. (2001) 'Human Security: Paradigm Shift or Hot Air?', *International Security*, 26 (2), 87–102.

Parish Flannery, N. (2017) 'Mexico's Avocado Army: How One City Stood Up to the Drug Cartels', The Guardian, www.theguardian.com/cities/2017/may/18/avocado-police-tancitaro-mexico- law-drug-cartels.

Parker, A. (2013) Address by the Director General of the Security Service, Andrew Parker, to the Royal United Services Institute (RUSI), Whitehall, 8 October.

Parry, Jonathan (2017) 'Legitimate Authority and the Ethics of War: A Map of Terrain', *Ethics & International Affairs*, 31(2), 169–189.

Paskal, C. (2010) *Global Warring: How Environmental, Economic and Political Crises Will Redraw the World Map*. London: Routledge.

Pattison, James (2010) *Humanitarian Intervention & The Responsibility to Protect*. Oxford: Oxford University Press.

Peoples, Columba (2011) 'Security after Emancipation? Critical Theory, Violence and Resistance', *Review of International Studies*, 37(3), 1113–1135.

and Vaughan-Williams, Nick (2010 and 2015) *Critical Security Studies: An Introduction*. London: Routledge.

Philip P. (1993) 'Introduction' in Philip Pettit (ed.) *Consequentialism*. Aldershot, Dartmouth Press.

Pirages, D. (2013) 'Ecological Security: A Conceptual Framework'. In Rita Floyd and Richard A. Matthew (eds) *Environmental Security: Approaches and Issues*. Abingdon: Routledge, 139–153.

and DeGeest, T. (2004) *Ecological Security: An Evolutionary Perspective on Globalization*, Lanham: Rowman and Littlefield Publishers.

Pogge, Thomas. W. (2008). *World Poverty and Human Rights*. Cambridge: Polity Press.

Poland, T. M., and McCullough, D. G. (2006) 'Emerald Ash Borer: Invasion of the Urban Forest and the Threat to North America's Ash Resource', *Journal of Forestry*, 104(3), 118–124.

Posner E. (2003) 'Do States Have a Moral Obligation to Obey International Law?' *Stanford Law Review*, 55, 1901–1919.

Price-Smith, A. T. (2002) *The Health of Nations: Infectious Disease, Environmental Change, and their effects on National Security and Development*. Cambridge, MA: MIT Press.

Rachels, James (1986) *The Elements of Moral Philosophy*. New York: McGraw-Hill/ Random.

Rasmussen, M. V. (2006) *The Risk Society at War. Terror, Technology and Strategy in the Twenty-First Century*, 166–168.

Rawls, John (1971) *A Theory of Justice*. Cambridge, MA: Harvard University Press.

Raz, J. (1986) *The Morality of Freedom*. Oxford: Clarendon Press.

Reichberg, G. M. (2008) 'Just War and Regular War: Competing Paradigms'. In David Rodin and Henry Shue (eds) *Just and Unjust Warriors: The Moral and Legal Status of Soldiers*. Oxford: Oxford University Press, 193–213.

Rengger, N. (2013) *Just War and International Order: The Uncivil Condition in World Politics*. Cambridge: Cambridge University Press.

Reus-Smit, Christian and Snidal, Duncan (2008) *The Oxford Handbook of International Relations*, Oxford: Oxford University Press.

Rigby, A. (2005) 'Forgiveness and Reconciliation in Jus Post Bellum'. In M. Evans (ed.) *Just War Theory: A Reappraisal*. Edinburgh: Edinburgh University Press, 177–202.

Roberge, J. M. and Per Angelstam (2004) 'Usefulness of the Umbrella Species Concept as a Conservation Tool', *Conservation Biology* 18(1), 76–85.

Robinson, Paul (2008) *Dictionary of International Security*, Cambridge: Polity Press.

Rodin, David (2002) *War & Self-Defense*. Oxford: Oxford University Press.

(2007a) 'The Liability of Ordinary Soldiers for Crimes of Aggression', *Washington University Global Studies Law Review*, 6, 591.

(2007b) 'The Problem with Prevention'. In Henry Shue and David Rodin (eds) *Preemption: Military Action and Moral Justification*. The Hague: TMC Asser Press, 143–170.

(2008a) 'The Moral Inequality of Soldiers: Why *jus in bello* Asymmetry is Half Right'. In David Rodin and Henry Shue (eds) *Just and Unjust Warriors: The Moral and Legal Status of Soldiers*. Oxford: Oxford University Press, 44–68.

(2008b) 'Two emerging issues of jus post bellum: War termination and the liability of soldiers for crimes of aggression'. In Carsten Stahn and Jann K. Kleffer (eds) *Jus Post Bellum: Towards a Law of Transition from Conflict to Peace*. The Hague: TMC Asser Press, 53–75.

and Henry Shue (eds.) (2008) *Just and Unjust Warriors: The Moral and Legal Status of Soldiers*. Oxford: Oxford University Press.

Roe, Paul (2004) 'Securitization and Minority Rights: Conditions of Desecuritization', *Security Dialogue*, 35(3), 279–294.

(2008a) 'The "Value" of Positive Security', *Review of International Studies*, 34, 777–794.

(2008b) 'Actor, Audience(s) and Emergency Measures: Securitization and the UK's Decision to Invade Iraq', *Security Dialogue*, 39(6), 615–635.

(2012) 'Is Securitization a "Negative" Concept? Revisiting the Normative Debate over Normal versus Extraordinary Politics', *Security Dialogue*, 43(3), 249–266.

Roos, R. (2012) 'CDC estimate of global H1N1 pandemic deaths: 284,000', www.cidrap.umn.edu/news-perspective/2012/06/cdc-estimate-global-h1n1- pandemic-deaths-284000.

Rothschild, Emma (1995) 'What is Security?', *Daedalus*, 124(3), 53–98.

Royal Society, The (2009) 'Geo-engineering the Climate: Science, governance and uncertainty', http://royalsociety.org/uploadedFiles/Royal_Society_Content/pol icy/publications/200 9/8693.pdf.

Rubenstein, Jennifer. (2007) 'Distribution and Emergency', *Journal of Political Philosophy*, 15, 296–320.

Ryan, Cheyney (2008) 'Moral Equality, Victimhood, and the Sovereignty Symmetry Problem'. In David Rodin and Henry Shue (eds) *Just and Unjust Warriors: The Moral and Legal Status of Soldiers*. Oxford: Oxford University Press, 131–152.

Salter, Mark B. (2008). 'Securitization and Desecuritization: A Dramaturgical Analysis of the Canadian Air Transport Security Authority', *Journal of International Relations and Development*, 11(4), 321–349.

   (2011) 'When Securitization Fails: The Hard Case of Counter-Terrorism Programs'. In T. Balzacq (ed.) *Securitization Theory: How Security Problems Emerge and Dissolve*. Abingdon: Routledge, 116–132.

   and Can E. Mutlu (eds) (2013) *Research Methods in Critical Security Studies: An Introduction*. London: Routledge.

Sandin, Per (2009) 'Supreme Emergencies Without Bad Guys', *Philosophia*, 37(1), 153–167.

Sarat, Austin (2009) *Mercy on Trial: What It Means to Stop an Execution*, Princeton University Press.

   (2010) 'Introduction: Towards New Conceptions of the Relationship of Law and Sovereignty under Conditions of Emergency'. In Austin Sarat (ed.) *Sovereignty, Emergency, Legality*. Cambridge: Cambridge University Press, 1–15.

Schimmelfennig, Frank (2005) 'The Community Trap: Liberal Norms, Rhetorical Action and the Eastern Enlargement of the European Union'. In Frank Schimmelfennig and Ulrich Sedelmeier (eds), *The Politics of European Union Enlargement: Theoretical Approaches*. London: Routledge, 142–171.

Scruton, Roger (2007) 'Can Terrorism Destroy Democracy?' *The Observer*, 30 September, www.guardian.co.uk/theobserver/2007/sep/30/featuresreview.review10.

Sea Shepherd (2018) Mission Statement, https://seashepherd.org/mission-statement/.

Searle, John R. and Vanderveken, D. (1985) *Foundations of Illocutionary Logic*. Cambridge: Cambridge University Press.

   Security Dialogue (2004) Special section, 'What Is Human Security?', 35.

Sen, Amartya (1999) *Development as Freedom*. New York: Knopf Press.

Serwer, D. (2013) 'Acknowledging Wrongdoing' *Security Community: The OSCE Magazine* 2, 26–27.

Shaw, William H. (1999) *Contemporary Ethics: Taking Account of Utilitarianism*. Oxford: Blackwell Publishers.

Shepherd, Laura J. (ed.) (2013) *Critical Approaches to Security: An Introduction to Theories and Methods*. London: Routledge.

Shue, Henry (1980) *Basic Rights: Subsistence, Affluence and US Foreign Policy*. Princeton, NJ: Princeton University Press.

   (1988) 'Mediating Duties', *Ethics* 98(4), 687–704.

(2008) 'Do We Need a "Morality of War"?'. In David Rodin and Henry Shue (eds) *Just and Unjust Warriors: The Moral and Legal Status of Soldiers*. Oxford: Oxford University Press, 87–111.

and Rodin, D. (eds) (2007) *Preemption: Military Action and Moral Justification*. Oxford: Oxford University Press.

Simmons, A. John (1999) 'Justification and Legitimacy', *Ethics*, 109(4), 739–771.

Singer, J. David (1958) 'Threat-perception and the armament-tension dilemma', *Journal of Conflict Resolution*, 2, 90.

Singer, Marcus G. (1977) 'Actual Consequence Utilitarianism', *Mind*, 86(341), 72–73.

Skleparis, Dimitris (2016) '(In)securitization and Illiberal Practices on the Fringe of the EU', *European Security*, 25(1), 92–111.

Smilansky, Saul (2004) 'Terrorism, Justification and Illusion', *Ethics*, 114, 790–805.

Soanes, Catherine (ed.) (2000) *The Oxford Compact English Dictionary*. Oxford: Oxford University Press.

Solomon, S., Qin, D., Manning, Z., Chen, M et al. (2007) 'Summary for Policymakers'. In *Climate Change 2007: The Physical Science Basis. Contribution of Working Group I to the Fourth Assessment Report of the Intergovernmental Panel on Climate Change*. Cambridge: Cambridge University Press.

Sorell, Tom (2003) 'Morality and Emergency' *Proceedings of the Aristotelian Society* New Series, Vol. 103, 21–37 .

(2013) *Emergencies and Politics: A Sober Hobbesian Approach*. Cambridge: Cambridge University Press.

Sperling, James and Webber, Mark (2017) 'NATO and the Ukraine Crisis: Collective Securitisation', *European Journal of International Security*, 2(1), 19–46.

SpielOnline (2016) 'Abstimmungen in drei Ländern: Die Ergebnisse der Landtagswahlen im Überblick' 14 March, www.spiegel.de/politik/deutschland/w ahlen-2016-die-ergebnisse-der- landtagswahlen-im-ueberblick-a-1082093.html.

Steinberger, Peter J. (2002) 'Hobbesian Resistance', *American Journal of Political Science*, 46(4), 856–865.

Steinhoff, Uwe (2007a) *On the Ethics of War and Terrorism*. Oxford: Oxford University Press.

(2007b) 'Torture – The case for dirty Harry and against Alan Dershowitz'. In David Rodin (ed.) *War, Torture and Terrorism*. Oxford: Blackwell Publishers, 97–114.

(2009) 'What Is War – And Can a Lone Individual Wage One?', *International Journal of Applied Philosophy*, 23(1), 133–150.

Stritzel, Holger (2007) 'Towards a Theory of Securitization: Copenhagen and Beyond', *European Journal of International Relations*, 13, 357–383.

(2014) *Security in Translation: Securitization and the Localization of Threat*. Basingstoke: Palgrave Macmillan.

and Sean C. Chang (2015) 'Securitization and Counter-Securitization in Afghanistan', *Security Dialogue*, 46(6), 548–567.

Taureck, Rita (2006) 'Securitisation Theory and Securitisation Studies', *Journal of International Relations and Development*, 2006, 9(1), 53–61.

Terriff, Terry, Croft, Stuart, James, Lucy and Morgan, Patrick M. (1999) *Security Studies Today*. Oxford: Blackwell Publishers.

Tesón, Fernando R. (2005) *Humanitarian Intervention: An Inquiry into Law and Morality*, 3rd edn, New York: Transnational Publishers.

and Bas Van der Vossen (2017) *Debating Humanitarian Intervention: Should We Try to Save Strangers?* Oxford: Oxford University Press.

Thomas, P. A. (2016) 'Biological Flora of the British Isles: *Fraxinus excelsior*', Journal of Ecology 2016, 104, 1158–1209.

Thorme, M. (1990) 'Establishing Environment as a Human Right', *Denv. J. Int'l L. & Pol'y*, 19, 301.

Timmermann, V., Børja, I., Hietala, A. M. et al. (2011) 'Ash Dieback: Pathogen Spread and Diurnal Patterns of Ascospore Dispersal, with Special Emphasis on Norway', *EPPO Bulletin*, 41: 14–20. doi: 10.1111/j.1365-2338.2010.02429.x.

Trombetta, Maria J. (2011) 'Rethinking the Securitization of the Environment: Old Beliefs, New Insights'. In Balzacq, T. (ed.) *Securitization Theory: How Security Problems Emerge and Dissolve*. London: Routledge, 135–149.

UNDP (1994) *Human Development Report*, Oxford: Oxford University Press.
    (2013) Human Development Report 2013 Kiribati, http://hdrstats.undp.org/images/explanations/KIR.pdf.

UNESCO Institute for Statistics (2013). Data Centre, http://stats.uis.unesco.org.

Uniacke, Suzanne (2007) 'On Getting One's Retaliation in First'. In Henry Shue and David Rodin (eds) *Preemption: Military Action and Moral justification*, Oxford: Oxford University Press, 69–88.
    (2014) 'Self-Defence, Just War, and a Reasonable Prospect of Success'. In Helen Frowe and Gerald Lang (eds) *How we fight: Ethics in War*. Oxford: Oxford University Press, 62–74.
    (2018) 'The Condition of Last Resort'. In Larry May (ed.) *The Cambridge Handbook of the Just War*. Cambridge: Cambridge University Press, 98–113.

United States Government (2018) Executive Order 13780: Protecting the Nation From Foreign Terrorist Entry Into the United States Initial Section 11 Report, www.dhs.gov/sites/default/files/publications/Executive%20Order%2013780%20Sect ion%2011%20Report%20-%20Final.pdf

Valls, M. (2016) 'Migrant Crisis: EU at Great Risk, Warns France PM Valls', www.bbc.co.uk/news/world-europe-35375303.

Van Evera, S. (1997) 'The "Spiral Model" v. "The Deterrence Model"'. Unpublished document, http://web.mit.edu/17.423/www/Archive98/handouts/spiral.html.

Vidal, J. (2015) 'With 90% of the UK's ash trees about to be wiped out, could GM be the answer?' *The Guardian*, 31 October.

Vié, J. C., Hilton-Taylor, C. and Stuart, S. N. (2008) 'Wildlife in a Changing World: An Analysis of the 2008 ICUN Red List of Threatened Species'. Gland, Switzerland: ICUN.

Villumsen Berling, Trine (2011) 'Science and Securitization', *Security Dialogue*, 42(4), 385–397.

Vuori, Juha A. (2008) 'Illocutionary Logic and Strands of Securitization: Applying the Theory of Securitization to the study of Non-Democratic Political Orders', *European Journal of International Relations*, 14, 65–99.
    (2011a) 'Religion Bites: Falungong, Securitization/Desecuritization in the People's Republic of China'. In Thierry Balzacq (ed.) *Securitization Theory: How Security Problems Emerge and Dissolve*. Abingdon: Routledge, 186–211.
    (2011b) 'How to do Security with Words: A Grammar of Securitization in the People's Republic of China', unpublished manuscript, University of Turku, Finland.

(2014) *Critical Security and Chinese Politics*. Abingdon: Routledge.

Vyas, K. and J. Forero (2016) 'FARC Rebels to Disarm in Deal With Colombia', *The Wall Street Journal*, 23 June.

Wæver, Ole (1989) 'Security, The Speech Act: Analysing the Politics of a Word', unpublished paper, presented at the Research Training Seminar, Sostrup Manor, revised Jerusalem/Tel Aviv 25–26 June 1989.

(1995) 'Securitization and Desecuritization'. In Ronnie D. Lipschutz (ed.) *On Security*, New York: Columbia University Press.

(1997) *Concepts of Security*. Copenhagen: Institute of Political Science, University of Copenhagen.

(1999) 'Securitizing sectors? Reply to Eriksson', *Cooperation and Conflict*, 34(3), 334–340.

(2003) 'Securitisation: Taking Stock of a Research Programme in Security Studies', unpublished manuscript.

(2004) 'Peace and Security: Two Concepts and Their relationship'. In Guzzini, Stefano, and Dietrich Jung (eds) *Contemporary security Analysis and Copenhagen Peace Research*. Abingdon: Routledge, ch. 5.

(2009) 'What exactly makes a continuous existential threat existential?' In Oren Barak and Gabriel Sheffer (eds) *Existential Threats and Civil-Security Relations*. Lanham, Lexington Books.

(2011) 'Politics, Security, Theory', *Security Dialogue*, 42(4–5), 465–480.

(2015) 'The Theory Act: Responsibility and exactitude as seen from securitization', *International Relations*, 29(1), 121–127.

and Buzan, B. (2007), 'After the Return to Theory: The Past, Present, and Future of Security Studies'. In Alan Collins (ed.), *Contemporary Security Studies Today*. Oxford: Oxford University Press, 381–402.

and Buzan, B., Kelstrup, M. and Lemaitre, P. (1993) *Identity, Migration and the New Security Agenda in Europe*. London: Pinter.

and de Wilde, Jaap (1998) Security: A New Framework for Analysis. Boulder CO: Lynne Rienner.

Waldron, Jeremy (1999) *Law and Disagreement*, Oxford: Oxford University Press.

(2002) 'The Constitutional Conception of Democracy'. In David Estlund (ed.) *Democracy*. Oxford: Blackwell, 51–83.

(2010) *Torture, Terror and Trade-Offs: Philosophy for the White House*. Oxford: Oxford University Press.

Walt, Stephen M. (1991) 'The Renaissance of Security Studies', *International Studies Quarterly*, 35(2), 211–239.

(2018) 'US Grand Strategy after the Cold War: Can Realism Explain it? Should Realism Guide it?', *International Relations*, online first.

Walzer, Michael (1977) *Just and Unjust Wars: A moral Argument with Historical Illustrations*, Fourth edition, New York: Basic Books.

(1992) *Just and Unjust Wars: A Moral Argument with Historical Illustrations*, 2nd edn. New York: Basic Books.

(2002) 'The Triumph of the Just War Theory (and the dangers of success)', *Social Research*, 69(4), 925–942.

(2004) 'Just and Unjust Occupations', *Dissent*, www.dissentmagazine.org/article/?article=400.

Watson, Scott (2013) 'Macrosecuritization and the Securitization Dilemma in the Canadian Arctic', *Critical Studies on Security*, 1(3), 265–279.

Wendt, Alexander (1999) *Social Theory of International Politics*. Cambridge: Cambridge University Press.

West, Niels (2004) *Marine Affairs Dictionary: Terms, Concepts, Laws, Court Cases, and International Conventions and Agreements*. Westport, CT: Greenwood Publishing Group.

Weston Pipper, J. (2016) 'An End to FARC's "Revolutionary Tax"', *The Atlantic*, 5 July.

Wheeler, Nicholas J. (2000) *Saving Strangers: Humanitarian Intervention in International Society*. Oxford: Oxford University Press.

White, Randall and Judith Heerwagen (1998) 'Nature and Mental Health: Biophilia and Biophobia'. In Ante Lundberg (ed.) *The Environment and Mental Health: A Guide for Clinicians*. Mahwah, NJ: Lawrence Erlbaum Associates, 175–191.

WHO (2016a) Western Pacific Region Kiribati statistics summary (2000–present), www.who.int/countries/kir/en/.

(2016b) Zika virus factsheet, www.who.int/mediacentre/factsheets/zika/en/.

Wight, Colin (2006) *Agents, Structures, and International Relations: Politics as Ontology*, Cambridge: Cambridge University Press.

Wilhelmsen, Julie. (2016) 'How Does War Become a Legitimate Undertaking? Re-engaging the Post-structuralist Foundation of Securitization Theory', *Cooperation and Conflict*, p.0010836716648725.

Wilkinson, Paul (2010) 'Terrorism'. In Myriam Dunn Cavelty and Victor Mauer (eds) *The Routledge Handbook of Security Studies*. Abingdon: Routledge, 129–138.

Wilkinson, T. M. (2007) 'Contagious Disease and Self-defence', *Res Publica*, 13, 339–359.

Williams, B (1988) 'Consequentialism and Integrity'. In Samuel Scheffler (ed.) *Consequentialism and Its Critics*. Oxford: Oxford University Press.

Williams, M C. (2003) 'Words, Images, Enemies: Securitization and International Politics', *International Studies Quarterly*, 47, 511–531.

Williams, P D. (2013 and 2008) *Security Studies: An Introduction*. London: Routledge.

Wolfendale, J (2017) 'Defining War'. In Michael L. Gross and Tamar Meisels (eds) *Soft War: The Ethics of Unarmed Conflict*, Cambridge: Cambridge University Press, 16–32.

Wolfers, A. (1952) 'National Security' as an Ambiguous Symbol. *Political Science Quarterly*, 67(4), 481–502.

Wood, G D. A. (2014) *Tambora: The Eruption That Changed the World*. Princeton, NJ: Princeton, University Press.

Wolff, S. (2011) 'The Regional Dimensions of State Failure', *Review of International Studies*, 37(3), 951–972.

York, C. (2013) 'Barack Obama justifies Prism NSA surveillance programme, saying it saved lives', *The Huffington Post UK*, 19 June, www.huffingtonpost.co.uk/2013/06/19/prism-obama-germany- merkel_n_3464613.html.

Zedner, L (2009) *Security*. Abingdon: Routledge.

Zupan, D (2008) 'A Presumption of the Moral Equality of Combatants: A Citizen-Soldier's Perspective'. In David Rodin and Henry Shue (eds.) *Just and Unjust Warriors: The Moral and Legal Status of Soldiers*. Oxford: Oxford University Press, 214–225.

Index